1

CONCHITA

CONCHITA

A Mother's Spiritual Diary

Edited by
M.M. Philipon, O.P.

translated by
Aloysius J. Owen S.J.

ALBA · HOUSE   NEW · YORK

SOCIETY OF ST. PAUL, 2187 VICTORY BLVD., STATEN ISLAND, NEW YORK 10314

Library of Congress Cataloging in Publication Data

Conchita, 1862-1937.
  A mother's spiritual diary.

  Translation of Journal spirituel d'une mere de famille.
    1. Conchita, 1862-1937. 2. Catholics--Mexico--
Biography. 3. Spiritual life--Catholic authors.
I. Philipon, Marie Michel, 1898-
II. Title.
BX4705.C742A3313   282'.902'4 [B]   78-1929
ISBN 0-8189-0368-6

Nihil Obstat:
Daniel V. Flynn, J.C.D.
Censor Librorum

Imprimatur:
Joseph T. O'Keefe
Vicar General, Archdiocese of New York
Jan. 25, 1978

*The Nihil Obstat and Imprimatur are
a declaration that a book or pamphlet is considered
to be free from doctrinal or moral error. It is not implied
that those who have granted the Nihil Obstat and
Imprimatur agree with the contents,
opinions or statements expressed.*

*Produced in the United States of
America by the Fathers and Brothers of the
Society of St. Paul, 2187 Victory Boulevard,
Staten Island, New York, 10314, as part of their
communications apostolate.*

4 5 6 7 8 9 (Current Printing: first digit).

© Copyright 1978 by the Society of St. Paul

To the Mother of the Incarnate Word, whose life was most simple and most divine.

LETTER OF

HIS EMINENCE CARDINAL MIRANDA

Archbishop-Primate of Mexico

We have known the Servant of God, Concepción Cabrera de Armida. We have met her in Rome and in Coyoacan. We have read her works. We have heard much about her virtues. She was a most beautiful soul, most simple, charming in the eyes of God and men.

It was here in this country the Servant of God lived. Here she prayed, loved, suffered and furthermore, founded, through her union with Christ, works in Mexico which are flourishing marvelously.

A mass of documents has passed through our hands. This concludes the phase of the diocesan process for the cause of the beatification and canonization of the Servant of God.

These priceless documents, in addition to her admirable writings, contain the testimonies of countless persons who lived close to her and who knew of her exemplary life, a life sanctified by the virtues proper to her state of life, as well as by her responsiveness to the calls of the Holy Spirit, the submissiveness of a pure and generous soul.

These documents of such great worth are even now in the hands of the Holy See. The supreme decision on the heroicity of her virtues which will lead to her glorious achievement—if it is for God's glory—the process of beatification and canonization, will be left to the judgment of the Vicar of Christ.

Now it is up to us to pray that, if God wills, we may behold her one day, on the altars, interceding for us.

When we contemplate the starry skies we rejoice to see appear on the horizon one after the other, the most distant stars. Our pastoral duty impels us to invite all of our diocese to fix their gaze on the horizon and to behold a new star which is beginning to rise, its orbit traced providentially by Him who has adorned our heavens with so many and so precious stars. This new star is the Servant of God who is beginning to shine in our sky with the wondrous and supernatural charms of grace. Let us follow that star attentively in its ascent and let us look at it with wide-open eyes so that our souls may be flooded by the light of its example: that light is called to shed its rays on the pathways of Christian life.

It is well to consider especially the life of this privileged soul from the domestic angle where, we saw her, with great admiration, in her home, with simplicity and fidelity, sanctifying herself by carrying out her mission as wife and mother. Following her step by step in her domestic life, we praise the Providence which has reserved for our times and especially for our country, the illumining of minds for discerning the incomparable treasures of wisdom, of strength of soul, of love which Christian family life holds.

On projecting the example of her life over our country, it is a joy and a consolation to think of the immense good it will bring about in all the families of Mexico.

Let us pray that God glorify His Servant.

MIGUEL DARIO CARDINAL MIRANDA
Archbishop-Primate of Mexico

Preface

The Church possesses an astounding treasure in the innumerable varieties of its apostles, doctors, spiritual teachers, its types of holiness in men or in women, not only in the past, but in our epoch and in all times.

After the apostles and saints of the east, after a St. Augustine, a St. Catherine of Sienna, a St. John of the Cross and a St. Teresa of Avila, we are presented with a Don Bosco and a Pere de Foucauld. Closer to our times, alongside the virginal figures of a Thérèse of Lisieux and of a Maria Goretti, at this moment it unveils to us an exquisite Mexican young girl, pure and lovely to look at, mother of nine children and grandmother of numerous offspring. She spent her life on earth with simplicity, surrounded by her family and friends, involved in the daily routine of her social milieu, a woman like other women, but in the depths of her soul shone an extraordinary apostolic flame, a heroic zeal to imitate Christ and to be identified with the Crucified to save men with Him. It reveals to us one who loves the Church passionately, offering herself as a victim to it, an incomparable model of a wife, a glory for the laity of whose mission in the Church and of whose call to the highest sanctity she reminds us. She never lived in cloister yet nonetheless inspired the founding of two religious congregations: one of women, the Contemplatives of the Cross, the other of men, the Missionaries of the Holy Spirit. It was she who left behind her a message for the renewal of the world through the Cross.

For too long holiness has been considered a monopoly of religious life and of the priesthood. Numerous conciliar Fathers of Vatican II reacted against this discretionary concept. It is the whole Church, every member of the Mystical Body of Christ, who should be holy. The People of God is *a holy nation*, a people of priests and of kings (Ex 19:6). The Sermon on the Mount is a charter of perfection for everyone, without exception. The Church of today needs saints everywhere, not only in the cloister and at the foot of the altar, but in the family, in places of work, in every sector of human activity. Holiness is a call of God who addresses Himself to all men.

The laity in particular is called today to witness before the whole world to an outstanding holiness. Does not God give us an example of this in this mother of nine children on her way to the altars?

Conchita lived on earth, simple and joyous among her own, wholly given over to God in the secret recesses of her soul in which dwelt the Holy Spirit, living in an intense apostolic splendor radiating from the horizons of the Church, *creatrix of a new style of holiness accessible to all.*

What strikes us most about Conchita is the many facets of her life. She fulfilled all the vocations of woman: fiancee, wife, mother, widow, grandmother and even, by a special indulgence of Pius X, without ever being deprived of her family status, died canonically as a religious in the arms of her children.

She addresses herself to all categories of the People of God, to lay and to married people, to priests and to bishops, to religious and to all consecrated lives.

She treats not only of the relations of the soul with God but also deals with all the great themes of Christianity: God, Christ, the Mother of God, the mystery of the Church, the eternal meaning of all human life. Her *Spiritual Diary* with its sixty-six manuscript volumes equals in amplitude the *Summa* of St. Thomas Aquinas, ascending effortlessly and often without transition from the most lowly household occupations to the Generation of the Word in the splendors of the Trinity. By the profundity of the sublimeness of her writings, Conchita rivals St. Catherine of Sienna or a Teresa of Avila. One of the Commission charged with examining her in 1913 in Rome declared: "She is extra-ordinary of the extraordinary!"

Mexico, March 3, 1972
on the 35th anniversary of the
death of Conchita.

Contents

Introduction

We present the posthumous work of the great spiritual theologian, Marie-Michel Philipon, O.P., a theological work on the spirit and doctrine of the Servant of God, Maria Concepción Cabrera de Armida. He entitles it simply: *Conchita, a Mother's Spiritual Diary*. This study took up most of his time during the last years of his life, for he realized it would bring us a spiritual message of capital importance, a gift of Providence for *the Church of today*.

The first contact Father Philipon had with Conchita's life and doctrine took place during a voyage he made to our Scholasticate in Mexico. He arrived in 1954 to give a series of spiritual conferences.

His intuitive talent—as he himself said—discovered this great treasure for the Church. It aroused in him the desire to make her known, especially to his European readers.

For quite a few reasons not only the publication of his book was delayed but also its elaboration. Not the least reason was the problem of understanding a foreign language, considering the style so characteristic and so personal of Conchita's writings, as well as the overpowering task of bringing together such massive documentation.

Yet God, in His Providence, opened the way and the Father's spirit of obedience was decisive in the matter. Prominent ecclesiastics and his religious superiors let him know he would render a service to the Church by making known Conchita's spiritual doctrine, especially today when there is coming about, a certain neglect or loss of the meaning of essential Christian values.

Father Philipon returned several times to Mexico to become acquainted in depth with the environment. He also, in keeping with his method, wanted to collect some authentic testimonials from living witnesses, and so, once he had an over-all view, he set himself to edit the work. When it was almost completed, the Lord willed to call him to Himself.

The first part, which he entitled *The Story of her Life* was fully edited by him. The first two chapters of the second part, "Great Spiritual Themes," i.e., "The Mystical Writer"—which he might well have wanted to revise somewhat more, but which we present fully respecting the text—, and "The Doctrine of the Cross," which he called the central chapter, are entirely from his pen. He only failed to point out some perspectives on the last three themes, *The Virgin of the Cross, The Mystery of the Church* and *The Abysses of the Trinity.* When he was in the course of writing about Mary, God called him, but he left behind some notes, outlines and a choice of texts. I have only taken over the responsibility of putting them in shape, and making them available because of the spiritual wealth which they contain, and I say this publicly out of an elementary concern for literary honesty.

Quite simply, I admit why I was induced to do what I have done and make this resolution.

I knew Father Philipon in 1954, when I was prefect of studies in our Scholasticate. There came about a deep affinity of thought between us, and from this moment on he chose me as his main assistant and counselor, due to my knowledge of Conchita's writings.

After lengthy conversations, he told me again and again humorously and sincerely: "I keep my full freedom and my own way of thinking." In his notes he wrote: "I have spoken with Father de la Rose hundreds of times." That is why I think I know his innermost thoughts wholly objectively and why I have taken on myself the responsibility of finishing this work, following, with the greatest fidelity, his thinking which I know perfectly.

Father Philipon intended to write a prologue to explain some principles of method for clarifying the meaning, the intent and the limitations of his work.

Everyone knows that this is as a rule the last page an author writes when he himself judges his work as a whole. Fortunately he wrote the main ideas, ideas which would have been expressed most carefully and elaborated in his own personal literary style.

I present below his notes which I think essential for the understanding of his posthumous work.

"I did not want to write about Conchita. Despite myself I was impelled by the force of events, that is by Providence. Prominent ecclesiastical personages who knew Conchita or who were acquainted with her doctrine, convinced me to write.

"Without the slightest pretense of wanting to say everything, rather on the contrary in full awareness of the partial and imperfect nature of this book, I have simply wished to respond to the manifest call of God and be the pen which endeavors to present the spiritual message of an admirable daughter of the Church of God.

"The fundamental document: *The Account of Conscience* is not a biography but a *Diary*, and not a complete one which jots down day after day all the happenings of human existence. Rather it is a *Spiritual Diary* which only relates mainly the intimate relationships she had with God. These relationships she faithfully wrote down during more than forty years in obedience to the formal command of her spiritual directors.

"A unique, providential fact which permits us to follow step by step from the age of thirty-two to seventy-five, the progressive ascent toward God of a privileged soul, a soul of exceptional heroism, endowed with a spiritual message for the whole Church and for all men of today, a soul which had received from God the mission of recalling to the world that apart from the Cross, there is no salvation.

"There is seen *no literary concern* in this veracious account in which we find scattered and at random in the course of her life, most sublime mystical elevations in close proximity to the daily concerns of a mother and the recipes of a perfect mistress of her household. While she is writing about the generation of the Word and about God's eternity, here she is called to come to dinner. Happily she hastens to sit down at table with her children, but when dinner is over, she goes back to her writing and continues taking down what the Lord says about the abysses of the Trinity and the other mysteries of God.

"Her diary does not report everything but it does explain everything. We must begin with the psychological and concrete data whence sprang the mystical intuitions and the spiritual doctrine. Both are inseparable. Whence we have two complementary parts: *Her Life Story*, thence *The Doctrine, the Great Spiritual Themes.*

"It was impossible to say everything and to set within one single volume the myriad of pages of this mystical author, seemingly the most prolific of contemporary literature.

"Did we manage to express the essence of a Spiritual Diary which has at least sixty-six thick bundles of manuscripts? We had no other ambition, no better intention than that of revealing to the world the inexhaustible riches of the Cross and of the mysteries of God contained in these writings. We think they constitute one of the present day treasures of the Church of Christ.

"*This Church alone will judge it*, for the Lord has entrusted to it to bring men to God and He has granted it, with the help of His Spirit, the gift of an infallible discernment of spirits.

"We submit unreservedly this attempt to recall to the world the mystery of the Cross which is set at the innermost center of the Gospel and at the heart of the Christian mystery.

"To be sure, on certain points, before this life and doctrine of a Mexican woman who spent her days far from Europe, there is aroused a feeling of surprise and a questioning of its suitability for our modern way of thinking.

"The danger lay in modifying what she wrote according to our contemporaneous categories which, besides, will very soon be outmoded. We are ever annoyed at and distrustful of what we read about Chinese thinking or Hindu mysticism by a Westerner. There is always a danger it is Europeanized and consequently altered. We do not modify a Chinese thought without deforming it.

"It seemed to us preferable and truer to bring the reader into a personal contact with the original by way of a translation as faithful as possible, expressive of Conchita's psychological reactions and her characteristic mentality, for Conchita's Spanish text is filled with Mexicanisms.

"Mexican folklore is fashionable today. Radio, TV have taken on a more and more planetary sense which makes us better understand and feel the resemblances and differences which bring together or separate men, their civilizations and their cultures, the various expressions of their religious sentiments.

"Vatican II has made us experience that the Catholicity of the Church is not uniform but is unity amid variety. Never have men measured, with such comprehension and objectivity, at the same time their basic unity and their legitimate diversities. Christ was an oriental. Nonetheless all men recognize themselves in this man.

"The same holds true for all the saints of Catholicism. No matter what their origin, their race and the color of their skins, no matter what their social class and the forms of their culture or even of their illiteracy, we feel ourselves *one* with them in Christ.

"Conchita, a Mexican, is a saint of our own. She is our sister in Christ. She has become through her apostolic zeal and her heroic immolation the spiritual mother of a multitude of souls who, as did she, want to walk in the footsteps of Christ to be crucified with Him and save men with Him.

"Conchita is close to us. This daughter of Mexico is bound by the communion of saints to all her brothers and sisters in Christ. She is a model for all, not in her personal and inimitable charisms but in her love for Christ, in her life offered up for her Church.

"It is in this spirit of Catholicity, her example and her writings are to be approached. Then it is, we marvel at the multiform riches of the capital grace of Christ.

"Let us distrust our Cartesian, Hegelian, existentialist and western mentalities. The center of the Church is in Rome, but its radiance extends no more to Europe alone than to all the countries of the Universe.

"Conchita is a witness of this Catholicity. Her message is addressed to priests and religious souls but also to the laity. She is a model for all.

"Thus appear to us the designs of Providence."

Such were, then, the notes and comments brought together by Father Philipon.

ROBERTO DE LA ROSA,
Missionary of the Holy Spirit

Part I.

THE LIFE STORY OF A WIFE AND MOTHER

"My life unrolls before my eyes—the joys, the sufferings, my marriage and my children, and the Works of the Cross."

CHAPTER 1.

DAUGHTER OF MEXICO

"I have grown like the grass of the fields."

Land of Volcanoes; the Family Environment

Conchita is a daughter of Mexico. She is to be seen vividly in her Mexican environment, in this land of violence and antithesis, a land of volcanoes but also the land of Veracruz, the *Nation of the True Cross:, and of Our Lady of Guadalupe.* Throughout her life there will be seen the contrast of a life more and more divine under the most ordinary appearances. One word was ever on the lips of those who had known her and whom I questioned during my first sojourn in Mexico: "simplicity." Conchita has an evangelical *simplicity.*

She spent her childhood and adolescence in the "haciendas" and on the "ranches," sailing in a boat along the streams, jumping into the water or pushing her companions and her father's employees into the water, laughing heartily, mingling with everyone, passionately fond of music and song, endowed with a fine voice. Later on, she will compose the first hymns of the Cross, and she herself will sing them while accompanying them on the piano. She is young, jolly, fascinating and will have, down through her last years, a tremendous influence on everyone about her.

She tells us in her diary, spontaneously and with incomparable aplomb, about her early years living with her family.

"My parents were Octaviano de Cabrera and Clara Arias. Both were from San Luis Potosi where they were married and where I was born. My mother was very ill and so could not nurse me. She made every effort to assure that I would be nursed. One day she almost died. The doctor, in this emergency, ordered that I be sent far from town to a big farm. There, out of compassion for me, the porter's wife offered to nurse me, entrusting her own son to a wet-nurse. She saved my life. Her name was Mauricia. I loved her dearly and, upon reaching the age of reason, I realized more fully all I owed her. Later my mother told me that on the way to the farm, she was afraid to uncover my face, thinking at every moment she had a dead child in her arms (*Aut.*, 1, 6-8).

"My birthplace was San Luis Potosi where I was born in a house owned by my parents, a house opposite the Church of St. John of God. There I was baptized. I have always lived in that house save for some short times when we had to leave while it was being renovated. I lived there until I got married. There my son was born when, for reasons of health, I was staying there. It was there that my father, my sister Carlota and my brother Constantin died (*Aut.*, 367).

"My parents were excellent Christians. At the haciendas each day my father presided over the recitation of the rosary in the chapel, with the whole family, the farm workers and some county folk present. When he did not do so, because of some urgent task, he had me take his place. At times he returned before we finished saying the rosary, and, on the way out he would scold me for lack of devotion. He said my "Our Fathers" and "Hail Marys" would go along with me to Purgatory and that no one there would want them, they were so poorly recited.

"My father was very charitable to the poor. Any time he saw someone in need he could not refuse to help them. He was so jolly and so frank. I helped him die a good death. And he himself was so brave. He himself prepared the altar for the Viaticum, begged pardon of his children for any bad example and disedification for which he might have been to blame. Then he took us into his arms one after another, kissing each one and gave each one a piece of advice. In his will he requested that we bury him without any commemorative plaque, without a tombstone, not even with a name on the grave but only a simple cross. Despite the pain it caused us we carried out his last request, his dying wish (*Aut.*, 365).

"My mother was a saint. She was an orphan when she was only two years old. She suffered much. She married when she was seventeen. She had twelve children: eight boys and four girls. I was the seventh, born between Juan and Primitivo, the Jesuit.

"My mother passed on to my soul love of the Most Blessed Virgin and of the Eucharist. She cherished me with all her heart and was quite broken-hearted when I got married. However, she told me that my husband was an exceptional person and that not everyone was like him. She had to undergo great suffering. She passionately loved poverty. She performed a great number of hidden virtues and her martyrdom was ever unknown to all. She had an attack and was unconscious for twelve hours. By dint of prayers, God granted her time to confess. A second attack resulted in death. I assisted her to die and then laid her in her coffin (*Aut.*, 366).

"I only attended three schools: as a tiny child, at the home of some little old servants, named Santillana; Later, but only for a short time, at Madama Negrete's; finally at a school run by the Sisters of Charity. When they were expelled, I was still very young, being only eight or nine years old. My mother did not want to send me anywhere else. Some teachers came to the house to instruct us and teach us music (*Aut.*, 1, 23).

"My instruction remained very elementary, not due to any fault on the part of my parents but because of my stupidity, my laziness and also on account of so many changes and travels at that period of my studies. Above all I became addicted to music for playing the piano and singing was my great delight. I wasted many an hour of my life in so doing! May God forgive me!

"My mother taught us how to run a household: from scrubbing the floor to embroidery. At the age of twelve I was already put in charge of the expenditures of the house. At the hacienda —farm— the cows had to be milked, the dough kneaded, and meals prepared. My mother never let us be idle. She was very watchful and insistent we keep busy. We surely did: mending, darning, all kinds of sewing, preparing hors d'oeuvres, sweets and pastries. Besides my mother taught us ever to be humble and not to give way to vanity. Poor momma labored beyond belief to train us properly, and made every effort possible to teach us not to be selfish. Quite a few Sundays, inviting us to take a walk, she brought us to the hospital to see the dead and the dying. From my earliest years, as soon as one of our friends fell seriously ill, we had to watch over and take care of that friend in every possible way. She also had me attend men, women, children, rich and poor when they were dying and this taught me not to be afraid, but rather to help them by my prayers, clothe them and keep them neat and clean.

"Neither my father nor my mother could stand affection. When I was only six, I got on a horse by myself. The horse was frightened, reared and threw me off. Disregarding my tears, my father made me take a drink of water and then get back on the horse! In this way I no longer had any fear of horses. I was so proud I rode the most spirited ones, those which no one else could master. I have always been extremely fond of horses. How many times here in Mexico, when my husband took me for a ride, the only thing I noticed was the horses! As for people, they all looked alike (*Aut.*, 15-16).

The First Delights of My Soul

"Thanks to God, the Lord granted me good dispositions but I am to blame for not having cultivated them as I should have. From my tenderest childhood, I felt in my soul a strong inclination toward prayer, penance and, above all, purity (Aut. 1, 10). Penance was always a joy as far back as I can remember. When I learned to read, I shut myself up in the house library. I only picked out the *Christian Annals* and out of the numerous volumes, I only read those pages where there were accounts of the penances performed by saints. I enjoyed reading about them and hours flew by during which I found out what mortifications they practiced. I was very envious of them and tried hard to find out how to imitate them (*Aut.*, 1, 2).

"While riding about the countryside with my father and my sister Clara, I spent hours reflecting on how I could manage to live in a mountain cave all by myself, far from everyone, giving myself up to penance and prayer whenever the spirit moved me. I was delighted at the thought and pondered it in my heart. Sometimes along the road—we often stayed at my mother's hacienda—I would ride along meditating very slowly, word for word, prayers to our Blessed Sacrament or to the Blessed Virgin, prayers which I had learned by heart. My childish heart found ineffable delight in all this. Up to the time of my marriage, I thought that everybody did penance and said prayers and when they did so they did not let anyone else know. I was very much surprised on learning this was not so but rather a lot of people hated mortification. My God, why is this? (*Aut.*, 17-18).

"I made my first confession when I was seven or eight. I was told to confess grievous sins. So that is what I did although I had not committed any, as I realize now. The priest had to bend over to see me for I hardly reached the grill of the confessional. He scolded me harshly and gave me four rosaries as a penance! It was an awful lot for a little girl! (*Aut.*, 24-26).

"I made my first Communion on the feast of the Immaculate Conception, on my tenth birthday, December 8, 1872. On account of my tepidity and thoughtlessness I do not remember anything special except an immense interior delight and a great pleasure to wear a white dress. Since that day my love of the Eucharist has ever grown and, from that period on, I have fervently loved to frequent the sacraments. When I was around fifteen or sixteen, I was permitted to receive four or five times a week, and, soon after, every day. I was happy, so happy when I could receive! It is an absolute necessity of my life. How often, on returning from a dance or from the theater, I received Communion the next day without any feeling of guilt. At night I would think first about the Eucharist, then about my fiancee. How often when

I received and visited the Blessed Sacrament I said to Jesus: 'Lord, I feel so unable to love You, so I want to get married. Give me many children so that they will love you better than I.' This did not seem out of place to me, rather a legitimate prayer to quench the thirst of my soul, my desire to love Him more and to see Him loved even better by beings proceeding from my being with my blood and my life (*Aut.*, 27-29).

An Elegant Amazon

"I grew rapidly, in fact so rapidly that I fell ill. The doctors prescribed some treatments during my stay in town, one being I should ride horses. Harness was sent from the hacienda and I rode every morning with one of my brothers. I lived so secluded in San Luis, a sparsely populated town, that even there where I had spent the greater part of my life, no one knew me. They thought I was the wife of the brother who rode with me. I was thirteen and knew very few people, even very young ones. The first day I was called *miss* I turned pale and started to cry. I was glad to be still a child and was horrified at their regarding me as a young girl. At home I used to wear a short dress, in town a long one. The young governor of the State liked to talk with me and courted me. As for me, I told him stories and was at a loss what else to say. How naive!

"At this time and while I was riding, the man who was later to be my husband, as he himself later on told me, met me for the first time" (*Aut.*, 67-69).

Fiancee at the Age of Thirteen

"I did not like dances, but as soon as you wore a long dress you had to attend. It was the custom. I recall when the first dance was held at home, on December 12. It was time and I did not want to get dressed for the dance. I preferred to go to bed but I had to go because I had promised. So I went. It was on this occasion one of my brothers introduced me to my future husband. On December 24 I went to another dance. There he was. When he spoke to me I almost died, he paid me such compliments and made such outlandish statements! I was very embarrassed. However, it was very nice to see so many men come up to me and invite me to dance. I was so ashamed for I did not know how to treat them. They all liked me very much. But I was going steady with Pancho, yet they kept on courting me. I did not know why. One day, just for fun, I counted some twenty-two suitors, quite rich ones, but I loved only Pancho and never cared for anyone else (*Aut.*, 69-70).

"I am going to tell here how I fell in love with my intended, whom I married many years later.

"On January 16, 1876, I was taken to a family dance (at San Luis they danced a lot), where he proposed and I immediately responded to his feelings. I had never heard love spoken of and here I am hearing him say that he would suffer a great deal if I did not love him and that he would be very unhappy if I did not feel the same toward him and a thousand other things of the sort which, at first, left me cold. I did not believe I was capable of inspiring tenderness and my heart was overcome. I found it amazing that anyone could suffer because I did not love him. I told him then that I also loved him and it was not worthwhile to suffer for so little a thing.

"On returning home, I was upset and felt a weight on my heart. A strange thing had just happened to me. I felt a certain disquiet and was even somewhat afraid. I forbade Pancho to write to me. He complied until May when we met occasionally outside since my family rightly thought I was too young. We were engaged for nine years before we married. I must gratefully say that Pancho never took advantage of my simplicity. As a fiancé he was always correct and respectful. On my part, from the very first letter, I strove to raise him up to God. I had the satisfaction of seeing him ever inclined to piety. I spoke to him about his religious duties, about love of the Blessed Virgin. He, in turn, sent me prayers, religious poems and a copy of the *Imitation of*

Christ packaged in a very pretty case . . . I urged him to frequent the sacraments as often as possible. Later, I never stopped being concerned about his soul (*Aut.*, 70-72).

"My betrothal never troubled me as an obstacle to my belonging to God. It seemed to me so easy to combine them both! When I went to bed and was alone, I thought of Pancho, then of the Eucharist which was my greatest delight. I went to Communion every day and it was on those days that I saw him go by. Thinking of him did not hinder me from praying. I made myself look as lovely as I could and I dressed myself elegantly to please him. I would go to the theater, and to dances for the sole purpose of seeing him. Nothing else did I care for. But in the midst of all this I never forgot God. I dreamed of Him as constantly as I could and He drew me to Him in an indescribable way.

"Under my silken gowns—I did not care whether they were but of cotton—at the theater and at the dance I wore a belt of haircloth, delighting in this for the sake of my Jesus (*Aut.*, 1, 73-74).

Longing for God

"At the heart of this ocean of vanities and festivals, I felt within my soul a burning desire to learn how to pray. I inquired, I read, I kept myself as much as I could in God's presence. This was enough to begin seeing a great light shed on the nothingness of worldly things, on the vanity of existence, on the beauty of God. I felt a great love for the Holy Spirit. When I went to bed I held my crucifix and, not knowing what was happening to me, felt a profound interior emotion. My heart fixed itself on Christ in an inexplicable way. Christ drew me to Himself, absorbed me, enchanted me. Soon all dissolved in tears. Then this experience passed and I returned to my life of tepidity, of vanity and of folly. This caused me much suffering. Even in the midst of adulation, recreation, festivals, I felt emptiness in my soul, and seemed to hear a voice saying: 'You were not born for this, your happiness is somewhere else.'

"When I recall these things, it seems to me I should have had a religious vocation but I never, so to say, had heard of such words and never paid close attention to it. On reading the *Christian Annals* I was quite enthused over the religious mentioned, but I never knew any of them and thought they were no longer alive. Many a time I and my cousins played at being nuns. For a long time I would kneel down, feeling in my soul God's delight. Soon, however, my cousins lost interest with this game and played with their boy friends.

"Vocation, Virginity! I had no idea what these words meant. I thought I was destined to marry without any other question than to do so, although I had no concept of its divine grandeur and its obligations. My confessors spoke to me of no other way of life. My uncle, who was a priest, was the only one who used to read to me beautiful passages about virgins and martyrs, but it never crossed my mind, that could be for me.

"I thought that once I was married, I would be wholly free to practice my penances. I felt glad and at peace. One day I went to confession at the Church of Santa Maria del Rio. A wonderful priest gave me this advice which impressed me very much: 'There is in your soul a great docility. It is absolutely necessary for you to choose a confessor.' Only then did I learn that my soul was docile. Under the impulse of this priest, I think my soul made some progress.

"Thus in the midst of my miseries and vanities and at the same time amidst God's calls, I spent many years of my life. At dances I was highly regarded. Was it due to my candor? Scarcely had I arrived, my dance card was filled with the names of dance partners, but how tiresome dancing so much! It is said there are great risks dancing, and now I understand. . . .

"Dressmakers complimented me on my figure! I was moved by vanity but felt no real pleasure on hearing this. I followed the trend. I was glad to be affable with my fiancé, with simplicity, nothing more. I was only concerned with how I was dressed and looked during the few minutes Pancho passed by or came to visit me. Hardly had he turned the corner, I removed my finery. Ear-rings, jewelry and rings all made me feel embarrassed. Mama felt the same way. I recall the day of my engagement, the feast of Saint Raphael, October 24, 1884. Pancho gave me a golden bracelet which he fastened on my wrist. It had a lock and though it caused me considerable pain then, I have never taken it off for many years.

"Everything ephemeral, everything under a false light, vain and factitious, left me. Never did material things satisfy my heart, I felt something else, very great in the depths of my heart. I experienced an immense void which I imagined must be filled by my marrying so good a man as Pancho who loved me so dearly. This was the object of my desires and of my prayers to God, St. Joseph and the Most Blessed Virgin (*Aut.*, 1, 75-81).

Tragic Death of Her Brother Manuel: Starting Point of a New Life

"A terrible blow took me away from the world and its vanities to bring me close to God. My brother Manuel, the eldest of all my dearly beloved brothers, was suddenly shot to death. His brains were blown out by a bullet while he was entertaining a friend, Don Pancho Cayo. Don Pancho insisted on wearing his gun to dinner. As he sat down at the table the trigger of his gun caught on something and the bullet passed through Manuel's cheek and came out of his head. It was a terrible tragedy but an accident. My brother fell down dead. He left behind his wife and three children.

"As soon as we heard what had happened, we took the road to Jesus-Maria. When my mother learned of the death of her son, she fell down on her knees and prayed before giving way to her grief. The tragedy occurred at two o'clock in the afternoon and, around six o'clock I was close by the corpse.

"My parents were almost out of their minds but resigned and

accused no one. Don Pancho was in despair. My brother Primitivo who was present when the accident happened, walked back
and forth on the terrace, as thunder boomed and lightning flared,
completely overcome. Thence sprung his vocation. Good Lord,
what a tragedy! For me, the blow though cruel was salutary for
my poor soul so confused and distraught. And this was true for
the whole family. I returned home in sorrow, resolved to give
myself wholly to God, to think more intimately about Him, to
detach myself more fully from the trends which led me toward
the vanities of the world. I have always been afflicted by my
extreme sensitivity. My soul is affected not only on the occasion
of a death but even by simply the absence of someone. As a
tiny child, when my father and my brothers came and went, how
many tears did I shed! Yes indeed, my soul has suffered much
because of my sensitivity. I think that on this point I have never
been understood. My heart has been the source of my greatest
sufferings, despite an appearance of coldness and indifference
(*Aut.*, 1, 82-85).

Growing Like the Grass of the Fields

"My God, how little I have understood Your graces, Your
favors and the singular predilection in which You have enveloped my poor soul. . . I have always felt the inclination to write.
From the age of sixteen, I composed an account of the existence,
filled with God, which we lived at *Peregrina*. I tore most of it up.
In that hacienda, prayers were said every night. At nightfall,
I felt my soul ascend far from the earth, seeking God ardently.
It was the favorite hour in which I felt myself flooded by something, yes, by this Other thing which I could not define but
which elevated me above the earth and turned me resolutely
towards the heavens. . . .

"A tranquil life and a happy one but one which, as far as I
was concerned, I did not find wholly to my liking because Pancho
was not there, Pancho who was staying at San Luis" (*Aut.*, 1,
101-103).

On hearing her, we think of the poet's words: "Only one is wanting to you and so you think the world is empty" (Lamartine).

Chapter II

WIFE AND MOTHER

"To be wife and mother was never a hindrance to my spiritual life."

My Marriage

Her life as a young girl passed without ado, awaiting future happiness.

"The day finally came when I received a formal proposal of marriage. My mother wept. My father asked me: 'What do you think?' I answered him that I accepted Pancho's proposal because I loved him. Though he was not rich, I preferred him to all the others. He was so good! I say again to him, *never did my love for him, so full of tenderness, hinder me from loving God.* I loved him with a great simplicity, as wholly enveloped in my love for Jesus. I did not see there was any other pathway for me to come to God. . . .

"The eve of my wedding, I was given a white dress. I cannot express how fearful I felt on seeing it. It was very expensive, very elegant and along with it I was given a complete trousseau: magnificent ear-rings with gleaming pearls, a cross studded with diamonds (which later on became the stance of the monstrance of the cloister), a necklace, some jewels, (which did not impress me much for I have always been quite indifferent toward jewelry) and finally, a great number of gifts, and a lot of clothing. . . And I, what did I feel? I felt great sorrow, a strange fear and an indescribable suffering. I married Francisco Armida on November 8.

From midnight of November 7, until 8 a.m., I prayed with all my heart. I recited fifteen decades of the rosary, up to the moment when I was to make a contract with obligations. I was still unsure about many things. At about 6 a.m., Pancho and I received Communion at the Church of St. John of God. Right after, both of us returned home, to get everything ready. I prayed to Jesus to help me be a good wife and make happy the man He was giving me as a companion. I put on my white wedding dress embroidered with orange blossoms. Later I offered up part of my dress to the Immaculate Virgin and the rest I used to decorate the prie-Dieu of my future children on their First Communion and to fashion pillows for the poor on Christmas Eve. They placed a veil and a crown on me. Thus garbed, I knelt down to ask for my parents' blessing. They gave it to me whole heartedly but in tears. We left in a carriage for the church of Carmel, which was magnificently decorated with white flowers.

"The ceremony was performed at 8 a.m., presided over by my uncle, Canon Luis Arias, my mother's brother. I attended Mass with great devotion, then I returned to my parents' home for the customary greetings and for the civil ceremony. Somewhat later we went to get our pictures taken. Finally, we went to the *Quinta de San Jose* where there was a banquet and a dance up to midnight (*Aut.*, 1, 104-108).

"I remember that at the wedding banquet, when toasts were being made, I got the idea to ask him, who was now my husband, to promise he would do two things for me: allow me to receive Communion every day and never to be jealous. Poor soul! He was so good that many a year later, he stayed home with the children waiting for me to come back from church. During his last illness, he asked me whether I had gone to receive Our Lord. God must have rewarded him for this favor which made up my whole life.

"When evening came my brother Octaviano called me. He wanted me to leave with Pancho right away, without my mother being aware we were leaving. I felt terribly uneasy. Silently and in tears, awfully confused I left. Pancho consoled me but I was very upset on going off alone with him. We finally arrived at our house, brilliantly lighted and filled with white roses (*Aut.*, 1, 110).

"My husband was always a perfect model of respect and tenderness. Many priests assured me that God had chosen him for me as an exceptional favor. He was a model of a husband and of virtue (*Aut.*, 1, 111).

" One month after my marriage, December 8, I celebrated my twenty-second birthday but I was already not well, not knowing how long the illness would last and unable to receive Communion. How many things happen in one's life! I had come into this house, filled with flowers and brilliantly lit and nine months later, I left it in the middle of the night, fleeing in terror from a fire, never to come back" (*Aut.*, 1, 112).

With My Husband and My Children

"On September 28, 1885, at 9 p.m., on a Monday, my first child was born. I offered him up to the Lord with all my heart before his birth and as soon as he came into the world. His father, as soon as he was born, fell on his knees, sobbing and thanking God. The Lord enabled me to nurse him for eight months, then I had to wean him. I had quite a few difficulties with him. He did not want a wet-nurse and so had to be fed donkey's milk instead, evidently the most like mine!

"Here is another bit of nonsense I relate with a laugh. I wanted his first word to be 'mama,' but it was 'cat.' This hurt me, being as naive as always. This child; as soon as his father made him study, was perfect. I can only say that he was studious, smart, very upright, with self-respect, ever properly behaved, impetuous but kind-hearted. It seemed to me that the Lord destined him for marriage (*Aut.* 1, 114-115).

"My husband followed a schedule for leaving and returning home from work. I took advantage of this for speaking to my Jesus, for spiritual reading and for doing penance, removing my haircloth belt at the moment he was about to arrive. Once he noticed it and was annoyed. He said I had enough suffering with my children, with nursing them, and with my illnesses. As for me, I felt sure this was not enough, but had to look for even further opportunities for suffering. Later on I shall tell how the Lord took care so that I was not seen while I was writing. My confessor forbade me, for three years, to impose any penances on myself. I did what he told me (*Aut.* 1, 129-130).

"In 1887, on March 28, on a Monday at midnight, my son Carlos was born. I was able to nurse him. He was a very lively child, intelligent and precocious. He lived only six years and died of typhoid fever on March 10, 1893. In the midst of his sufferings, he said: 'May Thy will be done on earth as it is in Heaven.' He suffered a great deal and died without being confirmed. My sorrow has never left me. His death was heartbreaking for me, and I felt such pain as I had never felt before. I could not tear myself away from him, but the voice of obedience speaks and immediately I made the sacrifice of leaving him behind.

" In these very days, there had been inflation, and my husband's business was so badly affected that he had to borrow some money to pay for his son's burial. At this period the Lord overwhelmed me with humiliations and financial difficulties. May God be blessed for everything!

"After Carlos' death, my soul felt strong desires for perfection. Scruples tormented me. My conscience reproached me for having told him the medicines he took were pleasant to the taste when they were not. I only wanted him to take them. I did not know how to overcome these scruples. Finally, as a last remembrance, I kept one of his garments. I felt my heart was attached to it. One day the Lord gave me the inspiration to make the sacrifice of giving it up and gave me the grace to do so. Only a mother could understand my feelings. I called a poor child to come in and I dressed him in Carlos' garment. On doing so I felt such sorrow as if my child had been taken away from me again (*Aut.* 1, 131-132).

"On January 23, 1889, my son Manuel was born at San Luis Potosi, in our house on Rosario Street where we had moved. To the sound of *Hail Mary's*, during the recitation of the Angelus this child who has cost me so dear was born. It was at this very same hour that Father Jose Camacho died. As soon as I heard of his death, I offered my son to the Lord sincerely, with all my heart. Some time later, I fell ill, but thank God, I was able to nurse him until he could walk. I wanted him christened Manuel because of my great devotion and love for the Holy Eucharist. It is celebrated on *Corpus Christi*. Manuel has always been very kind. He is simple, joyful, humble and docile and, after his childhood, much inclined to virtue and to the things of the Church. He was enlightened by the Spirit, beyond his age, as to detachment and the vanities of the world. I recall that when Manuel was around seven, his father was at table surrounded by his children and told them he could hardly wait for them to grow up to help him pay the expenses of the household. Manuel answered: 'I will help you, of course, but spiritually, in what concerns the soul, since I was not born to earn money, which is of the earth and a vanity.' Pancho and I looked at each other surprised at his answer.

"He passed through some periods of awful scruples. He was always very pious, without human respect, full of candor and simplicity. He was the most affectionate to me of all my children, even to extremes.

"God called him, listening to my prayers and his. Since he began to speak, together we asked for the immense grace of a religious vocation. The day of his First Communion and on great holy days, he fervently renewed this prayer. The Lord heard him. He entered the Society of Jesus November 12, 1906. He took his vows on December 8, 1908, when he was nineteen years and eleven months old (*Aut.* 1, 135-138). [He died a holy death in 1955 at Gijon, Spain, at the Immaculate College].

"My soul continued feeling strong desires for perfection. It aspired to attain something beyond, which eluded it. It experienced days of great fervor with intimate and very strong touches of divine love ever accompanied by sufferings which in some way or other have never left me.

"Was this virtue? I myself have often asked this. Since my

childhood, my soul has loudly called out for knowledge of virtues in order to practice them. I would spend long moments reflecting on this, lamenting my not understanding what I wanted to accomplish.

"One day on the feast of Corpus Christi, I went to the Cathedral to visit the Blessed Sacrament. Suddenly the Lord enwrapped me in a prayer of tranquility. Now I realize this is what it was. At that time I could only be aware that these effects were divine. Inflaming my soul, the Lord said to me: 'I promise that one day you will know the nature of virtues for I will place a great number of them within your reach, ones most of which are unknown to you.' I was completely astounded, not knowing what He meant. Who would have told me that ten years or even more later, the Lord would dictate to me more than 'two hundred virtues and vices' (*Aut.* 139-141).

"Worldly life wearied me very much. I had accustomed my husband, an excellent man, to come home early and find everything there without having to seek elsewhere certain diversions, but he insisted that I accompany him on some occasions although, deep within me, it was against my will.

"I surrounded him with a multitude of attentions. When his birthday came, I gave him eighteen or twenty presents. He was very good. He always treated me most delicately and all that I did for him was but little compared with what he deserved. He helped me put the children to bed and lull them to sleep. His home and his children, there was all his happiness! (*Aut.* 142-143).

"I wished that God would give me a daughter and not so many sons. One after the other I had three boys. After Manuel, the Lord sent her to me, setting her apart for Himself. . .

"It was a Monday. She was named Maria de la Concepcion. Without knowing it, she made me suffer a great deal. Her father and I cherished her with a special tenderness. I offered her right away to the Lord, with all my heart, that she might be all His. I strove to keep her as pure as a lily until her total consecration to the Lord, as I will tell later. I was able to nurse her all the time required, thanks to God. She was an enchantment for her father and both of us showered her with blessings. When she was six months old, I thought she was going to die. This was very serious.

"Some years later she had an attack of typhoid fever for forty days and, constantly hung between life and death. Her First Communion was her Viaticum. I offered her to the Lord as a bud to open up in the heavens if that was His divine will. But the Lord did not take her. He destined her to become His spouse on earth. . . During Concha's illness, the Lord dictated to me all those virtues He had promised me some years before.

"Concha was an angel, extremely pure, filled with hidden qualities and virtues. Modesty was her dominant note. How many virtues I saw her practice in the bosom of the family and in the intimacy of the home! She was a jewel, a pearl, a precious 'shell,' a lily. . . At fifteen she made a vow of virginity and at seventeen and a half she entered religion. . . A pure jewel not made for this world. . . . The Lord chose her for Himself (*Aut.* 1, 144-149).

"When we were married, my husband had an explosive temper, but as soon as the shock was over, he was quite confused. At the end of several years, he changed so much that his mother and his sisters were astounded. I think that this was the work of grace and of my personal efforts, the poor soul, constantly rubbing against the harsh flint that was me (*Aut.* 1, 151-152).

Relatives and Friends.

"The Lord made me undergo painful humiliations by my sisters-in-law. He willed that I appear in their eyes as useless and not very agreeable. No matter what I did, I never could please them. This went on for many a year, but with God's grace I managed to control myself. . . . This torment was quite beneficial for me, the more so since my husband often agreed with them. This resulted in my being able to forget about myself and brought me to think I was capable of nothing neither in my relations with others, nor with myself. When I spoke, no matter at what cost at first, because of my pride, I always praised my sisters-in-law, even before my own husband and my father- and mother-in-law, blaming myself. Thanks to God, I thus overcame my pride. I never let my husband have the least suspicion of the slight difficulties I felt on the part of his family. I did so, not out of virtue of course, but to maintain peace. I offered this up to the Lord. In the course of time this manner of behavior owned me, on his part, a great unmerited esteem.

"My father-in-law always liked me very much. For a long time he had not frequented the sacraments. I begged him to do so and made arrangements for him to go to confession. God granted me this grace and a short time later, he suddenly died.

"My mother-in-law admitted much later that at the beginning of my marriage she did not like me at all, but later, she felt great affection for me. This was true. She took my part even against her husband. She came looking for me and I spoke to her of God, teaching her as well as I could how to meditate. She was such a pure and simple soul and so good, though uneducated. She profited from everything. I was broken-hearted at her death. At first she did not frequent the sacraments, but later she began to do so and became very fervent, marked by her suffering (*Aut.* 1, 152-154).

"In the evening, at nightfall, I went to the church of St. John of God and there, close to the tabernacle, I emptied my heart close to Jesus. I offered Him my children, my husband, those of the household, asking Him for light and prudence for carrying out my duties" (*Aut.* 1, 156-157).

Her life was spent normally among the duties of her household and her social obligations, without being able to avoid unforeseen circumstances.

"One day, I had to go and visit a priest. On returning in the evening I was taken by surprise as there was no carriage nor trolley in sight. I was very upset and the time passed on. I decided to return on foot. I thought of several directions I might take. I did not know the way, and went into a shop to ask directions. Without my being able to avoid him, a man came out who frightened me. He offered to guide me. He came very close to me smelling of wine. We went along together ever moving on. Aware of the risk I ran, I commended myself to the Blessed Virgin. It was night. My husband had invited a friend for supper and here I was so far away! My God! I did not know where I was going to wind up. Never in my life had I felt such anxiety in a matter like this. At last, the Holy Virgin heard me. On turning onto a street, a trolley was coming along. I did not know in what direction I was going. I broke away from his embrace as he tried to stop me. I jumped onto the trolley. I was saved!" (*Aut.* 1, 42-43).

Spiritual Ascent

For understanding Conchita there is no need to look for extraordinary phenomena. Hers is a run of the mill holiness. A brief statement in her *Diary* reveals to us her state of soul as a young married woman: "Upon seeing, despite my husband's great goodness, marriage did not correspond to what I regarded as life's fullness, instinctively my heart drew closer and closer to God, seeking in Him what was wanting in it. The inner life of my soul had grown in spite of all the joys of the earth" (*Aut.* 1, 112-113). In the very bosom of the greatest joys of love, she feels the limitations and the ephemeral nature of all human love.

The true life of the saints is entirely "hidden now with Christ in God" (Col 3:3). The effects may be seen in their external behavior and often they themselves let us know the principal secret thereof. . . As for Conchita, we have her *Diary*. It is the key to everything. It enables us to follow her from the age of thirty-one to seventy-four. It is the main guide we shall use, without neglecting complimentary sources. She herself has let us know about her family life, the exceptional favors and graces she received since her most tender childhood, the tragic death of her brother Manuel, the veriable point of departure of a new life which directs her resolutely toward God, the profound influence Christ had over her whole being from the very first days of her marriage and her constant ascent toward perfection by way of the least things that happened in her home. In the daily course of this existence of a woman, to all appearances like that of all others, God prepares for the Church and for the world a great saint.

"Your Mission Will Be to Save Souls."

Something that happened unexpectedly furnished her the occasion for spending long days of silence, prayer and contact with God. For the first time in her life, she went to make a retreat, the "Spiritual Exercises" preached and directed by Father Antonio Plancarte y Labastida, later Abbot of Guadalupe. It was 1889 and Conchita was twenty-seven. Married, the mother of a family, a house mistress, with an exacting and somewhat jealous husband, she could not make a closed retreat. "I took part in it, coming and going, since I could not leave my children alone" (*Aut.* 1, 150-160). She hurries to get there in time for the instructions, spends as many moments as she can in silence and recollection, then hastens back home. Yet the Holy Spirit reaches souls as He wills. In Conchita's heart there arose, under the impulse of the Holy Spirit, an apostolic flame which will soon spread throughout the whole Church. In her simplicity and humility, at first she will never suspect the extent of God's designs. Her outlook did not go beyond that of a woman living an ordinary life in her home. God Himself is going to open up to her the horizons of the Redemption. "One day when I was getting ready with all my soul for all the Lord would ask of me, at a certain moment I clearly heard in the depths of my soul, without any doubt at all, these words which astonished me." He told me: 'Your mission will be to save souls.' I did not understand how I would do this. It seemed so strange and impossible. I thought there was question simply of sacrificing myself for my husband, my children and our servants. I made very practical resolutions, filled with fervor, redoubling my desire to love Him who is my love beyond measure. My heart had found its refuge and peace in solitude and prayer. But now I had to return to the world and my duties, having to pass through fire without burning myself, while at the same time this flame glowed more and more in my heart. The zeal to share with others the joy of what I had learned, devoured me and ardently increased.

"Now, precisely, at this time, I had to go for a while with my children to the country, to 'Jesus-Maria,' the farm of my brother Octaviano, which was near San Luis. As soon as I arrived, I decided to bring together women from the neighborhood, to give them some 'spiritual exercises,' explaining to them what I had learned. This brother of mine who was always very kind to me and who cherished me most fondly, agreed to this right away. Some sixty women assembled. It did not even come to my mind the least thought of becoming confused, or if I might be wrong or erroneous in what I said, or even whether this could be pretension or pride on my part. I felt within me a fire that burned and I desired to enkindle in other hearts this flame. This is all that mattered. So we began the 'spiritual exercises' in the chapel of the hacienda. I sat on a low chair in front of them and, just as 'in the kingdom of the blind the man with one eye is king,' these poor women enjoyed very much what I told them. They wept, filled with contrition, even wanting to confess their sins to me, which, of course, I would not let them do. At the end of the exercises several priests came to hear their confessions and they fervently received Holy Communion. I was very happy to speak to them of my Jesus and of His very blessed Mother! The days passed rapidly and hours flew by while they carried out such sweet occupations. At times Octaviano came to hear me and God helped me not to stumble while I was speaking. All this was done, of course, behind closed doors" (*Aut.* 1, 159-162).

Conchita looked for a director in order to make more certain progress toward God: "I felt myself filled with the desire of perfection. I had a vague idea of the gate, the way, the path on which I should await my Jesus. While I was pondering these projects, humbling myself, I spent many a day in desolation, anguish and darkness. . . I thirsted for the divine, with a burning thirst for Jesus but I felt myself crushed and as it were, lost on

the road of obscure faith and without hope. I spoke at length
to a priest about what was so deeply disturbing me, about my
ideal of perfection ever running through my mind. Doubtless the
Lord did not want him to understand. He talked to me about
poetry, nature, what touched on God but never about God
Himself! And the world strove to win me over, with creatures
to attract me. I recall I spent my time now and then looking
through journals of fashion, and remorse flooded my soul until
the day the Lord told me not to look at them any longer" (*Aut.*
1, 198-199).

Deceived and saddened at having come to a priest and received but banalities when she had come to him seeking God, she
redoubled her prayers. The Lord then sent her Father Alberto
Mir, S.J., who helped her very much, in the course of the first
ten years, in her ascent to God.

J.H.S.

The love of Christ animated each day more and more Conchita's heart and the least significant actions of her life. She
loved her husband and children passionately but as it it were "enwrapped in this same love" (*Aut.* 1, 105).

When but a child, at the family hacienda, and after she was
older, at her brother's farm, she had noticed that the owner's
mark was branded with a red hot iron on the cattle. She dreamed
she too would have branded on her flesh the effigy of Christ. A
similar case is found in the life of the saints, as, for instance, that
of blessed Henri Suzo, a Dominican. An even more similar case
is that of St. Jeanne de Chantal. When she was a young widow
her family asked her to remarry. To put a stop to this, she with-
drew into her bedroom and engraved over her heart the Name
"Jesus." The scars were still there when she died, while there
only remained a blurred last letter, an "S." St. Francis de Sales
made it quite clear that had he been there he would never have
allowed her to do it. Saints are at times more admirable than im-
mitable. The same might be said of Conchita.

"By dint of many a plea, I got my director's permission to engrave the initials on the feast of the Holy Name of Jesus, January 14, 1894. . . I cut on my bosom in large letters: J.H.S. No sooner had I done this than I felt a supernatural force which threw me, face down, on the floor, my eyes filled with tears and a burning flame within my heart. Vehemently and zealously I then asked the Lord for the salvation of souls: *Jesus, Savior of souls, save them, save them!*

"I remember nothing more: souls, souls for Jesus! That was all I desired. . . The ardor of my soul far surpassed the burning sensation of my body and I experienced an ineffable joy on feeling I belonged wholly to Jesus, just as a branded animal to its owner. Yes indeed, I belonged wholly to Jesus, to my Jesus who will save so many poor souls called to bring Him glory. Enraptured, I spent the rest of the day with an ardent desire of solitude and prayer but awaiting a visit I was to receive" (*Aut.* 205-206).

Such an act as this is dependent on the order of charisms and on the folly of the love in imitation of a Crucified God. It is explained by the exceptional mission of the foundress of the Works of the Cross called to be spread throughout the whole world. Thérèse of Lisieux, Conchita's favorite saint, however, used another way for proving to Jesus her loving folly, dreaming the love which refuses nothing, is in the Church. We must take into account people's temperaments, their personal grace and the mission of each one. It is the same Spirit which expresses itself in letters of fire and blood but also, no less forcefully, in absolute fidelity to the least sacrifice. In Christianity, heroism of the lowest is united to heroism of the highest in the transports of the same Spirit of Love.

The monogram inaugurated a new phase, the repercussions of which were felt on her *personal life*, on her *apostolic radiance*, and, in a charismatic way, through *divine illuminations for the benefit of the whole Church.*

This is so in the economy of salvation. Privileged actions sometimes extend their salvific effect on the whole Mystical Body of Christ. This was so, to a unique degree, of Mary's "fiat" which saved the world. With due proportion, the least human act has its effect on the history of the world and can only be adequately measured at the Last Judgment.

Spiritual Wedding with Christ

Conchita was the first beneficiary of her heroic act of total belonging and consecration to Christ through a gift of her blood.

"It seems to me that with the monogram, the Lord opened a door to lavish on me His graces. From that day on how He pursued me! What attention! What tenderness! What astounding kindness toward a miserable creature such as I! He never left me alone neither by day, nor by night, neither when I was praying nor when I was not. He kept telling me: 'I want you to be all mine! You are Mine now but I want you to be even more so Mine!' He said over and over: 'Come. I want to be spiritually married to you. I want to give you My Name and prepare you for great graces' " (*Aut.* 1, 208).

Monsignor Luis Martinez, Archbishop of Mexico, her last spiritual director, places at this period the singular grace of her spiritual wedding with Christ. Theologians have not ended their discussions on the unpublished case of a woman, wholly bound to conjugal life and mother of a large family, authentically elevated by the Lord to higher mystical states. God is the master of His gifts.

A New Stage: Joy in Suffering

A second result, even more marvelous, produced in her spiritual life, was that of experiencing joy in suffering. Thus Christ Crucified enjoyed on the summit of His soul the Beatific Vision, at the same time by His physical and moral sufferings He was "the Man of Sorrows" (Is 53:3).

After the monogram, Conchita is flooded with graces and divine favors. She wants to be like Christ on the Cross. She has but one desire: "to sacrifice all for Him, with the greatest joy, for Him alone and out of pure love . . . would want to be an apostle, going about the world, proclaiming, manifesting and making known Him who is Jesus!" (April-May 1894). She would give her life to bring Him "an atom of glory" (*Aut.* 2, 7). She lived "wholly in God and always in God" (*Diary*, April 2, 1894). She rendered an account to her director of this state of her soul: "I feel as if I were transported into another atmosphere ... I can neither think nor move myself save in God, within God. In me, God is all within me and I am all in Him, in a sphere of light and divine things" (*Diary*, April-July 1894).

Now Conchita knows it by experience: the divine union is inseparable from suffering. To the measure she approaches Christ, the Cross rises higher and higher on the horizon. In her there takes place a profound confusion: "There are priceless moments during which I feel—a strange phenomenon—as it were a joy at the heart of suffering. My soul tastes of delights till then unknown. Without lessening in the least, pain takes on a feeling of suavity which engenders the act of abandonment to the divine will and happiness in pleasing Him. . . I have never felt like this. *I have experienced today in my soul an extraordinary thing: union in suffering*" (*Diary*, April 30, 1894).

"Very rarely had I experienced within me such effects: rejoicing at the heart of suffering! That seemed incredible to me who had turned my back on it, tried to avoid it countless times despite the attraction God had given me toward hidden suffering. How could I not but be amazed that, from evening to morning, I might well say, suddenly, when the soul is engulfed in pain, at these very moments, almost of despair, there comes a gentle breeze, changing parching arid suffering into a pleasant freshness, without other desire than to please the Beloved, without dreaming any more about the pleasure of future goods. No, all this becomes or appears secondary in comparison with the joy of pleasing Him. Oh, the wonders of grace! My soul loses itself in these spaces up to now unknown to me in my wretchedness, and which I thought I would never be able to reach. These favors, in truth, are gratuitous and unmerited. What bounty on the part of God, bounty without limit, immense, infinite as Himself!

"I believe the union of suffering is stronger, more indestructible than that of love, the one producing the other. Union on the Cross makes spring from the soul the most sublime and selfless love. It is the purest love, without admixture of egoism or self-love. The love of suffering is the love of Jesus, solid and authentic. May no one deprive me of this quite hidden treasure, one which is mine. . . Yes, I want to hide my pain. It is now the treasure which unites me with this other treasure: my Jesus. I am ready to drink my chalice down to the last drop. . . Yes, Lord, solely for covering You with glory, no matter how wretched I am" (*Diary*, May 2, 1894).

Apostle of the Cross

The monogram which came to transform her personal life, prepared Conchita for her apostolic vocation of the Cross. What is remarkable in the inscribing of the Holy Name of Jesus on their bosoms by St. Jeanne de Chantal and Conchita, was the different meaning of their deed of love. For St. Jeanne it was the supreme affirmation of her unique love for Jesus Christ. For Conchita it was the unexpected explosion and we might say, the eruption of her inner fire, of her indivisible love of God and of men. It is right, then, for her religious family to date the birth of the Works of the Cross from the monogram.

Some time after the monogram, while Conchita was praying in the Jesuit church at San Luis Potosi, her native town, there suddenly appeared to her the Holy Spirit, the Spirit of Love, illumining and enkindling from on high all the Works of the Cross.

"I was meditating devoutly on God, when all of a sudden I saw a vast tableau of very vivid light, growing brighter and brighter at its center. A white light! And most surprising, above this ocean, this abyss of light with its thousand rays of gold and fire, I saw a dove, an all white dove, its wings spread, covering I know not how, this whole torrent of light. I understood that there was here a vision most elevated and impenetrable, profound and divine. It left me with an impression of suavity, of peace, of love, of purity and of humility. How can the unexpressible be expressed?

"Two or three days after this vision—an inexplicable thing—I saw, one afternoon, in the same Jesuit church—a happy afternoon—I saw again a white dove in a large hearth whence flared brilliant and sparkling rays of light. The Dove, once again with its wings outspread, was perched at the center, and beneath It, at the bottom of this immensity of light was a large Cross, a very large one, with a heart at the center (*Aut.* 1, 211-213).

"The Cross seemed to float in a twilight of clouds of fire from within. From below the Cross there flared myriads of rays of light, which could be clearly distinguished from the white light of the Dove, and the fire of the clouds. They were like three different grades of light, how beautiful!

"The heart was alive, beating, human, but glorified, surrounded by a material fire which seemed to glow, and sparkle as in a hearth. Above it there flared other different flames, like tongues of fire of a higher quality or grade, I shall say. The heart was surrounded by luminous rays, longer at first and then becoming smaller, distinguishable from the flames which were below, and from the dim light and the most brilliant disc which encircled it.

"The flames which blazed up from the hearth ascended rapidly as if dispatched with great force, covering and revealing the tiny crosses fastened within the heart.

"The thorns which encircled the heart hurt us on seeing them as if they pressed against this so delicate and tender heart.

"I was able to describe all this because, many a time, day and night, this very beautiful Cross was presented to me, though without the Dove. What does that mean? That is what I asked myself. What does the Lord wish? I rendered an account to my director. At first he told me to disregard this, then, inspired by God, I think, he wrote me a letter for my soul in which he said: 'You will save many a soul through the apostolate of the Cross.' He simply wished to speak of my sacrifices, united to those of the Lord. He never thought that this formula could designate the name of the Works of the Cross. As far as I was concerned, on reading this, I only knew what I felt: this name must characterize the Work which the Lord began and of which I was now speaking" (*Aut.* 1 214-215).

God came to choose this young woman, married and the mother of a family, a simple lay person, to make us be mindful of the mystery of salvation of the world by the Cross.

"The Lord told me: 'The world is buried in sensuality, no longer is sacrifice loved and no longer is its sweetness known. I wish the Cross to reign. Today it is presented to the world with my Heart, so that it may bring souls to make sacrifices. No true love is without sacrifice. It is only in My crucified Heart, that the ineffable sweetness of my Heart can be tasted. Seen from the outside, the Cross is bitter and harsh, but as soon as tasted, penetrating and savoring it, there is no greater pleasure. Therein is the repose of the soul, the soul inebriated by love, therein its delights, its life' " (*Aut.* 1, 216-218).

Here we have the prophetic announcement of the contemplatives of the Cross. All are consecrated to a life of immolation of love: "I was praying, when, all at once, there was presented to my interior view, a lengthy process of nuns, bearing a great red cross. . . They passed along two by two, looking at me often on going by. Some days later, the Lord told me: 'There will also be a Congregation of men, after this foundation for women, but I will speak to you of this later, at a more opportune time.' There are now some four hundred nuns in Mexico, in Guatemala and in Spain" (*Aut.* 1).

The message of the Cross was to be introduced to the whole Church: "Yes, this apostolate of the Cross will spread to the entire world and will give Me great glory."

Finally the Lord reveals to Conchita that she will have to continue in the Church the work of Margaret Mary. Here is what she says to her director in reference to this: "Father, I hesitate to tell you this, but it was Jesus Himself who evoked the memory of Margaret Mary. He told me that He had chosen both of us, one for one thing, the other for another, that is, one to reveal His Love and the other to reveal His suffering. . . Do you understand me?" (*Diary*, May 1894).

In a letter to Father Jose Alzola, Jesuit provincial, Conchita expresses this more clearly. "The Apostolate of the Cross is the work which continues and completes that of My Heart and which was revealed to Blessed Margaret Mary. I tell you that this does not mean only My external Cross as a divine instrument of Redemption. This Cross is presented to the world to bring souls toward My Heart, pierced on that Cross. The essence of this Work consists in making known the *Interior Sufferings* of My Heart which are ignored, and which constitute for Me a more painful Passion than that which My Body underwent on Calvary, on account of its intensity and its duration, mystically perpetuated in the Eucharist. I tell you, up to this day, the world has known the love of My Heart manifested to Margaret Mary, but it was reserved for present times to make known its suffering, the symbols of which I had shown simply and in an external way. I say again, there must be a penetration into the *Interior* of this boundless ocean of bitterness and an extension of knowledge of it throughout the world for bringing about the union of the suffering of the faithful with the immensity of the sufferings of My Heart, for their suffering is mostly wasted. I wish them to profit from it by way of the Apostolate of the Cross for the benefit of souls and for the consolation of My Heart."

"A month ago, while I was traveling, the Lord told me suddenly: 'The Work of the Cross is the continuation of that of My Heart. It includes likewise the continuation of the revelations made to Margaret Mary'" (Letter to Fr. Alzola, Jesuit Provincial, Nov. 4, 1899).

Transfigured Daily Life

Conchita is not to be thought of as a mystic with ecstatic eyes and fixed attitudes. Her children told me over and over again: "There was nothing more natural than her external appearance."

This is the point they stressed most of all. "Even in church, we felt she was with us."

We read in her *Diary* pages revelatory of her manner of conceiving Christian perfection in the true spirit of the Gospel. It is interesting to analyze also what she entitles her *Retreat resolutions* she wrote at the end of her Spiritual Exercises, ten days, from September 20 to 30, 1894. Conchita was thirty-two at this time. They are not resolutions of a nun but of a married woman, mother of a family and mistress of a household. Her director advised her to divide them thus: seventeen points concerning her relations with her husband; twenty-three for her daily conduct with her children; and a final page, seven points, for orienting her attitude in justice, kindness and charity toward the servants of the house.

Here are some extracts:

"My husband: I will make every effort not to lose his trust in me but rather to increase it more and more. I will keep myself informed about his business, I will ask God for light to make some sage suggestions. . . I will act in such a way that he will find in me, consolation, holiness, sweetness and total abnegation. Equanimity will be evident under all circumstances, to such a point that he will see God working through me for his spiritual profit. . . . Never in any way will I speak ill of his family, I will always excuse them, I will keep silent, and trust they will respect me. . . . I will reasonably be concerned about economy, that nothing be lacking to anyone, and to carry out myself many things which involve expense. I will be ingenious under all circumstances. I will give as much alms as I can. . . . As to the education of my children, I will so act that we will always be in agreement, energetically and correctly on both parts . . .

My children: I will be very much concerned and vigilant about them. . . . I will recommend that they should be charitable to the poor, and suggest they deprive themselves of what they have for their personal use. . . I will not weary them by overloading them with prayers and making piety tedious. On the contrary, I will make every effort to make it agreeable to them and they will practice it, especially in the form of ejaculations. . . I will study each one's character and will encourage them in so far as it is proper, without ever giving way to my natural affection. As a rule, I will never yield and, without swerving, I will not change my decisions and resolves. I will learn how to impose them on them and at the same time gain their confidence. . . I will arrange it so that they see certain acts of piety practiced by their father, so that his example benefit them in everything he does. . . I will make men out of my sons teaching them to control themselves in the least things, without ever offending God. May He deign to grant me it. Rather death, a thousand times, than sin. I ask this of the Lord with all my heart. . . I will act toward my daughter in a very special manner."

House-servants: "I will see to it they act morally. . . I will give them monetary assistance and, I myself will if I can, help them when ill. . . I will be very much concerned about their souls, giving them opportunity to hear sermons, instructing them in religion, and seeing to it that they carry out their obligation to hear Mass" (*Diary*, Oct. 6, 1894).

This is how Conchita appeared to us. This young woman, thirty-two years old, was a model wife, mother and house mistress. She composed a *"Rule of life,"* for herself, which guides her conduct, but not rigidly, with concern for fidelity to God and service to others out of love.

Here are some more notes evocative of the spirit which animates her: "I propose to do ever what is most perfect. I propose to seek in all things Jesus and His Cross, inconformity with His holy will. I propose in my actions to pursue the interests of Christ and not my own."

But then she adds realistically and with a fine sense of adaptability: "I will never be disquieted should circumstances prevent me from observing my '*Rule of life.*' I will go on tranquilly. I will be flexible in the face of difficulties, humbly . . . then onward, ever onward!" (Extract from her *"Rule of life,"* Aug. 21, 1894).

Her social relations brought her to meetings and a variety of

amusements, as a woman of the world and mother of a family.
She did not shun them. She went everywhere with a smile, but her
heart was all given over to Christ. "In a short while, I am going
to the theater. I who fled the world with all my heart and soul,
must go there with my husband. I will have to go smiling and
happy, taking great care not to show the least discontentment
lest it displease him very much. Here I am on the cross on all
sides. O Jesus, help me! Give me the grace to know how to
compose myself and keep my heart inviolably faithful, learning
how to control myself so that nothing betrays me in the presence
of those who cannot understand me" (*Diary*, May 17, 1894).

Now here is how she conducted herself during Carnival time:
"Yesterday, I could not write. In the afternoon, I had to agree to
go with my husband for four hours in an open carriage in the
midst of the uproar of a dreadful crowd. As much as I could, I
multiplied acts of love, reparation and penitence" (*Diary*, Feb.
28, 1900). She was not a worldly woman who walked amid the
follies of Carnival, she brought upon the men and women who
are madly enjoying themselves the eyes of the Crucified.

She only felt at ease in her home and in the circle of her
family and her friends. Then she became the life of the party and
everyone wanted to meet her. She was fully aware that her place
as mother and educator was above all with her children: "I must
form the hearts of my eight children, fight against eight temperaments, keep them out of harm, introduce them to good and to
make progress in it. A great deal of patience, great prudence and
a great deal of virtue are necessary for carrying out this mission
of mother in a holy way. In all my prayers, the first cry from my
heart is to ask graces for my husband and my children. It is ob-
vious I expect everything from above, from this infinitely boun-
tiful God and from Mary, the Mother of us all, to whom I have
entrusted and commended them in a very special way. She will
be their shield, their light, their guide, their dearly beloved protectress. A loving devotion toward Her will save them from all
the dangers of this wretched world, so full of perils. Oh Mother,
help us, clothe us all with the mantle of Your purity, never aban-

don us until our eternal happiness has been assured. O Mary, encompass Your purity around my children! May they never stain their soul, so much loved! May they ever be devoted to God! May He alone be their very breath and life. Oh Virgin, watch over, safeguard them! They are Yours before they are mine" (*Diary*, Aug. 16, 1899).

Thus Conchita's daily life passed, as that of all mothers, in an alternance of pains and joys: "Yesterday, I celebrated my thirty-seventh birthday. Externally, it was for me a day filled with all the satisfactions I could wish from my husband, my children and other members of the family, and yet sadness, emptiness, filled my heart, still in suffering and struggling to control myself. I had had the joy of seeing my children receive many prizes at school and of hearing them loudly applauded. Yet this produced in me movements of vanity and I did my best to overcome them. I offered up to the Lord all the presents I received, remaining in my cherished poverty. I tremble when I think of my weakness, the world offers us so numerous occasions to give in and I feel myself capable of anything. Yesterday, I renewed my total oblation to the divine will, abandoning myself without reservation into the hands of God" (*Diary*, Dec. 9, 1899).

There were many household concerns and many health problems weighed heavily upon her at times. It was either she herself or her children who were seriously ill and death came into her home. "According to His superior designs the Lord reminded me of the gates of eternity, at the edge of the tomb. Hardly able to write, I took up my pen again to continue my *Diary*. An attack of pneumonia almost brought me to the grave. I am now convalescing but am weak and in pain, as well as undergoing many troubles. My youngest daughter too almost died. Another child has a contagious disease, which deprives me of seeing my eldest. What a heart-rending sorrow for a mother! Blessed be Thou, Lord!" (*Diary*, April 21, 1898). "And Jesus placed many another cross on my shoulders. Only God's help enabled me to bear all this patiently. I saw death very near. I had to practice truly and in the innermost depths of my soul total abandonment of my being into the arms of God, detached from my children, I, wife and mother, and this cost me dear. I found a great peace, at each instant, in keeping myself in the presence of God.

"At times fear came over me and one night, nestling myself in His arms, I said to the Lord: 'I am afraid.' He answered, 'Do not be afraid.' 'Be calm.' His words came true and from that moment on, I felt a peace of soul and a boundless confidence, with the certainty that I was not going to die" (*Diary*, April 21, 1898).

Thus her life passed on, sicknesses and infirmities piled up. She bore her suffering alone in her heart and on her face ever a smile. "The Lord told me: 'Do not complain about your sufferings before strangers. Do not let them see how you are in pain, that would lessen your merit. Suffer in silence. Let me work in you and walk the earth silently and obscurely crucified' " (*Diary*, April, 1898).

Her home was filled with joy and animation. "Mama always smiled," her children told me. When, at the end of my first sojourn in Mexico, in 1954, after questioning them down to the most minute details, I stated to her children: "Your mama was a great saint and a great mystic," they straightway replied, "Saint or mystic, we do not know, but mother, the greatest mother that ever lived!"

The "Inner Cloister"

Where is the secret of such a life to be found? Undoubtedly in her love for God and in an unbelievable love for Christ. Her daily life is transfigured by faith. Nothing makes her stand out from those who are around her. She is a woman whose life resembles that of all others. God fashions in her a model for women of today who live in their homes, where they carry on their daily occupations, with evangelical simplicity, faithful to all their duties, generous, devoted, at times heroic without the slightest suspicion of it. It is a new type of holiness of which the present day world has need. The Lord told Conchita: "I want to make of you a saint known to Me alone. That is why I take care of you, advise you, direct you, watch over you. . . . I want you to be a mirror of hidden virtues . . . nothing external. I am tired of this reef on which a great number of souls which should be Mine either perish or run aground. You, if you are Mine, if you listen to Me, if you content yourself, if you pass by everything, letting yourself be held back by nothing. Finally if your eyes and your heart are constantly fixed on Me, you will achieve what I expect of you" (*Diary*, April, 1895).

The Master knew that his humble servant, responding to His call, would follow Him along the paths of a hidden life: "I want to be a saint. This aspiration without bounds never leaves me, despite the weight of my misery. My soul has the desire, a great desire of sanctity under this form. So it is that I ask it of the Lord with all my heart. I want an obscure sanctity, like to the shades of night, one which God alone might see. I want daylight to let be seen only something contemptible and common place. Even more, in my heart there burns the ardent desire that the world judge me as *a worm, not a man*, as *the scorn of men, despised by the people*" (*Diary*, Sept. 19, 1897).

In order to be able to remain united to God in the midst of external agitations and daily tasks, Conchita took refuge in her *inner cloister*, as did St. Catherine of Sienna in her *inner cell*, where she constantly found Christ through faith and love.

Under diverse forms, they are the same instructions for union that Christ gives to all His disciples, as in His Last discourse to His Apostles: "Live on in Me, as I do in you. No more than a branch can bear fruit of itself apart from the vine, can you bear fruit apart from Me?" (Jn 15:4-5). He said again and again to Conchita: "I do not want you to expend yourself externally with creatures. No, your mission is other than that. You must correspond with it with an extreme fidelity. No more useless conversation and words. You are to live cloistered in the very inner sanctuary of your soul, for there is where dwells the Holy Spirit. It is in this sanctuary you must live and die. There are your delights, your consolations, your repose. Do not look elsewhere for it, you will never find it. It is for this purpose I have created you specially. From today on, enter into the innermost regions of your soul, into those areas so unknown to so many others but where is found that happiness which *I* am. Enter into it never to leave it.

"And here is the path which will lead you there: *the inner*, of which I have spoken to you so many times, offering you as your Mistress, Mary.

"There, you will find absolute purity, you will measure the amplitude of this virtue in all its fullness. There, you will discover a divine reflection in the purity of the soul. There, will await you the gifts and fruits of the Holy Spirit for your own sanctification and, through you, for the glorification of God. There, your soul will put on the wings and the might to go and lose yourself in this immensity of God of which you have had some experience. A much vaster field of virtues awaits you there that you may practice them and that you may comprehend them on letting yourself be crucified.

Here is your cloister, your religious perfection.

"It is not enough to immure your body, to be a nun . . . The 'inner cloister' is essential for the sanctification of the soul wishing to be all Mine. You must never leave this inner sanctuary, even in the midst of your outside obligations. This constant interior recollection will facilitate these activities in the very measure you will practice them in God's presence. . .

"You seek perfection to come closer to Me. You have there a practical path to reach it. The pure and recollected soul lives in Me and I in it, not confusion and pride, but in interior solitude and in the sacrifice of contempt of self. . .

"There, in this sanctuary, which no one sees, is found true virtue and consequently the contemplation of God and the dwelling of the Holy Spirit" (*Diary*, Aug. 15, 1897).

Divine Illuminations

Conchita lived in the heart of the world, cloistered in Christ. Then new horizons opened up. Her heart expanded to the dimensions of the Church. "The Lord unrolled before me spiritual panoramas which left me mute in admiration. Suddenly I found myself involved in the most profound secrets of the spiritual life. I contemplated its ravishing beauties, its formidable abysses, its delights and dangers. I do not know for what purpose and in what manner He conducted me in these so unknown areas. . . Why do these flashes of interior light burst out in me at any moment at all? Why do the supernatural and the divine present themselves to me so clearly? At times I think that all this is purely natural and within the range of my intelligence but I know the rudeness and limitations of my spirit and I cannot but admit that *such illuminations are extraordinary* and graces from heaven, even though I do not know their purpose" (*Diary*, March 21, 1901).

God had predestined a simple lay woman, without scholarly culture, to illumine His Church. Therein, unquestionably, is the reason for these divine illuminations which astound us and which cannot be explained save by the special illumination of the Holy Spirit, supernatural intuitions touching on the most fundamental mysteries of Christianity. We shall cite but a few examples lest we render dull the simple relation of the film of her life, reserving for a second part, the account of her great spiritual themes. The Lord enlightened her about the paths of holiness, about the mysteries of the Church, about priests, and above all progressively about the mystery of God and the abysses of the Trinity, not speculatively and abstractedly, but ever in relation to her person and concrete life for helping her ascend to God.

Lights on the Immensity of God

Here are some of these dogmatic elevations on the immensity of God, on the essence of Him who is, on the Trinity and the Incarnation and on the eternal Generation of the Word.

"I received and experienced most vivid lights on the immensity of God. . . . I saw God so great, so infinite in each and every one of His attributes. I felt lost like a drop of water in this ocean, like an imperceptible atom on these vast horizons. I felt myself submerged in God. I embraced His infinite bosom, feeling myself overcome with the infinite thirst of my heart. I found my joy on feeling that nothing was lessened in God, ever like unto Himself. What a marvel! A marvel impossible to explain. I could only perceive and savor it. I experienced also an inexplicable spiritual joyfulness on scrutinizing my nothingness before His infinite altitude, on becoming aware of my impotence and of my weakness before His grandeur and omnipotence. I rejoiced in my nothingness and fragility, in my misery, feeling Him, my God, of such grandeur, of such infinitude for ever and ever, world without end. . .

At other times, I experienced this illuminating, formidable presence of my God within the innermost depths of my being, an infinite thirst, an irresistible and constant impulse toward this unique Being, who alone was capable of satisfying me. . . I felt inside me, a kind of harmony and resemblance to God Himself. And I said to myself: 'How can one doubt the existence of the soul and its immortality?' Those who do, poor things, have never experienced what I endeavored to express.

"At yet other times, I felt a soaring of the soul, like a great flame which rises ever higher, like to, I thought, a mass of steam which ascends and overcomes all obstacles, losing itself, being dissolved, in the object of its desires. 'God! God!', I said again and again. 'God! My God! . . .' This Being so great is all Mine. My Creator become my Redeemer. . . This life, wholly divine, eager to suffer and die to give me life on a cross . . . to die for me!

"Who would not have had their heart torn out on making such reflections! I had never felt so vehemently this immensity of God" (*Diary*, March 10, 1895).

"*I am Who Am.*"

With an impeccable doctrinal assurance, Conchita's spirit rises to the supreme summit of divine revelation where, according to Exodus (3:14) God manifests to Moses on Sinai His inmost nature as the God of the Covenant with His Chosen People. The scientific and architectural genius of a St. Thomas will discover in this privileged text "the sublime Truth" (*Contra Gentes*) which he will make the keystone of the arch of his *Summa theologica:* "I am existence itself." The entire Thomistic synthesis is ordered around this fundamental truth. If God speaks to a woman, if He reveals to her the secret of His Being, it is in order to establish consciousness of her nothingness and make of it the point of departure for her spiritual ascent. Had not the Lord announced the same basic truth to St. Catherine of Siena. . . ? At the debut of her divine visions, that is, at the time when Our Lord began to manifest Himself to the saint, He appeared to her one day while she was praying and said to her: "Do you know, my daughter, who you are and who I am? If you have this twofold knowledge you will be happy. You are she who is not. I am He who is. If you keep this truth in your heart, never will the enemy be able to deceive you, you will escape all his snares. Never will you consent to commit an act which is against My commandments, and you will readily acquire all grace, all truth, all clarity" (*Life* by Bl. Raymond de Capoue, Ch. X).

God spoke almost in the same way to the great Mexican mystic, who relates it in her *Diary*, still greatly perturbed by the revelation of this supreme truth.

"Eternally *I am: I am* covers all eternity. For Me there exists neither before, nor after, neither past, nor future. I cannot say *I have been* or *I shall be*, but eternally *I am.*

"Why do you tell me this, Lord, if I do not understand it?

"Before creation, at the bottom of My eternal Being, without beginning: I AM now. . . I AM eternally. I AM by My very self. Nothing was brought to Me. I bear in Me all the perfections and attributes which I produce from my own essence. I am blessed because I am eternal, ever enjoying within My own self, eternal Truth: Father, Son and Holy Spirit, the Whole in Unity, three Persons in one single substance, there is your God thrice Holy! Holy! Holy!

"And I, in truth, am confused. I cannot think, or reason and, then feel I am at such heights, I can but lower myself into the bottomless abyss of my nothingness. I close my eyes, I believe and I adore. . . !

"I believe there is no better lesson of humility than this. How can anyone believe, before God and in the presence of such grandeur, that he is something of grandeur, miserable atom that he is? How can he think he is something good in comparison with this goodness without limits? How can he declare himself perfect in the presence of such a light on these infinite perfections. How can he esteem himself pure, in the face of this eternal Truth. Oh what fools we are, we others, poor beings of this world, when we believe we are something or consider ourselves capable of the least thing!

"In truth, after I touched God and had an imperfect notion of His Being, I wanted to prostrate myself, my forehead and my heart, in the dust and never get up again" (*Diary*, Aug. 8, 1896).

Trinity and Incarnation

The Most Blessed Trinity also revealed Itself to her but by way of the Incarnation. It is ever thus with the mystics: through the humanity of Christ to the splendors of the Trinity.

"The Lord next elevated my spirit to the contemplation of the Incarnation of the Word. He made me understand most profound things in relation to the Most Holy Trinity of which He is the Second Person.

"The Lord told me: 'My Father existed from all eternity. He produced from the depths of Himself, of His own substance, of His very essence, His Word. From all eternity too, from the beginning, already there was the Word—God and the Father, who is God, the two Persons constituting but one same divine substance. But never, at any moment, were these divine Persons, the Father and the Son alone or only two. In this same eternity, but inspired by the Father and the Son, the Holy Spirit existed, reflection, substance, essence of the Father and the Son and, equally Person. The Holy Spirit is a divine reflection in the bosom of the same divinity, the reflection of Love in the bosom of Love itself. The Holy Spirit is the reflection of Light in the bosom of Light itself, the reflection of Life within Life itself and likewise of all the infinite perfections in the most intimate depths of eternal perfection. This communication of the same substance, of the same essence, of the same life and of the same perfections which form and are in reality one and the same essence, substance, life and perfection, constitute the eternal felicity of one and the same God and the endless complacencies of the august Trinity.'

"Oh! how great, immensely great is our God and, in Him what incomprehensible abysses for man and for angels! In the presence of this grandeur, I feel like the most miniscule atom, yet my finite soul on feeling capable of receiving a feeble reflection of this same greatness, dilates itself, filled with joy, contemplating the felicity, the eternity, the incomprehensibility of the immensity of its God.

"And is it there the Word is? I say to myself, greatly moved: It is from this throne He descends toward a poor atom of the earth. Oh my eternal God, how do I receive such condescension?

"Jesus continued: 'The Word, the Second Person of the Most Blessed Trinity, descended into the most pure womb of Mary and, conceived by the Holy Spirit, as I have told you at other times, the Word became incarnate and He has become man! A most profound humiliation which the Love of a God alone could bring about. The Word has made human nature His own. At the same time as His Body, He received a holy soul, a very pure soul which animated it. But on becoming man and on descending to earth, He no less remains a divine Person in His humanity as Redeemer.'

"I heard about this marvelous and sublime mystery, things so profound which I have to keep to myself alone, not being able to explain them to others, for want of words. . . .

"Tell me, Jesus, when I reflect on Your most blessed Incarnation, I ask myself, how did this come about? Would you be willing to explain it to me?

" 'In God,' the Lord deigned to answer me, 'although there

are three distinct Persons, there is but one will, one same substance, one same might. This will, this omnipotence brought about this mystery of the Incarnation of the Word, in this sense that the Holy Spirit, the Spirit of the Father and of the Son, is He who accomplished it . . . The Third Person is the bond of light and of Love, the divine source of all fecundity. Thus, when I myself was on the banks of the Jordan, before everyone, there appeared a dove, the symbol of the Holy Spirit. The voice of the Father was heard saying: *'This is my beloved Son. My favor rests on Him'* " (Mt 3:17); (*Diary*, Feb. 25, 1897).

Here we have the marvel of marvels:

The Eternal Generation of the Word

"One night, the Lord invites me to pray, raising my soul to these summits of the divinity which frightened me because of my great misery. This night, I resisted as much as I could. In punishment, my heart stayed in a glacial coldness.

"The next day, right after Communion, I felt a divine impulse. I resisted again, as much as possible, but not being able to meditate, I ended up by opening my soul to God, abandoning myself wholly to His will. Scarcely had I done so than I felt submerged in an abyss of light, of clarity, of some inexplicable thing which took away all my feelings, leaving my soul in suspense fixed on one single point, and this point was: God! God! abyss of purity and infinite splendors!

"There, I saw, (I rightly say: I saw, the better to express myself), I saw, I felt, what had never happened to me before: the eternal Generation. I did not know there had been in God a generation. I had never thought about it. An eternal Generation! A divine Generation! Oh, if I could express all that I feel in these words, which left their traces in my memory and in my heart. The impression I felt and experienced then about this divine Generation was so vivid that I still tremble at the thought and become as it were mute.

"I saw a large hearth with a most live and pure light. From

this increased light there burst forth dazzling rays of divine clarity. All was divine. It was one and the same divinity in an eternity without beginning. Then my soul, as it were transported to this place, contemplated this torrent of light, of fire, of life which came back so to say toward the very hearth whence it had come, as if flowing back and reflecting on itself. I do not know how to express myself. My God! In this dazzling splendor of light, of fire, of life, of one and the same divinity, I understand how there was brought about the Generation of the Word, of that Word which was from the beginning!

"I perfectly well know that none of these Three divine Persons is anterior to the other, but I cannot explain what I have seen nor can I explain the way in which I saw it.

In this production of the Word, endowed with all the perfections of the Father and forming two divine Persons in a single substance, one and the same will, one and the same might, one and the same beauty, one and the same light and one and the same love, in this unique instant there was established among these two Persons a complaisance, a felicity, a union of love, yes, as union which produced the Third Person, the Holy Spirit. He Himself brings all to perfection. He is the indispensable bond between the Father and the Son. Without Him, they could not exist. This indivisible unity is so fine, so perfect, so pure that it cannot be adequately understood on the earth not even in heaven, outside of God Himself. This divine Unity constitutes the felicity of the saints, the purity of the angels, the ardent flame of the seraphim.

"Oh Trinity! Blessed Trinity! Light of Light in which there appears not the slightest shadow, render me pure as crystal, pure so as to let the rays of Your divinity be visible in me. Oh eternal Generation! Oh Father, Son and Holy Spirit! I rejoice in the sublime secret of Your incomprehensible Felicity. I love you so that, if it were granted me to increase by an atom your beatitude, even at the price of my life and of my damnation—provided it be without sin I would do so. I do not know what I experience on contemplating this hearth of happiness in which They live the same Life! I saw the Three divine Persons, distinct but united in one and the same Center, one and the same love, one and the same substance, one and the same happiness and one and the same perfections" (*Diary*, July 17, 1897).

In view of such dogmatic elevations, I could not resist saying one day, at Rome, to his Eminence the Cardinal of Mexico, who personally knew the servant of God: "This is not only a woman but one inspired by God." He fully agreed.

"They Assure Me That My Spirit is of God."

Despite the personal discreetness of the servant of God in the founding of the Works of the Cross, this exceptional case of Conchita, involving many confidential matters, enthusiastically received or strongly opposed, could not fail to pose certain questions. The archbishop of Mexico was consulted. He ordered there be an examination into her life and writings. Conchita showed herself ever docile to the teachings and directives of the Church. "I believe in Her, in her divinity, in her indefectibility. I will shed my blood to defend the purity of her doctrine and of her dogmas." (*Diary*, March 31, 1900).

In October 1900, Conchita was examined by theologians and men of great qualification.

"October 1, 1900. Today, after a rigorous examination and after I prayed, the Very Reverend Mele, Visitor of the Congregation of the Heart of Mary, assured me that my spirt was of God and that he was ready to testify thereto."

The next day, October second, she simply says: "Today, Father del Moral, Visitor and Provincial of the Paulists, has confirmed that my spirit is of God."

Chapter III

WIDOW

"Oh night of solitude, of sorrows, of suffering! . . ."

The Death of My Husband

" On the seventeenth, at 6:55 p.m., the Lord took away from me the husband He had given me on earth for sixteen years, ten months and nine days. The Lord gave him to me, the Lord took him away from me. Blessed be His Holy Name! An interior presentiment on the night of the eleventh, had made me know, without understanding why, the Lord was about to ask me to sacrifice my husband's life, something to which my soul was disposed, but which my fleshly heart refused and which I rejected. In the course of this cruel interior sorrow, I was prostrate, offering myself to God's will, feeling grow in me, more and more, and clearly measuring it, the whole extent of the sacrifice.

"What struggles . . . what pains . . . what sufferings! This sword pierced my soul, without any assuagement, without any consolation. This very night, the Lord presented to me the chalice and made me drink of it drop by drop to the dregs. During these days, I visited the Tabernacle for sustenance and strength. Oh! If I had not been sustained by Him, then through my great weakness, I would have succumbed! I saw, I affirmed, moment by moment, that my husband was losing his life. What a model husband! What a model father! What an upright man! What finesse, what delicacy in his relations with me, so respectful in all his actions, so Christian in all his thoughts, so honest, so perfect in everything he did! My God! My heart is torn with pain and also with remorse that I did not reveal to him the secrets of my soul. To the measure that I saw our separation approaching, the tenderness of my heart toward him took on more and more considerable proportions. I felt I had no longer head, nor faith, nor reason, but only a heart. I experienced, as it were, horror for the spiritual life. What days I spent! What hours! What nights!

"Oh God's grace, of what are you capable! It is certain that during these days I could but pray thus: 'May Your will be done on earth as it is in heaven!' But from that moment on, I felt the force of the Holy Spirit for accepting the terrible blow which directly struck my heart and took away their father from my children (*Diary*, Sept. 27, 1901).

"I was already concerned with having him go to confession and receive Viaticum. I frequently recited the prayers of the dying and for the recommendation of his soul. I encouraged him in so far as I could, by ejaculatory prayers, acts of contrition, acts of love, hope and faith, in order to give him strength and courage. I said them over and over again with all my soul. In this way I spent hours until he expired, my soul suffering with him during his terrible agony . . . But no, I was not alone in my suffering. God was with me and sustained me.

"Four of my older children stood around his bed and saw him die. At this so solemn moment, I told them to be silent and two priests gave him absolution. Then, I recited the prayer of the deceased. My God! What my heart felt . . . You alone, You alone know. I fell right down on my knees and made to the Lord, with all my heart, the offering of perpetual chastity.

"After this I begged his pardon for all that may have offended him. Now that he saw all things, he must understand, it seemed to me, the reason why I did not reveal my spiritual secrets to him. After extreme unction, I had asked him to give his last counsels and blessing to each of his eight children, then, I asked him for his blessing, and we mutually pardoned each other. After he died, his children came up to him, one by one, and I asked them, before their father's corpse, to promise me they would be good and imitate his virtues to obtain a good death. Then with my eldest son, we laid him who was my companion in the coffin...

"Oh! A night of solitude, of sorrow and of suffering...." (*Diary*, Sept. 27, 1901).

Visit to the Cemetery

"What a sad day for my heart, the heart of a wife and mother, was this day, my husband's birthday.... Overcoming my feelings, I went to his tomb with my children to spend the morning there, right near his remains, praying and weeping....I recalled at that time how Jesus wept over Lazarus.... How real, my God, as a subject for meditation! That death is something terrible, something serious! Thinking of death one weighs time versus eternity, good versus evil, the passing and the ephemeral versus the real and the eternal. My God! How much I reflected, suffered and understood. The soil which covers him whom I loved so much, is still moist and has been recently turned. My children's and my own tears moistened this soil, this dust out of which we have been formed and to which we shall return. Then there passed through my imagination, in rapid flight, the years gone by and memories of them: sorrows, joys and dreams. In an instant all had vanished, like smoke at the breath of death.

"Oh! how ephemeral is life! How short our existence! How near to each other are the present and the past! What do we do when this time is not employed for God alone?" (*Diary*, Oct. 4, 1901).

Portrait of My Husband

"Here is a picture of what my husband was. He was very good, a Christian and a gentleman, honest, correct, intelligent and big-hearted. He was sensitive to adversity, full of tenderness toward me, an excellent father of a family, who had no other diversion than his children. They were his joy and he suffered greatly when they were ill. Very proper in his attitudes, refined, very polished in his manners, very attentive toward me, a home body, very simple, filled with deference and delicacy. He had a strong, energetic character, which, as time passed, he toned down. He showed great confidence in me, (he often spoke to me about his business, asking my opinion, even though it was worth nothing,) and an orderly methodical man.

"From the day after our wedding until his death, he let me receive Communion every day. I had laid down that condition on the day of our marriage. He kept his promise faithfully and took care of the children until I came back from church. Later, when he was gravely ill, he told me: 'Go to Communion.' I lived at the time opposite the church of the Incarnation. I left at the moment of consecration and quickly returned to be with him. I never read to him anything I wrote . . . At times he found me writing my *Account of conscience*. He said to me: 'They are spiritual matters I do not understand anything about them.'

"It was necessary sometimes to go with him to the theater or the dance, especially when we lived at San Luis. He never went alone.

"He had a great fear of death. When I read him some passages from the *Imitation of Jesus Christ*, we often came across the chapter 'on death.' He thought I did this deliberately. Two years before his death, I had the presentiment that he would not live very long. I told him this, begging him to profit by it for the good of his soul.

"He was somewhat jealous. When I was gravely ill, which happened on numerous occasions, he attended me day and night, not wanting anybody else to watch over me. Every Sunday he went to Basilica, the national sanctuary, to commend me to Our Lady of Guadalupe.

"Before dying, he made a general confession and his fear of death changed into perfect acceptance of the divine will. He said: 'To my mind, death is the moment I am failing most to my children but God knows what He is doing and I want to do His will.' I helped him die a good death. At that moment, my forehead resting on the forehead of him who was so good to me, I consecrated myself to God to be all for Him" (*Aut.* 1, 379-381).

Alone With My Eight Orphans

The first days of her widowhood were terrible for Conchita. Her doctors thought she was going to die. The thought of her husband followed her everywhere. "What consoles me most on recalling the tragedy which just took place, so cruel and heartbreaking for me, is not only that it was God's will, but also my husband's perfect conformity in accepting the divine will. So much the more since he himself, humanly speaking, judged that his mission was not yet fulfilled, leaving behind such little children. God knew what He was doing. When I told him my heart was crushed by sorrow, he answered: 'Why do you not think of God's will?'" (*Diary*, Sept. 27, 1901).

Another version, more detailed, has conserved for us the moving memory of her last intimate conversations with her husband. "He said to me: 'Concha, I am dying. . .' I replied, 'No, you are going to see God'" (*Aut.* 4:66). After having received Viaticum, he gave his blessing to his children. . . He insisted that I take special care of the youngest, Pedrito. . . Then, I asked him for his blessing, begging him to pardon me if I had ever possibly offended him. In turn, he did the same and asked me to bless him. I replied: 'I have always tried to please you. If God calls you, I want to carry out your last wish. What do you desire of me?' He answered, 'That you be wholly at God's disposal and at your children's'" (*Aut.* 4:60).

Her husband's death abruptly changed her life, leaving her at once courageous and desolate. "Today, my eldest became sixteen. Even when I control myself, I go through moments of despondency. My tears flow very often without my being able to hold them back. My heart of flesh recalls many a sorrowful memory. I suffer, drinking deep of sorrow. May God be blessed for all!

"The sound of my children crying over their father pierced my soul. . . My body is exhausted. Now it is that I feel wearied, for I never was far from my husband while he was ill neither during the day nor during the night, until he died. Some of the children became ill, the smallest above all. May the Lord sustain me with His cross" (*Diary*, Sept. 28, 1901).

On September 30, she sorrowfully wrote: "Today ends the month in which I have suffered most during my life."

In her despair, she turned to Mary: "Remember, Oh my Mother, that never was it known that anyone who had recourse to You was left unaided. I hope in You, I have confidence in You, I fly to You for protection. Mary, help me and my eight orphans" (*Diary*, Oct. 3, 1901).

Meeting with Father Rougier

It was precisely when Conchita had need of spiritual support that she met Father Felix Rougier. Each of them, in writing, has recounted this providential encounter from which was to be born the founding of the "Missionaries of the Holy Spirit," called by God to become, for the present epoch, the apostles of a renewal of the world by the Cross under the impulse of the Holy Spirit.

In Mexico, the Missionaries of the Holy Spirit preserve, as a precious relic, the confessional in which this encounter took place.

"On the third (Feb. 1903), I learned that there was at the church of the College de Filles (the name given the French parish) a priest, the Superior of the Marists, an affable person. This occurred around 4 p.m., and I became quite anxious to speak to him about the Cross.

"On the fourth, an interior force impelled me to go to this church. I went there. I pushed the button to let them know I was there. A priest, a stranger to me, whom I was just about able to see, came down. I went into the confessional and made my confession. I felt an extraordinary impulse to open up to him my soul, to speak to him about the Cross, the delights of suffering, the marvels of sorrow. I saw and I felt the echo of my feelings in his soul. I became aware that my words penetrated its depths.

I think that at that moment they were not my words. I perceived that I was speaking inflamed, fluently, in a way that was beyond myself. This came from the Holy Spirit.

"I spoke to him about the Works of the Cross and I felt that he was greatly enthused over them. I saw deep down into his soul and could fathom what was in his mind. I also understood that this soul would render to God a great glory of His Works. I sensed that he was blessed by the Cross, touched to the utmost depths of his soul. I sensed, too, that he was deeply impressed, piously affected in the vitals of his heart. I spoke to him about the cloister. Right away he asked me whether there were any in Mexico and whether there were any for men. 'No, there are none for men, but there will be,' I replied.

"I then returned home, very impressed by this surprising encounter, an encounter which seemed to be for the glory of God. None the less, I asked the Lord, for a long time that, if it was not according to His will, Father would not be able to find me nor even my address. By making inquiries, I do not know how, Father came. Without knowing each other we exchanged greetings. At once we began to speak of God and of the Works of the Cross. I continued seeing the impressions the Holy Spirit made on his soul and his desires for perfection. I suggested to him, if he wished, to offer himself up wholly to the Lord. He accepted, desirous of his perfection. I decided to write him this act of oblation for the next day. I invited him to be at the Monastery the following day, at ten in the morning, then we said goodbye" (*Diary*, Feb. 4, 1903).

The result of this encounter with Father Felix was that, through manifest signs, he became Conchita's spiritual director. Thus he became ever part of her life. At first he was the counselor of the contemplatives of the Cross at a difficult and delicate time when, for her first iron-fisted director who would suffer her to have no other director than he, God substituted an understanding and sage director who helped her greatly to ascend to God and in the direction of the nuns of the Cross. Father Felix, a Marist, faithfully rendered to his superiors an account of this unexpected meeting in which he believed God was calling him in a special way. The Father General of the Marists judged otherwise and made him stay in Europe. There Father Felix, with heroic obedience and faith as unshakable "as that of Abraham," waited, in silence, for God's hour.

God had placed close to Conchita a saint. When not having seen her for ten years, Father Felix met her again, his first words were simply: " I have not changed my opinion about the Works of the Cross." On his return to Mexico, at the very moment of his disembarking at Vera Cruz August 14, 1914, he met some Mexican bishops who (driven out by the persecution) were going to leave on the same ship. They knew him and loved him. They did not hide their amazement upon seeing him disembark, but Father courageously responded: "The Lord wants me to found His work during the agony of the nation."

Father Felix was no dreamer but rather a well-balanced, realistic man, with good common sense, as immovable as the rock of Monts d'Auvergne, his native place, and possessing the soul of a saint. Very Reverend Father Gillet, Master General of the Dominicans, who had known in Paris at Rome and in the course of his travels about the world, eminent personages, testified in 1938: "Of all the men I have met in my life, no one gave me so great an impression of sanctity as he."

Until the end of their lives Father Felix and Conchita worked together for the founding and development of the Works of the Cross. They mutually sought each other's advice, visiting each other while carrying out mutual projects, and in order to speak at length of God in as pure and holy a friendship, as that of St. Francis de Sales and St. Jeanne de Chantal.

The Divine Scalpel

By way of daily sufferings and joys, without anything special attracting attention to her life as a widow, entirely devoted to the education of her children, God carried on in this elite soul His work of purification and union. He was preparing in her a model for Christian homes. Her husband's death had crushed her: "I felt the divine scalpel in my soul cutting away all that attached me to the world." She understood right away that she must come close to God. It is there the true meaning of life is found." A powerful grace impels me to undertake, in my new state of life, a new way of perfection, of sacrifice, of solitude, of hidden life. . . . I understand that the Lord wants to purify me that I may be more His" (*Diary*, Sept. 27, 1901).

"All at once, I felt my existence change. A page had definitively been turned in the book of my life" (*Diary*, Oct. 9, 1901). "Now I realize how much my heart was attached to the world, how much I loved my husband, with a truly pure and holy love, but never measuring its extent, with not the slightest thought of its intensity until the moment I lost him. . . . In my life as a child, my family life, had so many imperfections! And in my life as a wife, how many regrets. I could neither be a daughter nor a wife. Let us see whether as a widow, I am going to seek my perfection and become a saint on carrying out the sacred duties of a mother" (*Diary*, Oct. 9, 1901).

The path of perfection for her was not that of a nun but of a mother, in the full sense of the word. By that path God was to bring her up rapidly to the highest summits of holiness.

Divine Favors

So she advances toward God. Her children keep her home. Without ever neglecting the duties of her state of life, she finds time to continue her apostolate of the Cross. She prays, writes her *Diary*, obeying always her spiritual director. She progresses toward God, now experiencing the light of consolation, now the darkness of desolation, now going through daily difficulties, now feeling joy. She is filled with divine grace, ever more and more. She confides to a bishop who was for her a father and a friend:

"Yes, the favors the Lord has deigned to grant me, despite my ingratitude, are innumerable.

"He carries me along, He envelops me in His immensity and

in His attributes. He unveils the mysteries, makes me feel and touch, I know not how, the mystery of the Blessed Trinity, the happiness of God within the communications of the three divine Persons, the eternal Generation, the sublime origin of the theological virtues and of virginity . . . this indivisible ensemble of the divine substance, of the Word, of the Holy Spirit, of grace, of light, finally the ineffable things which, if they are not from God, come from the devil, but in any case not from me.

"He communicates to me constantly lights for my self-knowledge which help me not exalt myself above my own wretchedness. At times I sense His presence, above all on receiving Communion, flooding me with His light, with His rays and purifying me. He has thus, by His divine voice, despite my resistance, dictated to me a whole treatise on perfect virtues and vices. He has bid me listen to Him, and even when I pretend not to understand, He does not let me rest until I have written it down fully.

"He told me that He has endowed me with the gift of purity and of humility and my confessors assure me that this is so, for surely, I do not know what impurity is. So I cannot take pride about it myself. It is solely divine grace. This comes from Him, from Him alone. In the midst of so many obligations, prior to his death, toward my husband, and after four years as a widow, toward my children, the Lord never lets me alone. He impels me, by the acceptance of sacrifice, to crucify myself, to desire suffering, martyrdom, to give my blood every day for the salvation of souls and for the Works of the Cross which bring Him such great glory.

"I have been ordered to have my spirit discerned by many Jesuits, two of whom are Provincials, by the Father Visitor of the Missionaries of the Heart of Mary, and by other priests, learned and virtuous men, and this with my confessor's permission. After I returned and after I asked them to pray, he enlightened me, and they all assured me that my spirit is of God, that the Works of the Cross come from Him, that I must have confidence and wait, taking the means offered me for achieving them.

"In the papers I have written on things so elevated that I do not understand them myself, for instance on the Word, on the Holy Spirit, on spiritual effects etc., they affirmed that there was no variance with the teachings and doctrine of the Holy Church which I love more than my life and to which I want to submit myself without reservation, with all my heart.

"I must follow the impulses of the Lord and keep practicing my way of life as a martyr, according to my vow of *ever suffering*, which the Lord had me make, several years ago, and which He helped me carry out.

"These are the divine favors. They are great but far greater are my sins and miseries. I do not understand how the Lord has made use of this poor instrument as a channel of His grace" (Statement made to Msgr. Leopoldo Ruiz y Flores, in 1905).

The Central Grace of Her Spiritual Life

When Conchita was forty, the hour arrived when the divine preparations were to be completed and end with the "central grace" of her spiritual life: *the mystical incarnation*. Throughout long years the Lord had given her a presentment of this grace of graces, the source of a multitude of other charisms and divine favors, all converging toward identification with the interior sentiments of the priestly soul of Christ.

Conchita returned time and again in her writings to speak of this signal grace but the principal account, the one closest to the event, the most immediate and spontaneous has been recorded in her *Diary*. Therein is clearly discerned three successive aspects: its preparation, its multiple consequences for her personal life and its apostolic radiance.

Preparation

"I want you to prepare yourself for the day when the Church celebrates the feast of the Incarnation of the Divine Word. On that day I descended to unite Myself with Mary, making Myself flesh in her most pure womb, for saving the world. This same day I want to unite Myself spiritually with your soul and give you a new life, a divine and immortal life, in time and in eternity.

"Prepare yourself, purify yourself, because the benefit I prepare for you is very great, immensely great. . ." (*Diary*, Feb. 17, 1897).

After she had understood this, on February 14, 1897 she felt a new force, an impulsion toward heaven, a great thirst for perfection and for purity of soul. She understood that she must be loved, and, year by year, she prepared herself for receiving what was promised her.

Conchita went on retreat March 20, 1906, avid for silence and recollection, resolved to be renewed. The retreat master was Father Mariano Duarte, S.J.

From the very first days, the Lord began to prepare Conchita for this supreme grace, in perfect keeping with her special vocation to the Cross. "Here I am on retreat. . . . Even now He urges me to practice virtues. Even now I feel His presence absorbs me. . . . Yes, oh my Life, speak to this heart which belongs wholly to You, speak to it in the solitude of Your cloister, in the atmosphere of Your Cross. From all eternity, by Your grace, you have made me come out of nothingness. . . . From my tenderest childhood you have drawn me to suffering. You have shown me the folly of love, but love of the Cross, you have transformed me into it" (*Diary* March 21, 1906).

"Lord, listen at this hour to the cry of my soul, during this retreat and this silence. This cry is most powerful, without any admixture of self love. You are going to listen to it then: 'Jesus, Savior of men, save them, save them, may they not perish! May they not fall into Hell. . . . May Your Cross hold them back and may the Holy Spirit sanctify them' (*Diary*, March 22, 1906).

While on retreat Conchita does not think of herself. She bears in her soul the anguish of the salvation of the world. She wants to save all men, her brothers.

"I feel in me, coming from heaven, a drive toward perfection, toward a new life" (*Diary*, March 23, 1906).

Fulfillment

Then, without undue emphasis, with evangelical simplicity, Conchita has described this sublime divine favor, carefully giving us the date of this major event of her life.

"March 25, the feast of the Annunciation of Our Lord: You have brought me to these holy exercises against every counsel of human prudence. You have given me health. You have also asked me from the first day, for the greatest sacrifices of the heart. You have then asked me to purify my heart of all the dust and affection of the world, so that I be all Yours. You desired me to belong wholly to You. Then you granted me contrition for my sins and the most vivid desire of purifying my poor soul as much as possible. All that is past. Yesterday I acknowledged all the faults of my life. Ever waiting, year after year, I expected today, trembling, what the Lord had promised me. I humbled myself, thinking that it was pride to expect to see come about what eight or nine years ago the Lord had offered or asked of me.

"Around a quarter after midnight, I rose, prostrating myself face down on the ground, I celebrated this sublime mystery of the Incarnation which, I know not why, ever filled me with wonder. At ten minutes after four, I stretched myself out upon *the roses* (thorns) for an hour. Then I wanted to make my meditation on the mystery of the Incarnation, but was totally unable to do so. According to the *Exercises* I was supposed to make my meditation on the flight into Egypt.

"Before Mass, prostrate before the tabernacle, I humbled myself as much as possible. I begged the Lord's pardon, I renewed my vows, I promised Him that I would never let my heart be taken over by the things of the world as I had done up to now. Thus, my soul empty of all else, I received Him in Communion. I wanted to say many things to Him, the *Incarnatus est*, but I did not know what to say when the moment came. In fact, at the first Mementos for the living and the dead, I was taken over by the presence of my Jesus, quite close to me, hearing His divine voice which said to me: 'Here I am, I want to incarnate Myself mystically in your heart. I carry out what I promise. In countless ways I have prepared you for this grace. The hour has come to carry out My promise: Receive Me.'

"I then felt an inexpressible confusion. I imagined I had already received Christ in Communion, but He, as it were, reading my mind, continued: 'No, no, it is not so. You have received Me today quite differently. I have taken possession of your heart. I incarnate Myself mystically in it never to leave. Sin alone would be able to separate Me from you. I likewise warn you, every creature that might come to occupy it, would lessen in it My real presence. By that I mean, the effects, for I cannot undergo any diminution.' He added: 'Therein is a very great grace which My bounty has prepared for you. Humble yourself and be grateful.' I dared say to Him: 'Lord, what You had promised me, what You had asked of me, was it marriage?'

"That has already taken place. Now there is question of an infinitely greater grace."

"Would it be, my Jesus, spiritual marriage?"

"Much more than that. Marriage is a form of more external union; the grace of incarnating Me, of living and growing in your soul, never to leave it, to possess you and to be possessed by you as in one and the same substance, without obviously, you giving Me life; rather, it is I, who communicate it to your soul in a compenetration which cannot be comprehended: it is the grace of graces.

"There you have a mystic union, one that is greatest and most sublime, the greatest that can ever be. It is a union of the same nature as that of the union of heaven, except that in paradise the veil which conceals the Divinity disappears, but since the Divinity never separates itself from Me, the union, the intimate encounter of nothingness with All is the same thing."

"I really and truly felt my union with Him living and throbbing in the depths of my soul, having the same effects the Eucharist produces but with greater intensity. However I said to Him: 'Lord, what if this was a figment of my imagination or a delusion?' He replied: 'You will discern all that from the results flowing therefrom.' He continued: 'What fidelity I demand of you! For you keep ever in your soul my real and effective presence. What grace of predilection! I have been prodigal toward you with My graces, for I have My designs on your soul.'

"I do not merit this, my Jesus."

"No one merits it. Love Me. This kind of union is most profound, most intimate and, if your soul remains faithful, it will be an eternal union. You thought you were going to die, when I granted you this favor which I had promised you. I communicate to you a new life. Aspire to live it. It is all pure and holy, the life of your Jesus. He Himself is He who is Life, your Word which, from eternity loved you and prepared you for this day."

"I felt my spirit innundated with freshness, peace, infinite delights, but was it true? Yes, certainly, year after year I saw myself humiliated by this promise which apparently was never carried out. I did not understand it all. My tears flowed, such condescension seemed impossible to me. What to do, yes, what to do to correspond to it? Lord, Lord, what will I do but humble myself and beg Mary to thank You for me and imitate You, repeating in my lowliness and nothingness: 'Behold the handmaids of the Lord. Be it done unto Me according to Thy Word' " (*Diary*, March 25, 1906).

Consequences

In Conchita's spiritual journey, the mystical incarnation held a central place. Hence the major importance for grasping the whole historical significance. This involved not only its preparation and fulfillment, but its consequence for the rest of her life. Conchita was the first beneficiary. She better understood the fuller meaning of her vocation and of her mission. She was to be a victim for the Church in union with Christ—Priest and Host. Conchita's entire spiritual doctrine is marked by this sacerdotal character. The mystical incarnation eminently realized the "royal priesthood" of all the members of the family of Christ.

"Upon increasing Myself in your heart I had My designs: to

transform you into Me, *the man of sorrows.* You must live out
of My life and you already know that the Word became incarnate to suffer, not as Word but in My human nature and in My
very holy soul. A mother gives her life to her child in whom she
communicates her own substance. . . . I will give it to your soul
but plunged in suffering. This union will largely be painful, making you like unto Myself, if you assent so to do. In this intimate
union there awaits you a path of suffering. Without thinking,
run along it. May the Holy Spirit be your strength. He has
played a great role in this mystical and real union with your
soul, learn to correspond with Him and you will be happy.

"What shall I do, Jesus? Live my life and be docile to my will.
That demands of you a perfect and total fidelity to each one of
my inspirations. That is frightening, Lord! If you love Me, you
will triumph over everything. If you do not get covered with
dust, you will be My repose and in a hidden life, recollected and
faithful, you will hear My divine voice which will ever sustain you.

"And I, on my part, felt born within me as it were a new life,
a total abandonment, a detachment from all created things, an
immense love" (*Diary*, March 26, 1906).

Right after the mystical incarnation, God inspired her with
the "Chain of love" (*Cadena de amor*) which was to raise up a
spiritual elite wholly consecrated to God, in the service of His
Church.

"You are at the same time altar and priest, for you possess the
most holy Victim of Calvary and of the eucharist and you have
the power to offer Him continually to the eternal Father for the
salvation of the world. Therein lies the most precious fruit of the
great favor of My mystical incarnation in your heart. I have
given you that which is the greatest in heaven and on earth:
Myself, and precisely for this purpose, I have wanted you to
start the 'Chain of love.' I have put in your hands a deposit of
immense value with which heaven may be bought. Alone, what
would you be able to do? But with Me, united to Me, by the
merits of this same price of ransom, the Word Himself, you will

be able to continue saving men, thousands and thousands of souls. You have nothing for yourself, but with Me, you possess all. Do you understand why this grace has now been given you?"

"Yes, My adorable Jesus, I now see that I will not be able to carry out my mission of saving souls save in possessing You and in offering myself to You."

"You will be My altar and at the same time My victim. Offer yourself in union with Me, offer Me at each moment to the eternal Father, with the so exhalted purpose of saving souls and of glorifying Him. Forget everything and above all forget yourself. Let that be your constant occupation. You have received a sublime mission, the mission of a priest. Admire My bounty and show your gratitude. Without your knowing it, I have given you what you desired so much, and much, much more than that: the ability to be a priest, not that of holding Me in your hands but in your heart and the grace of never separating Myself from you. Achieve the grandiose finality of this grace. As you see, it is not for you alone but universal, obliging you with all possible purity to be at one and the same time altar and victim, consumed in holocaust with the other Victim, the sole Host which may be agreeable to God and which may save the world.

"Thus grace is the echo of the cry of your heart which greatly has moved me and which has obtained the founding of the Works of the Cross, devoted to the salvation of the world. You asked me to save men. I have come anew into your heart for saving them. Through the intermediary of the Works of the Cross, millions of souls are going to be joined to this new spirit of My bounty. My heart will find therein a great consolation, my Church support, my Father His glory, and the Holy Spirit will find souls" (*Diary*, June 21, 1906).

This grace of the mystical incarnation, a grace of overflowing fullness will be for Conchita the sign of extraordinary lights designed to be spread throughout the whole Church. There took place in her something analogous to the sublime graces and charisms received by St. John of the Cross in the prison at Toledo. After terrible mystical nights and a transforming union, he came out another man, a saint, a teacher whose spiritual radiance and doctrinal synthesis are called to enlighten the Church to the end of time.

Likewise, Conchita's *Diary*, in this period following the grace of the mystical incarnation, has manifested an incomparable richness. Her grand spiritual themes have revealed an amplitude up to then unequaled, embracing in a striking and concrete synthesis the widest horizons of the mysteries of the faith.

The laws of religious psychology have shown us, there is in the lives of God's servants an indivisible point which clarifies and harmonizes everything.

Isaiah: In the case of Isaiah, it is at the moment when the vision of the transcendental holiness of Yahweh is revealed to the Prophet.

Mother of God: In the Mother of God, it is the day of the Incarnation of the Word, at the moment of the Annunciation, when Mary becomes by her "*fiat*," at one and the same instant the Mother of God and the Mother of men.

St. Paul: In the case of St. Paul, the point occurs during his conversion on the road to Damascus, when God the Father revealed to him the divine filiation of Jesus and His identity with all the members of His Mystical Body.

Nearer to our times, the apparitions of the Immaculate Virgin to Bernadette of Lourdes brought about in her soul a radical change. By way of a phenomenon of amazing imitation, by her actions and gestures, by her interior feelings, Bernadette manifested in her body, in her smiling, in her soul, a reflection of the Immaculate. Bernadette herself said, manifesting thereby the secret of her sanctity: "I want to live like the vision."

Likewise we know through *l'Histoire d'une ame*, that on the feast of the Most Holy Trinity, God revealed Himself to Thérèse de Lisieux, His face shone radiant with love and mercy, the dogmatic foundation of the spiritual childhood which has led a multitude of souls to offer themselves, as did Thérèse, to merciful Love in a total response of love.

The mystical incarnation, March 25, 1906, was for Conchita

the "central grace" of her life, the key to her spiritual doctrine and to her mission in the Church of God.

She was able to conclude: "My soul seems to awaken from a dream. It seems to me that on penetrating into my soul, my Word has brought me in a new measure, more secret and hidden, more intimate and more luminous, where the Beloved dwells. . . .

"Now I am going to go home to carry out my duties there and meet again creatures which deprive me of some time to spend with You and to maintain a certain indispensable contact with the world. Since that is what You wish, I wish it too. . . .

"I came here alone, I leave with Him" (*Diary* March 30, 1906).

Voyage to the Holy Land and to Rome

Many Mexican bishops, learning of the good offices of the Apostolate of the Cross and the fervor of the contemplatives, ardently wished there be a similar foundation of Priests of the Cross, of which Conchita was likewise the inspirer. They addressed a petition to Rome, motivated by the pastoral needs of Mexico. After some consideration, Rome granted the permission requested. But alerted by some defamatory and caluminous maneuvers, a telegram suspended the application of the rescript, until an examination had been made into the private revelations, linked to the founding of the Congregation of men.

By order of the Congregation for Religious, Conchita had to send to Rome nine volumes of her *Life* in which, utilizing her *Spiritual Diary*, despite her repugnance, in all simplicity and loyalty she revealed all the secrets of her soul and of her life to the supreme authority of the Church.

The Holy Father himself wrote to Msgr. Ramon Ibarra, archbishop of Puebla, her spiritual director, as to a brother and to a friend: "I have read your letter in which you express your regret for the delay in granting permission to found the Congregation of the Priests of the Cross. I beg you to forgive me as well as the Congregation for Religious, if in so grave a matter we have thought it our duty to proceed with great seriousness before granting approval. For the rest, we assure you that this matter will be promptly submitted to the judgment of the Sacred Congregation and that with God's help, a solution will be arrived at according to your desires and that of your brothers (in the episcopate). So have courage, for a work acceptable to God, despite all difficulties, cannot be stayed by any opposition. In this hope we give you the Apostolic Blessing. Dearly beloved brother" (March 10, 1910, Pope Pius X).

To hasten this definitive solution, at the opportune moment, Msgr. Ramon Ibarra decided to bring Conchita to Rome, for a direct examination, on the occasion of a Mexican pilgrimage to the Holy Land. So she left for Europe and the East. She chose to bring with her two of her children, delighted with this voyage: Ignacio, a sturdy youth of twenty and Lupe, a very pretty young girl of fifteen.

On this voyage at stake were the fate of the Congregation of the Cross and the return of Father Felix, as founder.

The Itinerary

To Conchita's mind, this long tour was above all a "Pilgrimage to Lourdes, the Holy Land and Rome," as is shown by the title of a detailed and quite humorous booklet in which she wrote the account. It was a very fine voyage in perspective, with an itinerary inspired by devotion but equally by tourism, culture and the desire of a solution by Rome of a matter for the future which involved a primordial work of the Apostolate of the Cross. The voyage was to last six months.

The Departure from Mexico

"August 26. At half past six in the morning, we left for Veracruz. I felt very bad about leaving my friends and relatives.

"August 27. Pancho and Elisa came to say good-bye. I received Communion at the parish church at half past three in the afternoon. The ship sailed majestically leaving the land behind. It hurt having to leave my children behind. Archbishops Ibarra and Ruiz, Bishop Amador and thirty-two priests prayed we might have a bon voyage and we sang the very moving hymn to the Holy Spirit.

"August 30. Arrival at Havana. Since I was not well, I did not go ashore.

"August 31. Vigil in honor of Archbishop Ibarra's saint's day, attended by the Captain" (*Diary*, Aug. 1913).

Enroute to Europe

The sea was very rough, awful, and all the pottery was smashed. Conchita became horribly seasick. "This must be one of the sufferings of Hell," she said laughing.

After ten days of a tedious crossing, they came to Cadiz, then passed through the Straits of Gibraltar with a splendid view, and arrived at Barcelona.

On September 22, marveling at the sanctuary of Notre Dame de Monserrat, a unique panorama, her daughter suffered an attack of appendicitis. They later rejoined the group of voyagers at Marseilles, on a German ship.

Egypt

"October 7: arrival at Alexandria. We go by express to Cairo. I kept saying to myself. 'Here I am, in the land trodden by the feet of and where lived, breathed and suffered the divine exiles, the Holy Family. My soul is filled with emotion. All along the way, I give thanks to God, admiring the camels, the palms, the Bedouins crossing the Nile several times, reminding me of the moving passages in Holy Scriptures. I remember, deeply moved, the Prophets, the Pharaohs, the Israelites, upon seeing the fertile fields of sycamores, oranges, acacias wheres the captives labored. I felt another milieu, another atmosphere which impregnated my heart with memories and raised my soul to God" (*Diary*, Oct. 7, 1913).

The following is a brief account of a visit to Cairo. "There was the University Al-Azhar, with its five thousand students, who were studying the Koran, and there were the Tombs of the Mameluks. We see a wonderful sunset over the Nile. Later, a Turkish ship brings us to Jaffa. 'Lord, I now approach the land where You dwelt, where You spread Your doctrine and Your blood, for me, miserable me' " (*Diary*, Oct. 13, 1913).

Jerusalem

"October 13. A happy and great day of my life! My God, may You be blessed! We moved on toward Jerusalem and passed through extensive groves of oranges and olives, meeting with numerous herds with their Turkish shepherds. Numerous camels were stalking along. We passed through Hebrew colonies and historical sites. When the Holy City came into view, we fell down on our knees. Personally I recited a *Te Deum*. When the train stopped, the Archbishop kissed the ground as did all the pilgrims with him. We arrived at the *Casa Nova*. In my room I began to pray giving thanks to God with all my soul.

"At three, singing and in procession, we made our visit to the Holy Sepulcher. What pious emotions! My tears flowed as I kissed it.

"October 14. I have seen Calvary! What impressions, my God! I, under the altar, my forehead in the opening of the Cross. My tears flowed abundantly. There, He pronounced the seven words, out of an infinite heart; there, He gave me Mary as Mother; there, they pierced His Heart. Thereon, the Beloved of my soul was nailed. I stayed there as long as I could. I did not want to tear myself away from this blessed place. I put my arms in the opening of the Cross. I did so in such a way that my tears fell within it. I touched the hardness of the rock. I saw with my own eyes the place where the Most Holy Virgin and Mary Magdalene stood at the foot of the Cross.

"I saw the place where they stripped Jesus of His garments, there where they nailed Him onto the Cross. We saw the place where my Love was found while waiting for them to crucify

Him. I kissed many a time the stone of annointment. Emotions followed one upon the other and my heart was too small to sustain them.

"In the afternoon, I returned to the mount where my Jesus taught the *Our Father*. There are some nuns (Carmelites) there and the "Our Father" is written in thirty-five languages on colored tile in the cloister. Then we went to the Garden of Olives and into the grotto of the agony. From there we went to the tomb of the Blessed Virgin which is near the garden. Joyously we visited it. It is from there that our Immaculate Mother was assumed into heaven, filled with joy" (*Diary*, Oct. 13-14, 1913).

"We stayed in the Holy City and visited other holy places nearby: Bethlehem where the Savior of the world was born in a cradle; Ain-Karin with its memories of John the Baptist and of the Magnificat of the Virgin Mary in response to the salutation of Elizabeth, her elderly cousin. Later, good-bye to Jerusalem and we departed to Jaffa, Nazareth and the other Holy Places of Galilee. Nazareth dominates all. It is the Virgin's town, the place where the greatest miracles were performed, where the most important event in the history of man and of the universe, the Incarnation of God, took place."

Nazareth

"October 25. Very early in the morning I went to the holy grotto where the Incarnation of the Word of God took place. I would not be able to explain what I felt. There is an altar and above it an inscription announcing: *Here the Word became flesh.* I was exuberant. I heard many Masses and the hours I could stay there, I spent happily in this so loved place!

"The Lord told me: 'It is not by chance that you have come to this place: My bounty has drawn you here to grant you another grace. Here you will consecrate yourself very specially to the Most Holy Trinity. The Mystical Incarnation in your soul is not an illusion, even though you do not know how to appreciate it. It is a reality which will spread over this cold world and very specially among priests in view of its holy purposes: love of the Word of God by the Holy Spirit thereby to honor the Father' (*Diary*, Oct. 25, 1913).

"The visit to the Holy Land was over in Damascus and in Lebanon. Now we were on our way to Rome passing through Beirut, Port-Said, Alexandria and Italy. In Italy we passed through Brindisi, Naples, Pompey, Capri, Sorrento, celebrated names in the history of the Mediterranean basin" (*Diary*, Oct. 1913).

Rome

"Finally we are in the Holy City. After Jerusalem it is the city in which I was most interested. It is here the outcome will be decided, the triumph or the defeat of the Works of the Cross. That decision will be final, definitive. Yet, why doubt since the Lord wanted me to come. He told me I would be subjected to humiliations and sufferings but that the Works would soon triumph. Faith and trust! God knows how to fulfill His promises and He never abandons anyone who trusts in Him.

"We arrived in the evening. Msgr. Ruiz was at the station and gave me the bad news about the situation here of the Works of the Cross. Patience and trust in God. I hope against hope! My God! What a City so full of memories! How many saints shed their blood here! It is the cradle of our religion. But all this is only the consequence of Jerusalem. If there had not been a Savior there, there would not be a Savior here, nor a Church, nor martyrs, nor confessors, nor anyone who would love God. I think of Nero, the Caesars, the pagan and Christian history of this center of Christianity.

"What an impression in my soul on arriving in this Holy City! After Naples, I came, saying prayers, and was thrilled at seeing this place of so many of my dreams, an awesome place, the place where the Church alone can approve of the Priests of the Cross. So here I am right close to the Pope. I can hardly believe it. I desire to see him and I tremble at the sole thought. My God, I am at Your disposal, even to martyrdom, if such be Your will" (*Diary*, Nov., 1913).

Pontifical Audience

"Yesterday, in the evening, I learned that the private audience with the Pope was scheduled for ten-thirty today. A wonderful surprise! The moment arrived, They called me and I presented myself to the Vicar of Christ on earth. I do not know what emotion I felt. The Holy Father was at his office with Msgr Ramon Ibarra in front of him. I knelt with tears in my eyes. He spoke to me. Finally, I regained my self-control and he asked me what I desired. 'I beg Your Holiness to approve of the Works of the Cross.' I expressed this while his hand was still touching my face.

"They are approved, do not fear, and I give you my very special blessing for you, your family and for all the Works."

"I said to him, 'Most Holy Father, I do not want to be an obstacle to these Works. Let them be apart from me and take no account of me.'

"I have spoken with Monsignor. Everything will be arranged this year."

"He looked at me with penetrating and gentle eyes, and I felt as if I was at the feet of Our Lord. He blessed me many times: 'Pray for me,' he said. He placed his hand on my head, and looked at me for a long while. I made bold to take his pectoral cross and kiss it, I kissed his feet and again he blessed me. I left radiant and joyous giving thanks to God. Oh what an unforgetable date! My God, may you be blessed" (*Diary*, Nov. 17, 1903).

Decisive Interview

Finally came the hour, so dreaded by Conchita, of an interview with Msgr. Donato Sbaretti, Secretary of the Congregation for Religious. He questioned her about her country, her life. Above all else he asked for explanations on the origins of the

Apostolate of the Cross and on the contemplative nuns. He asked her also whether she herself had written the manuscript volumes sent to Rome. He wanted to know whether she wrote with ease. "I answered him: 'Yes, although I do not know grammar.' But he would not believe it" (*Diary*, Dec. 7, 1913).

He had her state precisely the manner in which her visions of the Holy Spirit, of the Heart of Jesus, of the Cross of the Apostolate took place. Did she see all this with her bodily eyes? She gave him the account of the monogram, of the *dictates* of the Lord, of the division that occurred among the first sisters of the Cross. Conchita affirmed that she did not live with the nuns, but with her children. This satisfied him. . . . "I understood that on diverse points he saw quite clearly. I begged him earnestly that they do not require me to be part of the Works of the Cross, for I neither wanted to be, nor appear to be committed to them. I also told him that I would obey in everything the Holy Church" (*Diary*, Dec. 7, 1913).

Conchita wrote to Rome to Msgr. Sbaretti sending him, as he requested, the Spanish edition of her book "*Ante el Altar*" (Before the Altar), asking him to return her manuscripts, "intimate matters of her conscience," which she wanted back, leaving it, however, up to the decision of the Holy See.

"I tell you again, your Excellency, my greatest desire is to be a submissive and loving daughter of the Holy Church, obeying Her in all She will judge good to command. I have never wanted to deceive or delude myself, remaining ever disposed to follow God's voice in His Church, who is never deceived, while I can be. Thanks to God, I have always let myself be guided by obedience.

"I have no other ambition than to live a hidden, obscure life. I will follow with all my heart the path the Holy Church will lay out for me. I commend myself to your prayers, your Excellency, that I may be able to raise my children as good Christians" (Dec. 9, 1913).

In order to facilitate matters, in agreement with her, Msgr. Ibarra proposed the title *Priests of the Cross* be changed to *Mis-*

sionaries of the Holy Spirit, a change which Pius X personally approved.

"My soul is overflowing with joy. I think I am dreaming. My God, the God of my life, it has been eighteen years since you announced it to me. What pains, sufferings, penances, disappointments! What blood, prayers, calumnies, feelings of envy, persecutions, tears all this has cost. But it all is as nothing when I think that it was for purifying Your Works for Your greater glory (*Diary*, Dec. 22, 1913).

"While I was praying before the Blessed Sacrament, the Lord said to me: 'Thank Me. All is definitively concluded.' And right away I said the *Te Deum*" (*Diary*, Dec. 17, 1913).

Through Italy to France

The main purpose of the voyage was attained! After spending some ten days visiting places of art and religion in the Eternal City, the pilgrims visited Florence, the most artistic city in the world, Padua, Venice, Milan with its admirable cathedral. By way of Geneva, they reached France visiting Lyon and Paray-le-Monial, where she was drawn by her ardent devotion to the Heart of Jesus. "I would have loved to have stayed there for the rest of my life" (*Diary*, Jan. 9, 1914).

Now they moved on toward Paris. They arrived there at night, going along the grand avenues: "Paris, what a great city!" From Paris, Conchita went to Lisieux to entrust the Works of the Cross to *little Thérèse*.

Lisieux

"January 19. I went to Lisieux to visit the tomb of Sister Thérèse of the Infant Jesus, her convent and her house. It was snowing and unbelievably cold. I went to thank her since I had precisely commended to her all the Works of the Cross the cause of which had just triumphed. 'Little Thérèse of my soul, Thanks! Thanks!' We visited the monastery and her sister Pauline, now prioress, received us.

"January 20. We left Paris, Monsignor left this morning, the other pilgrims a bit later. Along with Mrs. Greville and Mrs. Paz Fernandez del Castillo, we took a night train and arrived in Lourdes at eleven in the morning" (*Diary*, 1914).

Lourdes

"January 21. We spent a bad night on the train. We arrived at Pau at eight o'clock and continued on to Lourdes. What a gorgeous panorama of snow-capped mountains! The Pyrenees are enchanting.

"We arrived at the station. We ate hungrily, then at once, we went on over a thick layer of snow. We visited the principal church, the Grotto and the beautiful Basilica of the Rosary. What lovely feelings! Here we felt the presence of the Blessed Virgin, her passage, her most particular protection. Kneeling in the grotto, we stayed contemplating this site in all its beauty, this place where Mary stood, in the course of eighteen apparitions. My mind went back to the past and my soul thrilled, recalling the number of graces and miracles lavished here.

"How often I remembered my mother who used to read to me enthusiastically, when I was a child, Henri Lasserre's book! How much she wanted to come to the scene of these religious events! My whole family dreamed of coming here with me, the most unworthy, the most miserable and so undeserving, the most indifferent. And here I am contemplating, marveling at this enchanted place. Thousands and thousands of candles were burning. The whole Grotto is black with smoke, even around the statue of Mary, located where Her apparitions took place. Only the rose bush, at the feet of the Virgin, keeping its freshness, flourished in the midst of the snow and smoke. What a marvel of God!

"We recited the Rosary walking along the ramps. We went to confession at the crypt. I prayed a great deal for the Works of the Cross, for my own, for poor Mexico. What sweet feelings! What charity on the part of Mary! At each hour the bells chimed the *Ave Marias* inviting us to glorify Mary. This produced an impression of enchantment. One feels so strongly here, Mary's presence, that there is no wish to leave" (*Diary*, Jan. 21, 1914).

In Spain With Her Son Manuel

The travelers took the train to Spain where her son Manuel awaited her. They enjoyed long hours of joy and togetherness. They went together to pray at Loyola and Manuel celebrated his twenty-fifth birthday with his mother. His brother Ignacio and his sister Lupe were there also. "How good God is to bring me here this day with him. We slowly walked about the countryside, with its beautiful scenery. On the bank of a stream I read him the diary of my voyage" (*Diary*, Jan. 1914).

On The Way Back

The entire group of pilgrims made their way back: there was San Sebastian, Pamplona, Barcelona, Valencia (Feb. 11). Then there was Malaga, Cadiz, Las Palmas, the Canary Islands, Puerto Rico (March 1), and Havana, Veracruz and Mexico (March 14, 1914).

On returning to Mexico, Conchita's first concern was to embrace her children. Then she hastened to the sanctuary of Nuestra Senora de Guadalupe, to thank the Blessed Virgin for her help in her triumph.

Conchita returned from Rome giving thanks to God. The Church had spoken.

Teacher of Her Children

The voyage to the Holy Land and to Rome has assured the future of the Works of the Cross. Conchita did not forget her duties as a mother, for in her eyes, they were her primary concern. She addressed to her director, Father Bernardo (Msgr. Maximo Ruiz), this capital statement one day: "It is a point about which I do not speak, I might say never, in my *Spiritual Diary*, namely about my children, when actually my concern to raise them occupies the greatest part of my life. I bear them constantly in my heart, and more so their souls than their bodies. Here is, pretty much the same prayer I make for each one of them, many times a day:

"Lord, preserve Pancho's righteousness, his balanced judgment with which You have endowed him. May he ever be as honest a man as his father. Grant him what is necessary for marriage, if that is for him, but free him from any relationships which are counter to Your divine will.

Lord, Ignacio worries me. He is so young and subject to danger. . . . Keep him in that purity of conscience which You have given him.

Lord, may Pablo be all Yours. Develop his humility and obedience.

Lord, may Salvador use his vivaciousness for his good and Your glory.

Lord, may this Lupe who is so lively, so well disposed to virtue, never fail to do what she should.

Lord, as to Manuel and Concha, those two souls so pure and so crucified for You, whom You have chosen from their youth, to adopt the better path, grant them perseverance, sustain them in their vocation. Make use of them for Your greater glory.

Lord, my two angels who are in heaven, Carlos and Pedro, may they ever attend You on Your throne.

Oh Mary, Mother of my soul, protectress of orphans, make Pancho's devotion to You ever grow. May it grow, too, in all my children. I give them to You as Your own. Cover them with Your mantle, keep them ever pure, keep them in Your Son's Heart, grant them good inclinations and love of the Cross. You know, I do not know how to educate them, I do not know how to be a mother, You know, Oh Mary. Shelter them in Your bosom, keep them pure for Jesus, Oh Mary, for Him alone" (*Diary*, Oct. 30, 1908).

Her life in union with God never estranged her from her family. On the contrary, never was a mother so mindful of her children as was Conchita.

The death of her first child, at the age of six, her little Carlos, left her crushed and bruised forever.

After she became a widow, the tragic death of her youngest child drowned in a pool in the garden of his home, caused her inconsolable anguish.

Pedrito's Corpse

"Tuesday of April seventh, a heart-breaking day for me:

"During Mass I was uneasy, interiorly urged, without knowing why, to go home. After a few household tasks were done, I started to sew. While I was sewing, suddenly I heard a voice which said to me: 'Pedrito is in the pool in the garden.' I thought he was calling me and automatically I repeated the same words: 'Pedrito is in the pool in the garden.' I ran, flew and the children who heard me, cried out to me: 'Yes, mama, he is here!' I did not see anything, for several instants I did not know what was happening to me. I took him in my arms, soaking wet, stiff . . . a corpse.

"A few minutes before, he had been at my side. The other children told me that on leaving the room, he told them that he was going to fetch some water for the pigeons. There were three servants near the pool, but no one saw him fall in. . . . I almost went out of my mind, trying as much as I could to resuscitate him, but in vain. His heart had stopped beating, and there was no pulse. His eyes had their pupils dilated and they were lifeless. My God! I felt my soul torn and, my son in my arms, I offered him to the Lord, in sorrow, bitterness, remorse, believing it was due to my negligence he was now dead. And I remembered how, at the moment of his death, that his father had left him in my care.

"Police officers came to make out an official report. Also a doctor and his assistant came, but all their efforts were in vain. I wrote my mother and Father Felix about what had happened, but the Lord willed I remain alone. My mother could come only five hours later and Father Felix only at night because he had not received my letter.

"I placed myself at the foot of my large Crucifix and there, bathing His feet in tears, prostrate, I offered Him the sacrifice of my son, asking Him that there be fulfilled in me His divine will. I spent the night, watching over the corpse of my son. At midnight I laid him in his little coffin. As I held him in my arms, he felt frozen. It was a terrible feeling" (*Diary*, April 7, 1903).

The Death of Pablo

Later on, it was Pablo who died in his mother's arms. He was a fine young man of eighteen, most pure, of whom she was specially fond.

"June 21, on the feast of St. Aloysius Gonzaga: Today Pablo received the last sacraments. This morning he wanted Father Pedro Jimenez to be called to whom he made quite willingly a general confession. When he had finished, his confessor told me: 'Do not ask that Pablo become well. He knows no evil, he is a pure soul. Let him go to heaven. He is a child, for in a few minutes he finished his general confession.'

"At half past three in the afternoon he received holy Communion, Viaticum and with fervor answering all the prayers. So as not to tire him, I had him make an act of thanksgiving somewhat later. He had a terrible headache, the result, it seemed, of typhoid fever.

"June 22. Today, Sunday, I had him removed from his room. He has a terrible fever. I was suffering very much but he was calm and resigned.

"Two or three days before he fell ill, after supper, he said to me: 'My little mama, very soon, you are going to see a dead man here.' I do not know what I felt then, but very early in the morning I got up to see whether he was dead. These days I frequently had a presentiment he would die and spoke to him while he was resting in bed, to see if he was alive. My God! Is it possible? Let this chalice pass from me! None the less Thy will be done not mine!

"June 25. He no longer recognized me. I stayed close by him. He cried out: 'I want my mama! Call my mama!' I do not know how I felt. I began to cry. His whole desire is to go and I, I sense death is coming. He never closed his beautiful blue eyes. For a few moments he fixed them on me. That look I keep in my heart.

"June 24. With a great effort, which was not my own, I helped him die a good death. I saw him agonize and expire, then, right after I had kissed his forehead, I began to pray. As soon as he died I put in his hands the crucifix I always wear over my heart. I took it away after I had laid him in his coffin. I opened his eyes, the color of the sky. I kissed his forehead and bade him farewell. Now he is no longer mine" (*Diary*, June 1913).

"Oh Mother of sorrows, Mother who understands a mother who has just lost her beloved son, at Your hands, through Your stainless heart, offer my own son to the Most Holy Trinity that in my name and as something God had given me, it may be glorified" (*Diary*, June 30, 1913).

Manuel, Her Jesuit Son

It is marvelous to see how solicitiously and affectionately this watchful mother followed each one of her children's lives, ever respectful of their personality and their liberty. Two of them from their youth had a religious vocation: Manuel and Concha.

Manuel was the first to leave. Conchita had dreamed of seeing him "a Priest of the Cross," but God is the master of vocations. Her son entered, at the age of seventeen, the Society of Jesus, where he received a solid foundation and spent himself valiantly, until his death, in the service of the Church; for the greater glory of God.

His mother encouraged her son in his fervor and their correspondence with each other showed them more and more united in affection at once human and divine. Once he had definitively made up his mind and she learned about it, she laid out for him the path of religious holiness: "I see grace working in your heart and I know not how to thank the Lord for His benefits. I do not know how to correspond to such great bounty? Give yourself up to the Lord, truly and with all your heart and soul, and never give up. Forget creatures, above all forget yourself. Avoid all that is not God to rise up to Him. Lead a life of full obedience, humility, and abnegation. Die to yourself. Live only for Jesus. May He reign in your soul.

"I cannot conceive of a religious who is not holy. We are not to give ourselves to God half-heartedly. Be generous toward Him. Life is too short not to sacrifice ourselves to Him out of love. Perhaps, and sooner than you think, temptations and conflicts will come to trouble you. Be firm and ever love the Cross, under whatsoever form it presents itself. It is always amiable for him, who, under its seeming rigor, knows how to discover God's will.

"It is evident that my maternal heart was afflicted, but I am happy to be able to offer to the Lord this sacrifice on behalf of your soul a thousand times more loved than your body. Pray, ever pray for me. . . . I have told the whole family about your decision. They will pray for you. Your brothers will write you later. I have wrapped you up in the mantle of Mary since your childhood. She will be your mother, love Her most dearly . . . keep your feet on the ground but your souls and heart; may they dwell in heaven. . ." (Dec. 9, 1906).

Some years later, on the occasion of her voyage to the Holy Land and to Rome, Conchita went to Spain to see her son. Mother and son rejoiced on seeing each other again. She found him very learned and spiritual. "We talked, laughed and cried, and thanked God" (January 1914). "When we had to say good-bye I suffered a great deal, for perhaps we had seen each other for the last time. He also wept. . . . Finally we parted: I was greatly pained, and renewed my offer to God out of love for him" (Feb. 2, 1914). Some days later she left the Iberian peninsula: "Good-bye Spain, there is where my son remains" (Feb. 19, 1914).

In December of 1919, Conchita learned that a part of her son's finger on the right hand had been amputated. Will he yet be able to become a priest? She admired her son who suffered "with the resignation of a saint" (March 4, 1920).

He was to become a priest, but the young Jesuit, had requested of his superiors, as a sacrifice offered to God on behalf of souls, that he be sent to the missions. He let his mother know about this and that his superiors had consented (Letter of June 1920).

My little and unforgettable mama:

I presume you have by now received my last letter and that you are not exactly undisturbed wishing to know just what I let you get a glimpse of in previous letters, to prepare you for it.

Now that all is arranged, you, after my superiors, are the first to know what I am about to tell you so that you, by your fervent prayers, will help me and, far from reproaching me, you will encourage me to make this sacrifice. From a purely natural standpoint, this may hurt and disappoint you, as it did me and quite painfully, but we are not to be concerned with that. We must, as we ought, view things with eyes of faith. Then, the news I am about to tell you will please you since it is about a beautiful sacrifice, God, I believe, has inspired me to make. After long years of probation, my superiors have fully approved it.

What is this about? I wanted to sacrifice to Jesus Christ, to Whom I owe so much, something that would cost me truly in order to render Him in return something for His innumerable favors. Under a divine inspiration, I then envisioned you, my family, my country, all of you, deeply rooted in my heart, the heart of a loving son. It was then, with a great spiritual impulse, I offered myself as a holocaust making a sacrifice of this so holy threefold love. Thus my dream of returning to you, to my brothers and sisters and the whole family, of treading this blessed land, sanctified by the presence and protection of the Virgin of Tepeyac, all this is over for me and unless you come by this way, it is only in heaven I shall see you again.

Sad news, is it not, mama? Yes, but only if we look at things from the standpoint of flesh and blood, but what a beautiful thing and worthy of my heart is this desire to love Jesus above all things.

I know you are going to cry when you read this letter. Your tears will fall into the very depths of my heart, the heart of a loving son. United with mine, you will know how to offer them up at the foot of the Blessed Sacrament, with those of your poor Manuel.

Dear little mama, it was you who showed me the way. From my earliest childhood I had the joy of hearing from your lips the demanding and salvific teaching of the Cross which I am now carrying out in practice. May God grant me to go on with It without ever stopping through the sacrifice of the sole thing I possess, my own life, for the glory of God and the salvation of souls. I shall be blessed if this be so.

Truly worthy of pity are the people of the world who, for money or for other more vile aspirations, take upon themselves similar sacrifices. It is for Jesus Christ and for higher aims we others do so. Thus we are and ought to be rather more worthy to be envied. As you know, little mama, absence makes the heart grow fonder. So you will be able to imagine how much my love for you, for my brothers and sisters and for the rest of the family has grown since I received this joyous news. We are happy in the joy of the Cross, the only really true happiness. Let us have but one desire: never to come down from it.

I will write you again in a short while. Tender and affectionate greetings to my brothers and sisters. And you, my unforgettable mama, send your blessing to your Manuel that, in his sacrifice, his joy be perfect.

Your loving son,

Manuel, S.J.

Conchita copied the letter in her *Diary*.

"Indeed, this letter caused tears to flow from my heart, but with God's help, I accepted and offered up this sacrifice to God, that of no longer seeing him on earth even when I will be able to go to Spain. I renounced the joy of attending his ordination Mass, hearing him preach, receiving Communion from him, making my confession to him and, who knows, being given the Last Rites on my death bed. May the Lord deign to accept my poor and imperfect sacrifice which makes my heart bleed. I am not worthy of such a son" (*Diary*, June 1920).

Conchita right away sent a letter to Manuel, a response so sublime that it showed the mother and son rivaling each other in heroism.

My dear son,

What will I tell you, after your letter announcing the news which I expected, knowing you so well? Tearfully, I offered up to God infinite acts of thanksgiving for His having given you the strength to carry out so great a sacrifice. I went up to the tabernacle, and put your letter close by it. I assure you, with all my soul I accepted your sacrifice of the feelings of affection, so deeply engrained in me. The next day, I bore the letter over my heart on receiving Communion, to renew my full acceptance.

Happy are you, my dear son, for having placed Jesus above flesh and blood, for having known how to raise yourself in an aura of faith above the earth. The little good you, in the forming of your heart, received from me, is not from me, but from God, who, in His infinite predilection, has chosen you for Himself from your tenderest childhood on granting you the religious vocation. I do not know whether you received one of my letters in which, having a presentiment of your sacrifice, I told you that Mexico needs a great number of workers and that there are vast regions in which Indians who are still pagans live, where the reign of Christ could be extended at the cost of great sacrifices and many privations, for instance, in Tarakumara or Muzquiz. I told you in my letter that, even on your coming back here, if you so wished, I would never see you any more. What you wished would be enough for me. Now superiors have sanctioned what you wished. It is clear, there is no doubt, it is the will of God. I accept it with all my soul, I venerate it and I love it.

Oh! Manuel, son of my heart, that which is the greatest thing after God, the sole divine thing the creature can do, is to love Him and to glorify Him in sacrifice of himself. Saint Ignatius' motto is the supreme formula of love: *to the greater glory of God*. How much this love is unknown on earth! Happy they who have received the light of the Cross. For the world, to love is to enjoy. In its egoism, it believes that love consists above all in receiving, in being consoled, indulged, satisfied, while love is nourished by the gift of self, and of immolation. Its food is suffering.

I will stop preaching. I only want to felicitate you a thousand times for having found the true road to heaven. Be ever generous toward God, out of pure love, and you will ever be happy on the earth as in the fatherland above.

Your brothers and sisters have undergone great sorrow, they will go to see you. Ask God that you will be able to see me again in heaven, although I be so little worthy of meriting it. I extend to you the remembrances of all your brothers and sisters, and with full approval of your decision, I give you my blessing.

Kisses from your mother, happy in her sacrifice (*Diary*, June, 1920).

Two years later, Manuel was ordained. Conchita's heart was filled with joy and pride.

Conchita received a beautiful letter from Manuel, which told of his ardent desire to be ordained, and many other things. It moved her deeply.

I shall never forget a single one of your intentions, nor our unforgettable papa, nor anyone of my brothers and sisters, on this day on which it is rightly said the Lord grants everything to His new priest. You know that, through the spiritual union which exists between souls and the Lord Jesus, we are not far apart. On this day, I promise you expressly, you and papa, as is right, will have the first and the best of my intentions. Then, there will be all and each one of my brothers and sisters, that Our Lord abundantly shed torrents of precious graces on this small corner of my soul, where, as the years pass, my heart loves more and more my unforgettable family. My dear little mama, you told me: "Remember, my son, when you hold in your hands the Holy Host, you will not say: 'Behold the Body of Jesus and Behold His Blood,' but you will say: 'This is my Body:, This is my Blood,' that is, there must be worked in you a total transformation, you must lose yourself in Him, to be "another Jesus."

Is not this the height of felicity on earth and in heaven?

As soon as I am ordained, now or later, mama dear, speak to me about it in your letters. Teach me to be a priest, teach me how great is the joy of saying Mass. I place myself in your hands, just as when I was a tiny child you hid me in your bosom to teach me the so sweet names of Jesus and Mary, for by penetrating into this mystery of love, of an infinite grandeur, I feel myself as a baby who asks for light, your prayer and your sacrifices. . . . (July 23, 1922).

The day of this sublime consecration as Priest of Christ draws near and the effusions of tenderness multiply in their correspondence.

There are hours in life, when one can say nothing, nor even feel as one should. Now is one of these moments for you and for me. It is up to you to make up for what it is impossible to put in writing. On this joyous day, you others and I will be united, and you above all my dear little mama and I, I and you, in an indissoluble and close bond which nothing will separate: neither distance, nor absence, nothing in this world. We shall remain united in the company, the holiest that can exist here below or in heaven above, the company of Jesus Himself. . . .

As soon as I will be a priest I will send you my first blessing, then I will receive yours on my knees.

All yours,

Manuel S.J.

On the day assigned, Conchita arose at night, keeping in mind the difference in time between Europe and Mexico, with the thought of assisting at Manuel's first Mass, and of receiving across space, his first blessing. *Te Deum laudamus* "I am the mother of a priest! I felt myself overcome. How was I to conduct myself, what saintliness, what life of gratitude, what plenitude of virtue would I have to practice! I can only weep and give thanks, asking all heaven to give thanks for me, so incapable was I of doing so, so wretched, so stained, so unworthy" (Letter to a friend, July 31, 1922).

For many more years mother and son will correspond. Conchita will tell him down to the least detail about the family, about each one of his brothers and sisters, about all that concerns each one of them, of the painful events going on in Mexico, of her unbreakable trust in God's mercy on her nation, heroic in the faith. They are letters of a mother, a friend, a confidant and of a saint which pours out her heart into that of her son.

Here is one of her last letters, perhaps the last.

"Today, on the feast of Christ the King, will be inaugurated the foundation of the Missionaries of the Holy Spirit at San Luis, your native place and mine! God be blessed! Send up your act of thanksgiving to Him: May it all be to His greater glory!" She speaks to him about the anti-religious laws and the threats of atheistic Communism. "Only the Virgin of Guadalupe can free us. Mexico is Hers and will ever be Hers. . . . Here I am at Morella, and deprive the Lord of a few minutes to write you. . . . Msgr. Martinez has given me the 'Exercises' as he does each year. This time he chose as the subject 'perfect joy in suffering.' Ask God that I profit from it. They may well be my last. I must prepare myself for a great voyage. As He wills!

"We hope God will calm passions and a world war will not break out.

"Become a saint. Life is too short to stop along the road. No matter what be the path we take to seek God, it always passes by the Cross. It is said that the Cross, written with a capital, was the Master's, while in small letters it is ours. Love it for it is the main instrument of our salvation." Conchita took some instants while on retreat for this urgent message: "Now the hour has come to be with Him. I am going to pray a lot for you. May He reign fully over your heart. May He fill up all the capacities of your soul. May He transform you into Himself, making of you, through Mary, another Jesus.

"Bless me and receive my poor blessing with my great tenderness. Your mother who never forgets you" (*Diary*, Oct. 25, 1936).

Her Daughter Concha, the Nun.

Concha, born after three boys, was Conchita's particularly cherished daughter. She was the joy of the home. Her father adored her. When at the age of six she fell ill of typhoid, she was only saved by the care and indefatigable devotion of her mother. She became a beautiful young girl but her soul remained entirely for God in inviolable purity. At fifteen she made a vow of virginity. Her personal charm irresistibly attracted to her a whole group of young youths who loved her passionately. For a while she was troubled and told her mother that she no longer wanted to enter the convent. A drama of love took place in her heart. Her mother respected her freedom but redoubled her prayers and penances: "Lord, if her beauty is an obstacle, take it away from her."

On returning from a retreat, Concha entered the house radiant: "Mama, I have chosen Christ forever."

An intimacy of soul, even more profound, developed between daughter and mother, until Concha's death. Concha became Sister Teresa de Maria Inmaculada. There was correspondence of more than three hundred letters witnessing to this, without counting numerous visits. Their souls vibrated in the communion of one and the same ideal of love of Christ and of sacrifice for the salvation of the world. Conchita's spiritual traits were spontaneously expressed in her daughter's soul. Was not her mother the providential inspirer and foundress of the contemplatives of the Cross?

Her mother never ceased praying for her. "May she be a perfect religious of the Cross!" (*Diary*, April 17, 1908).

"Grant her perseverance" (*Diary*, Oct. 5, 1908). When the novitiate left Mexico City for Tlalpam, her mother went with her daughter to the trolley. "I followed her with my eyes, reciting the Magnificat under my breath" (*Diary*, Aug. 16, 1909).

The visits filled both with great joy. "I saw Sister Teresa so happy" (*Diary*, May 3, 1908).

And so the years passed. Conchita was proud of her daughter and thanked God. "I am enchanted at Concha's virtue, Concha who is now Sister Teresa de Maria Inmaculada. I blushed with shame on seeing myself now so old and without virtue while she has made such giant steps forward" (*Diary*, Jan. 17, 1915).

On October 23, 1916, she pronounced her perpetual vows. "It is a day of unforgettable happiness! Teresa de Maria Inmaculada, my daughter Concha, has become forever the Lord's spouse! From the time she first spoke, I had taught her to say that when she grew up she would become 'the Spouse of Christ.' And here now this union is consummated, this union with the King of heaven and earth."

Sister Teresa made her entrance into the chapel, a lighted candle in her hand, pure, modest, trembling with emotion, radiant with joy. She pronounced her vows, in a placid and strong voice. She had a very beautiful voice. When she sang a solo, the "Veni

Sponsa Christi," her mother said to her. "I have felt an inexpressible joy, a profound humiliation and a boundless gratitude" (*Diary*, Oct. 23, 1916).

Her mother, marveling, contemplated Sister Teresa de Maria Inmaculada. "She is an angel . . . she will be a great saint" (*Diary*, Oct. 1916).

The young professed nun was charming. For her sisters who loved her much, she was a very sympathetic companion, faithful and smiling. She was very much appreciatd by her sisters of Puebla and of Monterrey. Her life went on without ado. One moment she went through a grave crisis about vocation but her love for Christ triumphed. Soon an illness overtook her in the very hot climate of Monterrey. She spat blood. There were very hard hours for the mother and the daughter. She was so ill that they transferred her back to Mexico City.

"Mother Javiera requested the archbishop to give me permission to stay near Teresa" (*Diary*, Dec. 11, 1925). "On the national feast of Our Lady of Guadalupe, December 12, they had her hold a blessed rose, brought from the Basilica, supplicating the Most Holy Virgin that Teresa would be able to receive Viaticum. She regained the use of her reason and the last sacraments were administered to her. She was conscious of everything. I do not know how to thank God. As for me, the main thing was that she receive Jesus! How fervently I asked this. She recognized me and said to me. 'My dear little mama!' Poor child! My soul burst, my heart was shattered on seeing her suffer so much! She repeated to Jesus: 'Behold my body . . .' 'Behold my blood.' I looked at her and I wept, offering her to the eternal Father, begging Him to take her if that was His will" (*Diary*, Dec. 12, 1925).

"At two o'clock in the morning, I went by car to get an oxygen balloon. My God! My God, do not let her die asphyxiated! She said: 'I do not want to despair.' And she entered into indescribable anguish, repeating: 'It is for souls, for priests, for the Works of the Cross! My God!' " (*Diary*, Dec. 17, 1925).

"Yesterday, December 19, at one forty-five in the afternoon, Teresa died! God of my heart, be a thousand times blessed!

"After twenty-nine days of illness and sharp pain in her whole body, the daughter of my life died. . . .

"She was an angel, a victim, a saint" (*Diary*, Dec. 20, 1925).

The Four Surviving Children

Three sons and one daughter, born of Conchita, are still living: Pancho, Ignacio, Salvador and Lupe.

Pancho is a handsome old man, straight as a die, flying by plane in the interests of the typewriter company he founded and still directs. He is a businessman, but above all a man of honor and a fine Christian. His brothers and sisters, who owe him a great deal, love him as "a second father." When his papa died, he was seventeen and courageously went to work to help his mother raise her seven other orphans. He went through many hours of difficulty, not hesitating to make long business trips in Europe and North and South America: United States, Brasil, Argentina, Bolivia, Chile, Peru. Conchita had utmost confidence in him and relied very much on him for the education of her other children.

Ignacio, after having raised a very fine Christian family, with his wife Chabela, dearly loved by Conchita, ended his life surrounded by the affection of his dear ones, in the house where his mother died, at San Angel. He prayed in memory of his mother who loved him so much and who said of him: "Of all my children, he is the one who was most like his father."

Salvador was the latest born boy. His mother watched over him with greatest tenderness, imploring God to have him find a wife who would make him happy. "Give a livelihood to my dear son Salvador" (*Diary*, May 31, 1924). After his marriage, Conchita wrote in her *Diary:* "All is over for me . . . But a mother always rejoices in the happiness of her children" (*Diary*, Sept. 24, 1929).

Lupe was a very proper and charming daughter. Salvador and

she were the two *enfants terribles* of the family, each having a big heart.

Conchita loved all her children and followed each one in his or her own life. I have never found on their lips the slightest reproach directed against their mother. She herself gave them the most beautiful testimonial when she said: "I am not worthy of the children God has given me."

Portrait of a Mother Drawn by Her Children

After 1954, I had the opportunity to talk with her children. Here was the living portrait of their mother such as comes out of the authentic testimonies, which I was able to collect, and to which I joined the oral replies to a questionnaire properly conducted, faithfully taken down in shorthand.

What impressed me most when questioning her children was their identical views about their mother despite each one's different temperament. All recognized the elementary nature of her early instruction in contrasting it with the sublimity of her writings. Pancho said: "Her instruction, at San Luis, was that of all young girls of the society of her times. There was only a question of finery, embroidery, piano playing etc. It was not then as it is today." Her son Ignacia, remarked to me that his mother was "highly intelligent." It is certain that with the feminine formation of the present-day world, Conchita would have stood out through her intellectual qualities, through her ability to synthesize, getting right down to the essential.

Christ, her Teacher, made up for everything and, under His *dictation*, her mystical genius developed. "All that she wrote was by divine inspiration," stated her eldest son.

Her daughter, Lupe, received from her mother true confidences about her intimate life with her husband. After the time of their wedding, she had been attracted to him by a great love. She saw in him a Christian spouse, of great morality, a person of strong character, in which time wrought a gentle change. "My mother has always fulfilled the obligations of her state of life.

She was very attentive and full of tenderness toward my father, ever submissive and seeking to please him in every way. My father was her sole love."

"For his part, my father was for her an exceptional husband. He in no way interfered, leaving her full freedom. He did not stop her from writing and left her in peace" (Pancho).

All her children testified to her fidelity to her duties as a wife and mother. "She looked on her marital relations with a great simplicity. Their conjugal life always went along peacefully. It was truly Christian, carried on with mutual understanding. I have heard it said that she never lost her baptismal innocence. There is no doubt she insisted strongly on purity in our education, but I also understood that she judged human things, without seeing sins everywhere. She judged all this as quite natural. She understood life, which was a good thing. Later, she spoke to me about my conjugal duties with my wife. I realized then that what she meant by purity was not ignorance" (Ignacio). This testimony of a father who had eight children deserves to be kept in mind.

"There was no affectation between them. They were perfectly sure of each other" (Lupe).

Housemistress

There was the same attestation on the part of her children about Conchita's perfect attitude toward the house servants and farm hands and other hired help who worked on the *haciendas* of Mexico at this period. I questioned an elderly servant and some employees, and all spoke with great reverence of Senora Concepcion Cabrera de Armida. She was most cordial with everyone, firm, sometimes annoyed but never offensive.

Her Style of Living

Pancho, the eldest, is still the main witness. She was a "marvelous" mother of a family. "We adored her, but as an ordinary mama, with nothing extraordinary about her. It is, I think, what

God intended. It would not have been comfortable living with a saint, with someone who had to be constantly shown veneration, without ever being able to be treated informally, as we did with mama. Everything about her was normal. Nothing was exaggerated in her behavior, no, never. For instance, when she attended Mass, certainly she showed great devotion, but just like everybody else. Do not imagine she spoke directly to the Lord in our presence. We others, did not have the slightest idea of anything."

"In her social life she enchanted everyone. She was most amiable and pleasant. She lived a family and social life which was quite normal, and this to such an extent that we, who lived so close to her, did not have any concept of her saintliness."

Mother and Teacher

Her children are constantly praising her qualities as wife, mother and teacher." There were nine of us. As the eldest child, I can state that my mother was under every aspect a model. First as a wife, for my father was demanding as to all that concerned the life of the home. As mother, she took care giving each one a complete formation on every plane: not only religious, but profane, cultural and social. After my father's death we were not rich. Her brother Octaviano helped us. She imposed on herself great sacrifices to assure our education in the best schools, with the Jesuits, for the boys and with the Madames of the Sacred Heart, for the girls. As the eldest brother I helped her in this difficult task. She was the first to give us a good example and corrected us severely but never losing her temper. Despite all the time she spent on spiritual matters, she never neglected her duties at home, as wife and mother. None of her children have gone astray" (Pancho).

"The most admirable thing in my mother's life was the naturalness and simplicity of her existence. Her prayer and her Communions seemed to me perfectly normal. She never used moments set aside for carrying out obligations for her prayer life. I never noticed any extraordinary phenomena in her daily behavior. I think my brothers and sisters will wholly agree. In society she was at ease with important people as well as with ordinary ones. I noticed nothing special as to what she ate, for it was what was eaten habitually in Mexican families. Everything in her life was absolutely normal. I must admit that throughout my mother's life, I was covered, as it were, by a veil which hid from me her saintliness. It was not until her death that we appreciated the mother we had.

"I cannot recall my mother without seeing her writing. She wrote books of which great quantities were sold. She also carried on a voluminous correspondence."

In conclusion, her eldest son used a magnificent word which revealed to us the secret of this life: "She loved Jesus Christ above all else."

Ignacio Armida has the same view as his brother, but in keeping with his own temperament. "I had the great pleasure of living with her for forty-two years of my life, being forty-four years old when she died. During the first two years of my marriage, I did not live in the same house with her but we had two neighboring houses and saw each other at the hour for dining." So we have here another testimony of exceptional value. Conchita had retired to her own house where she lived with her eight children, and died in their arms. "Mother was a very active woman. She received visitors all the time. There was nothing striking or unusual in her style of life. She had a very sweet character but was firm and energetic. When she had decided to act in a certain way, no human power could deter her. With her, one had to obey. This was also true of the works she undertook. She had her plan, her inspiration, her ideal and followed it to the end.

"Her life was most normal. Ever joyful, very much so indeed, she had a wonderful sense of humor and loved jokes. She had written a notebook full of them and would bring them out most gracefully and naturally. When she went to San Luis Potosi to her brother Octaviano's home, a prominent and rich person, who received many guests, mama was always the center of attraction.

She spoke to the guests, ably directing the conversation, turning them toward Christ. She entertained them most charmingly. If she was invited to come to a ranch for a ride on a horse, she was quite ready to do so. . . . She was ever with the poor. As soon as one of them died, even though an unpleasant person, she was there . . . helping in every way. In her eyes it did not matter. . . . I do not know whether one day she will be proclaimed a saint or not, but without any doubt at all, she was one of God's souls. She always had a pleasant smile, sympathy, and her blue eyes were the color of the sky! They were very penetrating. When she gazed with her eyes into yours, she looked deeply within.

"She had perfect equilibrium! Indeed, she was very well balanced. In difficult situations, her serenity pacified everything. No one can say she was unbalanced, nor that she was nervous, excessive or jealous. She was very sensitive to the sufferings of others, which to me seems a great virtue.

"With her, family life was not sad, painful, tearful. Of course, she suffered a great deal, but she kept it to herself.

"Here, Father, are the memories I have kept of my mother. She was a mama like yours, like all mamas."

Salvador, the youngest, said the same things in his own way. "There was a great equilibrium in her judgments. Many people consulted her. Never was there any self-deceit, nothing was eccentric about her behavior. Her life was most ordinary, the most normal in the world. When she became a widow, she went out often, visited people, other members of the family, relatives and friends. They often came to see her. She was very affectionate, but severely rebuked them when they did something that was wrong. She dearly loved the Blessed Virgin and frequently went to the Basilica of *Our Lady of Guadalupe*.

"I lived with her until I married when I was twenty-three. I can testify to her character. It was joyful, simple, balanced. Her charity toward others was truly admirable. Whenever she knew of anyone suffering she made every effort possible to help them.

"She was charitable toward everyone, even those who offended her or opposed her works. When she learned that certain persons were standing aloof or angry, she made arrangements to meet them. With those who were ill, members of the family or strangers, she was extremely tender, doing all she could to assuage their ailments. She always offered to assist the dying, to go to their funerals, even when there was question of persons of the family who did not esteem her. She lent herself voluntarily to perform all the services and chores of a servant. Everybody loved her."

Finally, here is the testimony of her daughter Lupe, who is ever refreshing and spontaneous. This testimony from a woman reveals many a detail that escapes a man. She too has kept remembrances of her mother which are as perfectly balanced as those of her brothers and sisters. She knew her intimately. "I always lived and slept with her, from my father's death until my marriage. She always seemed to me to be a most normal woman. She reprimanded me quite a bit. We never saw her go into ecstasy. She was a model mother-in-law. Once we were married, she never interfered by moralizing, but left us in complete freedom."

Her daughter Lupe, picked up one day a most important piece of confidential information which Conchita gave to her daughter-in-law, Salvador's wife. "I have always been very happy with my husband." On every point Lupe's testimony is like that of her brothers and sisters, concerning her qualities as wife, mother and mistress of her household, her warmth and her sociability, concerning her strength of soul when faced with the difficulties of life, and her great piety.

"Throughout her life she appeared to us endowed with an admirable natural spontaneity. During her married life her submission to her husband was absolute. She used to say: 'First of all, what pleases Pancho.' She was very attentive to him and full of amiability. She always paid the servants of the house what was due them. When I got married, she advised me to do likewise, indicating for me in writing the just wage I should pay them. She always showed her acknowledgment of the least things.

"Each one felt loved by her, even strangers who approached her." Her only fault, pointed out by Lupe, was a touch of gluttony. "She was very fond, perhaps overmuch, of candy." 'If I go by a jewelry shop, it is all the same to me, but when I go by a confectionery store in Celaya, my mouth waters,' she told me.

"She led an absolutely normal life, just like everybody else at home and in society. She laughed, told pleasantries, gossiped, played the piano, sang and amused her nieces and nephews even more than their own mama. She went through all this with a smile and gave me this advice: 'What God asks you to do, do it with a smile.' She told us time and again: 'Everything passes, except having suffered for God out of love.'

"As for me, I have always felt she was present at every moment of my life."

"And now, Lupe, do you feel she is ever present?"

"Yes, Father, she protects and watches over us in the shadow of the Cross."

Testament of a Mother

Conchita was frequently ill. Feeling herself more than usually in danger, she wrote an admirable letter to her children, the testament of a mother and a saint.

"If I die, if God now calls me, I exhort you, my children, to remain valiant Christians and full of faith, practicing with inviolable fidelity, the teachings of the Church, proud of being her members.

"Endeavor to carry out her precepts. Be generous toward Jesus who loves you so much, to whom you owe so much and who wants to save you. I implore you to pass on your faith to your children by your teaching and example, not shunning any sacrifice to assure them a Christian education, taking special care to form their souls and instruct them in their religion.

"Above all I exhort you to be united . . . union, union!" (Letter, June 28, 1928).

Mexico: a Terrible Persecution

There is, in Mexico City, at Tlaltelolco, "la Plaza de Tres Culturas," indicative of the three civilizations which explain the origins, the conflicts and the grandeur of the Mexican nation. Mexico, inheritor of ancient Indian civilizations, especially Aztec and Maya, enriched by Spanish colonization which came to mark it with a European stamp, evokes thus a great future due to the creative dynamism of modern ingenuity.

It is in this context that the story of Conchita's life must be set. She was a saintly woman, attached to her nation by all the fibers of her being, just as Christ, through His divine Presence, bore the traits of an oriental. Like Saint Rose of Lima, patroness of Peru, Conchita is only adequately explained by her milieu. We cannot understand her psychological reactions, the expression and forms of her piety and penitence save through the environment and customs of Mexico.

At the moment she had reached maturity, Mexico was undergoing a period of decisive change of which Conchita was the witness and of which we find the echo in her *Spiritual Diary*. In 1914 the revolution became anti-religious in character, which disquieted her soul, as a *daughter of the Church*.

"August 1914. This month began the anguish of war, and even worse a persecution about to inflict us. May God help us! I have no news about my brothers and sisters who are in San Luis, Oaxaca and at Queretaro."

"August 15. A day of anguish. They intend to requisition *la Casa de la Cruz*, (the convent of the contemplatives), to be used as general quarters and as a lodging for officers. Today some twenty thousand *Carranzistas* arrived. Some three or four times more are still to come. I felt in my soul a mortal sadness, as if Satan had entered Mexico. It was a terrible oppression. It is the scourge of God. The war unleashed against the Church, is accentuated. My spiritual director had to go into hiding. A persecution, a frightful one, draws near. God has put nearby us some neighbors, members of the government, who love the sisters and offer to save them."

"August 17. Things get worse every day. Horrible blasphemies, outrages, deaths, rapes and pillaging of homes occur. Gunfire is heard throughout the day. We are afraid to go out. A holocaust of priests exists. Religious have been expelled. The goods of the Church are going to be confiscated. There are forced loans and a thousand other pitiful things" (*Diary*, Aug. 1914).

Persecution of the Clergy

"The political situation worsens. A thousand excesses are all around us and blatant persecution of the clergy exists too. Oh my God! the God of my heart! In You we have put our hope, we shall never be confounded! Poor Mexico! It is the hour of God's chastisement and I hope we will learn to profit by it" (*Diary*, Aug. 27, 1914).

The Trial Will Pass

"Today we begin another month of a thousand anxieties. Puebla has been taken over by the anti-clericals. They have profaned this cathedral so dear to my heart! They expelled the canons and burned the confessionals. They have taken over the episcopal palace and committed thousands of vexations against the priests. Outrages and horrors are everywhere!

"When I complained to the Lord about what was happening to Puebla, He told me: 'The trial will pass' (*Diary*, Sept. 1, 1914).

In 1926-1927 the same topic appears in her *Diary* at the moment the persecution had reached its peak.

The Church of Mexico is Persecuted

"The Church of Mexico is combated, tyranized, persecuted. It is intended to reduce the number of churches and priests. Religious communities have been expelled, foreign priests sought out and hunted down with inconceivable savagery. The bishops are troubled and a great number of seminaries are closed. God of my heart, Word of God, have pity on Mexico! Virgin of Guadalupe, Mother filled with love and tenderness, obtain pardon for us" (*Diary*, March 9, 1926).

The Horrors of the Persecution Continue

"Today they came to see whether there were any nuns in the Mirto. They concealed Jesus and nothing happened. They saw the chapel was covered with dirt and said: 'Here there are no services held.' Hell is let loose against the Church. These last days, some priests who are prisoners arrive, brought in from other States to be concentrated here in the state of Mexico. The bishops are in great danger. Revolution and combats are all around us. Many youths are taken by surprise, are betrayed, and martyred. In the region of Leon, one of them who praised God and encouraged his companions to die for Him, had his tongue cut out before they shot him" (*Diary*, Jan. 6, 1927).

We Have a Great Number of Martyrs

"We already have a great number of martyrs in Mexico who are granting us favors. God be blessed! He knows how many there are. We must adore His designs. For God, everyone is a means which He uses, and how often it pleases Him to accomplish things counter to all human means in order to make His glory shine out the more. It is the hour of suffering and of prayer but we must also adore His delays, accept with love His designs, and hope against all hope for the triumph and peace that He, without any doubt at all, will bring us. Mexico will not lose the faith as long as it remains devoted to Mary" (Letter to a friend, May 26, 1927).

All these extracts from her *Diary* or correspondence during this period enable us to state that she judged all the events, even the most tragic, solely in the light of her faith. Instead of cursing the persecutors, she prayed and offered up her life for their conversion, entrusting them to God's mercy. Her ardent supplications especially for the priests, rose to God.

Offer Yourself

"Offer yourself as a victim for My priests. Unite yourself to My sacrifice for gaining them graces. It is necessary that in union with the Eternal Father, you accomplish your priestly role, offering Me to My Father for obtaining from Him grace and mercy for the Church and her members. Recall how often I have asked you to offer yourself as a victim, in union with the Victim, for My beloved Church? Do you not see that you are all Hers since you are Mine and that you are Mine since you are all Hers? Precisely, on account of this special union which binds you to My Church, you have the right to share in Her anguish and the sacred duty to console Her by sacrificing yourself for Her priests" (*Diary*, Sept. 24, 1927).

She often and courageously hides priests, bishops and men and women religious in her home.

She speaks not a word of recrimination or bitterness but manifests the purest Christian charity toward all. Since Her founding, the Church of Christ in all nations, undergoes hours of suffering, of persecution, of betrayal and of martyrdom. It is Christ, ever crucified in the members of His Mystical Body, who saves the world.

Solitude

"On returning from the obsequies of Msgr. Ramon Ibarra, my forehead pressed against the tabernacle . . . my heart torn, I offered myself to the divine will. Then there began for me the great 'solitude' and with it, the last stage of my life."

Upon the death of her director, February 2, 1917, the Lord Himself had announced to Conchita: "There remains for you to pass the last stage of your life imitating My Mother for obtaining graces for the Works of the Cross. Tempest will rise over them as over My Church, but they will triumph and will be your crown. Have courage, be brave! Carry on your mission, imitate the virtues of Mary in her *solitude*, virtues which brought about Her union with Me, Her obedience to My will and Her desire of heaven."

The route was traced by the Lord. Conchita carried out her existence on earth, as did the Mother of Jesus after His Ascension, in the solitude and isolation of the evening of her life. Twenty years of *solitude*, from February 2, 1917, to March 3, 1937, the day of her death.

She will see her external apostolate gradually diminish. From then on she will be an apostle by prayer and immolation. God will detach her from everything. She will know, more and more, solitude of the heart, and especially solitude of the soul, through an apparent remoteness from God, just as Jesus was abandoned by His Father on the Cross.

One year after another, each one of her children marry, leaving her more and more alone. It is the inevitable law of life, yet Conchita's sensitive heart suffered painfully, at times to excess. Her children surrounded her with affection and attention, but they had their own tasks, their own responsibilities in their new homes and in their struggle for existence. She feels more and more alone when evening comes.

Everything Passes

"I am in the most complete solitude of soul, but it is God's will and God, for me, is only there where His will is found. I do not understand anything any more, I am in chaos. This need to express my soul, my desires, my impressions, even on paper, all this has disappeared. I tend to keep secret my impressions, my tastes and even my sufferings and tears. I want to hide everything in Jesus. All is for Him alone. What a change has come over me! I clearly see that everything passes, changes, is consummated. On the earth, all is shadow, vanity and lies. The real, the true, what is of value, what endures, what is, is in heaven. The earth with all its things, all of them, are but a lever to raise oneself to Him.

All is lost in God: loves, sorrows, dreams, expectations, desires, aspirations, and all, all, disappear in Him.

"If I review my past life, if I consult my heart, I discover its affections. They have passed. Its desires, the most ardent ones, have passed. Its vanities and even its faults and disorderly acts, its excessive yearnings for such and such a thing, have passed, definitively passed. I loved my husband most dearly. It has passed. I ardently desired to be a nun, now that is all the same to me: to be or not to be, to die here or there, in a miserable courtyard, or in my house, alone or surrounded by others, loved or abhorred or despised. I have only one desire: that in me the divine will be done" (*Diary*, Nov. 16, 1917).

It would not be right to think that her heart, the heart of a wife and mother, is detached from all legitimate affections. On the contrary, the more Conchita advances in life and in divine union, the more human she seems to us. All her loves are then transfigured in Christ. Her heart is faithful to all the family anniversaries, to the least festivals and gatherings of her children, to their joys, their trials and tribulations. When their businesses were threatened in 1931 by the American financial depression, she begs God to save them, for they are honest, have worked hard all their lives, and are now struggling valiantly against the consequences of the devaluation of the dollar. "Illness is still afflicting me, in most sufferings and family troubles, seeing ruin of my children approaching, accompanied by humiliations. This tortures my heart, even though I have accepted it and welcomed it as the most holy will of God. Still, this does not take away the material pain I feel which involves a whole world of sufferings" (May 22, 1931). "There are deepest pains, as a sword pierces my heart. I have seen one of my sons weep when, after thirty years of labor, he saw himself threatened by the ruin of his business. The sight of his tears touched us all.

" Each one of my sons, besides the disgrace of the failure of his business soon to come, would find himself and his family on the street. . . . Lord I only ask You to give me the strength needed and to sustain the faith of my children" (*Diary*, May 28, 1931).

This wonderful mother, sixty-nine years old, consummated in holiness, sent up to God this cry of distress ardently begging Him: "I am pained on seeing my children suffer, it seems that God does not wish their businesses to succeed, and that they are threatened with disaster. Lord, may Your will be done, even though my heart is broken and crucified. For myself, Oh Jesus, I want nothing. Reject me! Leave me in wretchedness, abandoned and living on charity! I can no longer think of myself, but I cannot be unmindful of my children!" (*Diary*, Nov. 11, 1931).

How could God reject this cry of a mother, He, who, at the request of His own Mother, performed His first miracle at Cana? Her children's courage brought about a favorable change in their financial situation.

In this way painfully passed the last years of Conchita's life. After her last son's marriage, she noted sorrowfully in her *Diary:* "Now all is over for me. God gave me nine children. He has taken away all nine. May He be blessed! Two religious, the others dead or married, all, one after another have been snatched from my maternal heart. Ten beds, including that of my husband, are now empty and here I am now alone. Yet no, not alone, I have Christ who does not die, who does not part from me, and who will never abandon me.

"A mother, when her children get married, provides merely supplementary affection, but their mother is happy to make the sacrifice, her solitude. She rejoices in her children's happiness" (*Diary*, Sept. 24, 1929).

Conchita will never forget her husband. Year after year, on September 17, her *Diary* marks most faithfully the anniversary of his death.

"Here it is now three years ago since my husband died and my children have been without their earthly father. What sad memories! Lord, may Thy will be done on earth as it 'tis in heaven! My children have gone to visit his tomb. I, cannot go because my foot hurts. My heart struggles constantly. Truly, and literally, I water with my tears the bread I eat, the ground and my

Crucifix! Oh my Jesus! What You wish, that I wish too. . . . I feel so awfully alone. Oh Mary, my Mother, have pity on me" (*Diary*, Sept. 17, 1904).

"Twenty years a widow! Lord, preserve and increase the glory of my earthly spouse who was so good to me and who never hindered me from loving You. Fill with Yourself this father of my children, a model of a father, of a gentleman, of a man of honor and of a Christian" (*Diary*, Sept. 17, 1921).

"I have now been a widow for thirty-one years. Jesus took away my cherished husband whom He had given me on earth. Lord, increase his glory and go and greet him for me. Is it not so? You will surely do this for me, You who so kindly do things for me! There above, in heaven, with him are four of my children, Carlos, Pedro, Pablo, Concha. Oh Jesus, blessed may You be" (*Diary*, Sept. 17, 1932).

Thus Conchita lived on earth, ever faithful to her husband, her children and God.

The solitude of the soul surpasses the solitude of the heart. This solitude of the soul attains frightful proportions which make it more and more like to the innermost suffering of the Heart of the Christ and to His abandonment on the Cross, in the course of the last twenty years of her life. It was then that Conchita knew by revelation the immense merits of the *solitude* of the Mother of God, after the Ascension of Her Son, in the service of the Church militant (1917). It was then, too, that she received the *Confidences* of Christ about the grandeur and misery of the Priesthood (1927-1932). Finally, it was then that she brought together the supreme illuminations on the *consummation* of the whole universe *in the Unity of the Trinity*.

Christ's Countenance

When we look in retrospect at Conchita's life story, the uniformity of her spiritual itinerary, throughout all events God imprints on her the image of the Crucified. "My whole life is marked with the seal of the Cross" (*Diary*, July, 1925). It is possible to follow, throughout her existence, the progressive influence of the Crucified.

"Oh Jesus! let me die for You, desolate, abandoned, helpless, crucified" (*Diary*, 1893).

"The thought of the Crucified makes light for me all the corporal penitences and interior sufferings" (*Diary*, March-April 1894).

"I have met God on the Cross" (*Diary*, Aug. 26, 1894).

Since 1895, when Conchita was a young woman of thirty-three, the Lord clearly traced out the program for her spiritual life, she was to be a reflection of the Crucified.

A Mirror which Reflects The Crucified

"Jesus told me: 'As I am in My Father, making Myself *One* with Him, so I want you truly to be *One* with Me. I want you to be like a very clear mirror in which is reflected the image of Your Jesus Christ Crucified. I want you to reflect Me in yourself, as I was on the Cross. On your part, abandon yourself simply for receiving in you My image. I want you to be as I am, crowned with thorns, scourged, nailed to the cross in desolation, pierced, helpless. . . . Meditate one by one on all these things and be my living portrait in order that My Father may find in you His complacency and pour out floods of grace upon sinners' " (*Diary*, April 6, 1895).

The years passed by. All the graces God grants her, especially the mystical incarnation, tend to operate in her the transformation in Christ Crucified:

"I must reproduce in me Christ Crucified" (*Diary*, Sept. 16, 1921).

This is what God is going to carry out in her during the last years of her life and above all at the moment of her death. Physical and moral sufferings, illness, interior anguish, temptations against faith and hope, hours of abandonment will make her a reflection of the Crucified. Conchita consents to everything. She recalls this total identification with the Crucified on Calvary. She shares all the conditions of human flesh and old age but her soul is resplendent, more and more divine. "I am totally of Jesus! My body, my soul, my life, my sufferings, my time, may He dispose of all that is His, in full liberty, on behalf of priests" (*Diary*, Jan. 31, 1929).

After her last retreat at Morelia under her spiritual director, on "the perfect joy of suffering," Conchita returned to Mexico City, and spent the last three years of her life, now in bed, now in an armchair, undergoing atrocious physical suffering. She was afflicted by bronchial-pneumonia, erysipelas and uremia. She afflicted additional pain on her poor body, performing corporal penances out of her ardent love for Christ and for men.

In her soul there was a feeling of despair. Her prayer sought refuge in Christ's words in Gethsemane. She shared in the feelings of the Crucified, abandoned by His Father. For her, her Beloved Jesus has wholly disappeared. "It is as if we had never known each other," she said again and again to her innermost self. Two of her children, Ignacio and Salvador, each taking one of her arms, raised up their mother to ease her breathing. "She might well have been said to be Christ in agony on the Cross." There was even at the moment of death, a strange phenomenon to which her sons and Father Jose Guadalupe Trevino, M.SP.S., have testified firmly. The same testimony was given also by other witnesses.

The phenomenon took place on the death of Conchita, imprinting on her, as the seal of God on her personal vocation and her mission for the Church, a concrete and amazing synthesis of the spirituality of the Cross. Conchita's appearance was seen to change: no longer was there the face of a woman but the Countenance of the Crucified.

Part II.

GREAT SPIRITUAL THEMES

"All Mysteries are Found in Christ."

CHAPTER I.

THE MYSTICAL WRITER

"I am going to write out of obedience."

Blessed Raymond de Capoue, the confessor of St. Catherine of Sienna who did not know how to read or write, declared: "There is found in Catherine a doctrine which is even more admirable than her life." We only have three letters in her own hand, written toward the end of her life. She is a Doctor of the Church! By her words, her teaching and her example she illumines the Church of Christ until the end of time. The same may be said of Conchita.

Her basic education was elementary. She never received a literary or theological formation. From her maternal uncle, Father Luis Arias, she might have heard of the translation of Darras' "l'Histoire de l'Eglise. Conchita, personally, was very fond of reading, not for her cultural development, but in order to find nourishment for her soul. "All my life, I recall that I saw deeply and clearly into my soul. I greatly wanted to remember everything concerning the spiritual, for instance, mystical readings and sermons. If I cannot remember them, on account of my poor memory, still these truths penetrate the very depths of my soul. . . . This mystical meaning exists deeply hidden in my spirit and vibrates like a violin string at the slightest touch of things of God. . . . I have always liked to read and, in mystical books, I have found repose, light and relaxation" (April 1, 1894). Conchita has a mystical temperament, her most characteristic trait.

She always dreamed of writing. She had a vocation to be a writer. "I have always had an inclination to write. From the age of sixteen, I began the account of my life, wholly filled with God, when we lived at Peregrina. I have torn up most of it" (*Aut.* 102). Later on she will ask St. Teresa of Avila to obtain for her the grace to write.

Her directors order her to write her "*Diary*". . . Her first director, Father Alberto Mir, S.J., forbade all spiritual reading, except that of the *Imitation of Jesus Christ*, and at the same time ordered her not to read over what she had written.

Conchita obeyed most faithfully.

This order brings out clearly the special intervention of God and the Illuminations of the Holy Spirit, the interior Teacher.

As far as we can find out, Conchita received no human influence on her spiritual doctrine. The varied circumstances of her life led her to write numerous works, large and small, and a voluminous correspondence covering up to sixty-five years. Above all the Lord Himself, on many occasions, urged her to take up her pen: "Write, write, if you want to give Me glory" (*Diary*, June 18, 1900).

"Dictation" by The Lord

The better to inform her new and last director, Msgr. Luis M. Martinez, retracing her spiritual itinerary, Conchita drew up a balance sheet of the graces and charisms received from the Lord, throughout her life. "How often, how often my Jesus has spoken to me, *dictating* to me Vices and Virtues. Often He has spoken to me about the Holy Trinity, removing from my eyes the veil of mysteries. I see them as it were in a natural way, without them being called specially to my attention, just as they actually should be. Here I am now come to, or almost come to, the forty-fifth volume of my 'Accounts of Conscience' (*Diary*). In them is a whole mass of instructions, lights, counsels, God's secrets. Such condescension! I have heard Him some few times speaking to me in His natural voice, sometimes *dictating* to me and correcting me, at other times speaking to me in an interior voice holding in suspense my whole being, without the slightest possible doubt. Finally, *He can communicate Himself in a thousand ways!* So many graces for my poor soul: methods, counsels, particular instructions and manifestation of His will in so many ways" (July 3, 1925).

The term "dictation" by the Lord is to be understood in a loose, broad sense. It does not mean here, for instance a teacher expressing something word for word his pupil is to write. Rather it means a mode of divine illuminations adapted to the one receiving them according to his temperament, culture, the circumstances and modalities of his life which are so variable. The two basic laws of adaptation and of progress, found in the course of the historical development of divine Revelation addressed to the prophets and other inspired writers, are in due proportion found in private revelations. God makes the greatest allowance for the psychology of the subject. "In times past, God spoke in fragmentary and varied ways to our fathers through the prophets" (Heb 1:1). God did not speak in the same way to Isaiah and to Amos, to Teresa of Avila, to Angelo de Foligno and to Conchita. A decisive text of Conchita's *Diary* brings out the flexibility of the divine pedagogy.

"The manner in which I communicate Myself bears in itself the mark of Unity, since, in God who is One, thus go all things, simplified in every way. For example, right now, suddenly, I am reflected in your soul as in a crystal. There these divine rays are imprinted and you, under this impression, you see, you contemplate and you understand. Immediately, with the help of your intelligence, you put them in words, while I Myself, without you being aware of it, leave it to you to adapt yourself more or less exactly. Yet, from the illumination given you, I have left in you the substance, the essence, the image of the thing communicated. Then you transcribe it from your soul onto your intellectual faculties and thence transcribe it on paper. According to this manner of communication by God with His creature, there is, so to say, no error. There will be no admixture of human passions,

passions which obscure and deform to the point of obliteration, the traces of God in the soul. Therein lies a manner of God's communication which derives from His Unity, at one single stroke imprinting itself in a poor creature and, then, taking form in the language of the earth, even though, for that, I tell you again, divine cooperation remains necessary.

"When a soul humbly receives these communications and submits itself to them with indispensable purity of heart, without any admixture of passion, the divine impression is clear, transparent, luminous. There is no danger of self-deceit. It is evident that the divine, on passing into the human, takes on the form and color of the one who receives these communications. But this is quite secondary, the essence, the substance and form God willed to communicate remains identical.

"Since, in My bounty and in view of My sublime designs, I had chosen you as an instrument and a channel, never stain the mirror of your soul. Today more than ever, you must keep in it purity, lucidity and transparence, in order that the torrent of graces of the Holy Spirit be communicated" (*Diary*, May 16, 1913).

Conchita experienced the illuminating action of God and she was aware that it was God Himself who had communicated. " 'Listen,' Jesus said to me. . . ." Then she added: "Yes, I feel it is He who said it to me, I cannot say anything else" (*Diary*, March 3, 1894). She was aware, too, that it was His will that she write: "Write, I want you to write. . . . Write because I want you to . . . When I would not want you to, even should you want to, you will not be able to do it." And Conchita answered: "Let me tell you one thing: I am afraid to neglect my duties." Then Jesus: "If I saw it thus, I would not bid you do it. Find time, you can do it well. Arrange things before hand, do all that you can on your part and then write and pray" (*Diary*, March, 1894).

The Lord categorically answers her last doubts: "If (what you write) is from Me, it will be for My glory; if it is from the devil, you will be warned; if it is from yourself, you will be mocked, and you will profit from this humiliation."

The Lord alone is the Master of the times, of the place and of the modes of intervention. As He pleases He spends long months of silence. Then He suddenly turns up and Conchita must write, write, write. Often she is involved in family duties and social obligations, or due to interior impossibility to pray, must undergo terrible aridity and dryness. At other times, on the contrary, she reads the Trinity "like on open book" (*Diary*, July 18, 1906).

At times she has had enough and says so frankly. "I would like to stop writing, forget everything, turn the page, change my life. Such is, at this moment, the state of my spirit, submerged in temptations and sufferings." But she courageously has added. "I must control myself, with God's grace. I renounce myself without pity and keep on going, even though I may die in the struggle" (*Diary*, March 26, 1897).

The Lord knows He can rely on His faithful servant. Her heroic existence belongs to Him unreservedly in the service of His Church. He does not hesitate to appeal to the total giving of herself for as long as will be pleasing to Him, according to the designs of the Father. "Ask Me for a long life to suffer much and write much. . . ." He goes on, "there is your mission on earth. . . . You are destined for the sanctification of souls, most especially souls of priests. Through your endeavors many will be inflamed with love and suffering. Make the Cross loved, through the reign of the Holy Spirit. One day a constellation of holy priests will come, priests who will enkindle the world with the fire of the Cross. I make ready My ways. They will be formed to a singular perfection by the doctrine I have given you. I carry out what I said. You will be the mother of a great number of spiritual sons, but they will cost your heart many pains."

"I felt a great fire in my soul and I said to Him: 'What does it matter, Jesus, I want to be the mother. Give them to me. I receive them in order that they cover You with glory'" (*Diary*, June 29, 1903).

Conchita was at that time a young widow, forty-years-old. She joyfully accepted letting herself be crucified on her pen and suffer in a thousand ways for the glory of her Master until she was seventy-five. A long life as a writer, a long life of martyrdom above all. Not the slightest trace of literary vanity appears in her massive written works. If anybody had listened to her, not a single page of her *Diary* would be in existence today. In full sincerity of soul, she begged her first spiritual director to destroy it, as soon as he should learn of her death. "I come to ask you a favor, on my knees and with my arms crossed, in the name of Jesus, to whom you can refuse nothing. Is not that right? May no one at all, apart from you, look at these papers. Jesus, Jesus Himself, does not want me to destroy them today, but on my death, at the very moment, if possible, reduce them to ashes and dust, in the image of their owner. . . . Do you promise me this? Say 'yes' so as not to deprive me of the freedom to pour out here my conscience and all the rest" (*Diary*, 1894).

Her other directors were wise enough to forbid her to burn her writings. Msgr. Luis Maria Martinez, who directed her during her last twelve years and who was himself a spiritual writer, the most famous of Latin America, wrote her on April 4, 1929, "Neither you, nor I, nor anyone knows the treasures contained in the *Diary*. Many a man and many a year will be needed for exploiting them." On April 23 he wrote. "I think that you yourself cannot appreciate the wealth contained in the *Diary*. You know that as long as I am your director, I will never allow you to destroy a single letter of this *Diary*."

The whole collection constitutes an immense written work. More than a hundred volumes were submitted to examination for the Process of canonization. Conchita is the mystic of the Church who has written the most. Her *Spiritual Diary*, the "Account of Conscience," with its sixty-six tomes, constituting a collection more voluminous than St. Thomas Aquinas' *Summa Theologica*, remains the major work and, as it were, the synthesis of the whole. It is a treasure for the whole Church. God made use of a married woman, the mother of nine children and a simple laywoman, to recall to the present day world the Gospel of the Cross and the profound meaning of the principal Christian mysteries.

Chapter II

THE DOCTRINE OF THE CROSS

"The doctrine of the Cross—it is My Gospel."

The Gospel of the Cross

Every creative current of Christian spirituality has sprung from the Gospel. Thus there appeared, in the course of the history of the Church, monastic spirituality, that of the Mendicant Orders and all modern forms of the spirituality of action. For instance, Dominican spirituality is an expression, at once evangelical and original, aimed at continuing the mission entrusted by Jesus to His Apostles, "Go and teach all nations." All the values of the spirituality and organization of the Order of Preachers are intended for the evangelization of the world, according to the text of the first Constitutions drawn up by the Founder himself: "That the Brothers conduct themselves everywhere as men who seek their own salvation and that of their neighbor, in full perfection and in a religious spirit. As men of the Gospel, they follow the steps of their Savior, speaking only with God or about God" (Fundamental Constitution). The same is true of all religious families and of the greatest spiritual masters, the all-embracing asceticism of a *St. John of the Cross*, "Nothing, nothing, nothing, and on the mountain, nothing," is an eminent form of evangelical renunciation wholly dominated by the primacy of love. The "Ascent of Carmel" and the "Nights" take on meaning only in the light of the "Spiritual Canticle" and above all of the "Living

Flame of Love" which brings about, that throughout his whole work there breathes the Holy Spirit.

Likewise, Conchita's spiritual doctrine, the inspiration of the Works of the Cross, is entirely centered on love: *Amor y dolor*. Nothing the least bit dolorous is in the message of the Cross. It has the mission to recall to the world, a genuine mystique of love immolating itself to the image of the Crucified for the glory of the Father in the salvation of men. It is not a particular devotion but truly a "vision of the universe," a new expression of the Gospel of the Cross.

Basic Viewpoint: "Jesus and Jesus Crucified" in His Interior Sufferings as Priest and Host

All Christians are preordained, each according to his personal vocation and his mission in the Church, to express one of the aspects of the mystery of Christ. God the Father, one day told St. Catherine of Sienna, "I had two sons: one by nature, my Only Son, the eternal Word, the other by grace, your Father Dominic. He has received as his mission the office of the Word." As the Apostles of Christ, the Dominicans must be men of the Word of God. Each religious family imitates in this way Christ, according to its own specific grace: the care of the sick, teaching of the youth, Christian and social promotion and the thousand forms of active or contemplative life.

For Conchita, what was her particular way of imitating Christ? The documents of her *Diary* show us how one after the other the personal characteristics of His Son which the Father wished to imprint in her, were revealed to her under the action of the Holy Spirit. We can see how this divine pedagogy little by little formed in her the imprint of the image of Christ.

From her very childhood she was attracted by *Jesus;* then by *Jesus Crucified*, but in an original novel manner: by the *interior sufferings* of Christ, *Priest* and *Host*, Priest and Victim in His least actions, from His *Ecce Venio* to His *Consummatum est* on the Cross. An invitation to all men continually to offer Christ to His Father and to offer themselves with Him according to His same glorifying and salvific purposes. Here are the progressive stages of this identification with Christ: to be another Jesus, a Crucified Jesus, especially in the interior sufferings of Christ's Heart, Priest and Host, ever present in His Church through the Eucharist freely associating Himself with all the members of His Mystical Body, and continuing in each one of them by mystical incarnation, His mission of glorifier of the Father and savior of men.

Jesus

After St. Paul, every saint aspired to this identification with Christ, each according to his place and his mission in the Church. For Conchita, as for Teresa of Avila or Thérèse of Lisieux, the spiritual life is SOMEONE. It is Jesus! This married young lady, filled with love for her husband and her children, is irresistibly drawn by Christ, Master of her heart and supreme Ruler of all her loves. "Jesus, since I love You, whatever You wish, I will be happy. I would rather die a thousand times than commit one single deliberate venial sin. Ever to do what is most perfect, solely to please You, that is the sun which inflames all my actions. That is the brilliant light, the motive force, the ideal dominating my thoughts. The subject of my prayers and of all my aspirations will be constantly, day, night and always, one single resolve, carried out with all the energies of my soul. "My life, it is Christ. From today on exteriorly I will be Jesus Christ . . . and interiorly Jesus Christ" (*Diary*, 1894).

This Jesus Christ is not for Conchita the gentle *Little Jesus* whose robe changes color according to the liturgical season, as is done here below.

In the light of her faith, Conchita discovers in Jesus the eternal Word, the Only Begotten Son of the Father, the Head of the Church, the eternal Priest. She lovingly contemplates the infinite riches of the Incarnate Word, true God and true Man. She adores in Him the Second Person of the Trinity. She is dazzled by the generation of the Word and by the role of the Word in the inspiration of Eternal Love. She finds all in Jesus Christ. She groans in pain at the thought that a God died out of love for all the men who know Him not. As for her, her *Diary* is as full as her soul with this Sovereign and Theological Presence of Jesus. "The soul which has experienced this vision of union with Jesus cannot live alone" (*Diary*, Oct., 1893).

We understand her. . . . But she does not stop there. . . .

Jesus and Jesus Crucified

Among Christ's mysteries, it is the mystery of His Passion and Death which holds her entire attention. She fixes her gaze on the Crucified in order to have Him come into her life. *Contemplate in order to reproduce.*

"Christ is like a prism the light from which is refracted in varied luminous rays. Which is the color that should dominate in me? Here it is, to have nothing save Jesus and Jesus Crucified. . . . I must reproduce Jesus in me through the transformation virtues, bring about, that is by way of the Cross, that which makes us most like Him. Jesus wishes of me, not a Christ in the poverty of Bethlehem, not a Christ in the hidden life of Nazareth, not a Christ zealously active in His public life, but a Christ in the ignominy, the abandonment, and the crucifixion of Calvary and of the Eucharist. I must reproduce in me Christ Crucified" (*Diary*, Sept. 16, 1921).

This is clear, "I feel I was born to serve the Lord, crucified with Him, He told me that such is the purpose of the union sought by the Word: to be like Him through the Cross" (*Diary*, Feb. 26, 1897).

In His Interior Sufferings

On this subject there are countless texts. Without doubt, every form of Christian spirituality is marked by the seal of the Cross, but God reveals to Conchita the peculiar way she is to imitate Christ: above all, in the inner sufferings of His soul, that is, in

His interior Crucifixion. It is here we have a new aspect which will mark with a special seal the entire spirituality of the Cross. "I wish that above all, there be honored the interior sufferings of My Heart, sufferings undergone from My Incarnation to the Cross and which are mystically prolonged in My Eucharist. These sufferings are still unsuspected by the world. None the less I declare to you that, from the first moment of my Incarnation, the Cross already planted in My Heart, overburdened Me and the thorns penetrated it. The blow struck by the lance might have been some solace causing to gush from My Side a volcano of love and of suffering but I did not consent to that until after My death. I only receive ingratitude. That is why My Heart overflowing with tenderness will ever feel the thorns of the Cross. In heaven, as God, I cannot suffer. To find this Cross which above did not exist, I descended into this world and became man. As God-Man, I could suffer infinitely to pay the price of the salvation of so many souls. During My life, I never desired anything except the Cross, and ever the Cross, wanting to show the world That which is the sole wealth and happiness on earth, the currency which will buy an eternal happiness.

"By the Apostolate of the Cross will be venerated the interior sufferings of My Heart symbolically represented by the Cross, the thorns, and a spear. I draw hearts to the Cross. In these houses, in this '*oasis*' will be honored this ocean of interior sufferings today known to but very few. There, they will take My thorns and with them pierce their own hearts. They will lighten the weight of the Cross which burdens My Heart, themselves becoming living Crosses. Their lives will remain wholly secluded in the interior of the Cross of My Heart, venerating, alleviating, making their own these interior sufferings which, for thirty-three years, never left Me for a single moment. Here is the ideal of the Contemplatives of the Cross.

"I only remained on the Cross of Calvary for three hours, but on the interior Cross of My Heart, my whole life. The monasteries (Oasis) will venerate both of them but especially my Interior Cross which symbolizes these pains and these inner sufferings, so incomprehensible, which constantly oppress my soul. These sufferings remained hidden during My life. I smiled, I labored. Only My Mother was aware of this martyrdom which crushed My loving Heart. My external Passion lasted but a few hours. It was like a gentle dew, a comfort for the other Passion, terribly cruel, which tortured ceaselessly My soul!" (*Diary*, Sept. 25, 1894).

St. Thomas Aquinas taught the same doctrine: the interior and redemptive sufferings of Christ's soul were incomparably more painful than the physical pain of the Crucified of Golgotha. The intensity of the inner and hidden sufferings of Christ's soul, in view of the expiation of all the sins of men, is measured by His infinite love. Rightly, then, a Teresa of Avila, as did Conchita, professed an exceptional devotion to Christ's agony in Gethsemane "My Heart is filled with sorrow to the point of death" (Mk 4:34). It is in Christ's soul our destiny is carried out.

Christ: Victim For Our Sins

Very soon Christ revealed Himself to Conchita as the *Victim* offered in expiation for all the sins of the world. He thereby prepared her to offer herself with the same redemptive intent. This aspect of Host and of expiatory *Victim* is going to appear to her as one of the characteristics of the Crucified. Its express formulation is found in the very first volume of her *Diary*. "You Victim and I Victim, before you yourself are a victim for yourself and for the whole world and constantly" (*Diary*, 1893-1894).

"I want you to be truly one with Me. I wish you to be like a very clear mirror in which is reproduced the image of your Jesus Crucified. I wish you to reflect Me in you, such as I was on the Cross. On your part, abandon yourself simply to receive in you My image. I wish you to be as I am: crowned with thorns, scourged, nailed to the Cross, in desolation, pierced, abandoned... Meditate one by one all these things and be My living portrait in order that My Father find in you His pleasure and pour out His graces on sinners" (*Diary*, April 6, 1895). A most beautiful text which we have already mentioned apropos of her itinerary of transformation into Christ Crucified, seems to us equally suitable here.

Christ: Priest and Host

"The Church is one, one only Altar, one only Victim. . . . All souls, victims, should offer themselves in union with this great Victim" (*Diary*, June 20, 1898).

Through these concepts of *Victim* and *Host*, God will lead Conchita toward the supreme prerogative of Christ Crucified: His Priesthood, which constitutes as it were the keystone of the teachings of the Cross. This revelation will blaze forth at the moment of the *central grace* of the mystical incarnation. On that day, Conchita's full vocation will be clearly manifested to her.

The spirituality of the Cross has thus rediscovered and set in great relief the "royal priesthood" of the People of God, fifty years before Vatican II. "Here is the true priesthood: to be a victim with the Victim" (*Diary*, July 17, 1906). This spirituality, deeply within, has an essentially sacerdotal character, and joins with it the most basic vocation of the People of the Covenant: "a people of priests and of kings."

The Lord had told Conchita, some time after the mystical incarnation. "You are at once altar and priest, since you possess the most holy Victim of Calvary and of the Eucharist and since you have the power of offering Him constantly for the salvation of the world. It is the most precious fruit of the great favor of My mystical incarnation in your heart. . . . You are My altar and at the same time you will be My victim. Offer yourself in union with Me. Offer Me at every instant to the eternal Father, with the sublime intent of saving souls and of glorifying Him. Forget all and especially yourself. Let this be your constant concern. You have received a sublime mission. As you see, it is not for yourself alone but universal, obliging you with all purity possible to be at the same time altar and victim consumed in holocaust with the other Victim, the Unique Host, pleasing to God and able to save the world" (*Diary*, June 21, 1906).

From the mystical incarnation, Conchita became fully aware of this sacerdotal nature of her personal vocation and of her mission in the Church. "For me, to live is to be Christ.". . . In the measure of our union with Christ, we participate in His life and Christ grows in us in the measure in which we disappear.

"We must take Christ as Model, but each soul, each saint, reproduces Christ under diverse aspects. How is each one to imitate Christ? This is the secret of spiritual direction. To unite oneself to Christ as Model, is to live out of His life and to put on His likeness. Certain souls should model themselves on Him as the Christ Child, others as the Eucharistic Christ, others as Christ Crucified. . . . As for me I am to model myself on Christ under two aspects which are identical: *Christ Priest*—she stressed—and *Christ Crucified*. In any way Christ is Priest in reference to the Cross.

"The most sublime aspect in Christ is His Priesthood centered on the Cross. The Eucharist and the Cross constitute one and the same mystery. The first form of union consists in living the life of Christ by grace and the second by imitation. For me, I repeat, the aspect I must imitate, in virtue of the mystical incarnation, is His priesthood centered on the Cross. The monasteries of the Cross (Oasis) are but one vast Mass" (*Diary*, Dec. 28, 1923).

The Eucharistic Christ

This identification "of the Eucharist and of the Cross in one and the same mystery" reveals to us the last characteristic of Christ's physiognomy in Conchita's eyes. Her Christ Crucified is the Priest and Host Christ, immolated on the Cross, the state of victim of which the Eucharist perpetuates until the end of time, for the glory of the Father and the salvation of the world. The Eucharistic devotion is not something accidental. It is rather, the very "center" of its life. As for the Church, the supreme form of her devotion to the Crucified, is the eucharistic sacrifice, which is not purely a symbol but the efficacious memorial which renders the Crucified Himself present in His pilgrim and militant Church, in the trueness of His being and the reality of His substance, with His Body, His Blood, His Soul and His Divinity. With His Personality of Word, inseparable from the Trinity, the Crucified of Golgotha holds Himself day and night, raised above the earth, between God and men for the glory of the Trinity and the salvation of the world.

Christ glorified, ever present before the face of the Father in the bosom of His Church triumphant, the same Christ who once traveled along the roads of Samaria, of Judea and of Galilee, the same Christ born of the Virgin Mary, the true Christ of history, the Unique Christ is ever here among us. Hidden under the appearances of the Host, there is the Presence of the highest divine reality, the authentic Presence of the Eternal Incarnate Word, binding together earth and heaven, the cosmos and the Trinity. Conscious of this Presence, Conchita lived even in her home, quite close to her Christ, her Savior and her God, her *Supreme Love.*

Is it surprising that the texts are so countless in her *Diary* which treat of the most difficult and most profound problems about the mystery of the Eucharist? She comments on the words of the Consecration. "This is My Body. This is My Blood," with the mastery of a professional theologian. Her eucharistic doctrine, of impeccable orthodoxy, is found within the most sublime pages of her *Diary*, pages written under the *"dictation"* of the Lord.

God the Father therefore has revealed little by little to Conchita the characteristics of the true physiognomy of His Son Jesus, Incarnate and Crucified Word, who by His interior sufferings more than by His external Passion, saved us by the Cross, as Priest and Host, leaving to His Church an efficacious memorial of His real Presence and of His ceaseless action upon each one of us until the end of time, until the "consummation" of men in unity with the Father, the Son and the Holy Spirit. The Trinity is the Beginning and the End of this economy of salvation, but

Christ—Mediator, with His "royal priesthood," shared by His own, constitutes the keystone of His mission of glorifier of the Father and Savior of men.

In the great syntheses of human thought, secular or religious, is ever discovered a center of perspective, an angle of view, which brings together in the unity of one and the same outlook all particular aspects, down to the last detail. The basic viewpoint of the teachings of the Cross is incontestably *Jesus, and Jesus Crucified*. In this vision of synthesis of the mystery of Christ, the priesthood dominates all.

Primacy of the Holy Spirit

Before He left His Apostles, the Lord had promised them on the part of His Father not to leave them orphans, but to send them "another Paraclete, the Holy Spirit, to bring them to the fullness of truth.", and to sustain them in their combats by His invincible Force. The Acts of the Apostles clearly bring out this miraculous assistance of the Holy Spirit in the primitive Church, to such an extent that St. John Chrysostom calls "the Acts," the Gospel of the Spirit. In continuity with the patristic tradition, the great theologians of the Middle Ages have reserved to the Spirit of God an eminent place in their doctrinal systematizations. In his *Summa contra Gentiles* (IV, 20, 21, 22), St. Thomas Aquinas has left us a resume of this common teaching in three rightly celebrated chapters. After two centuries of pure deism, Vatican II has brought about a vigorous redressing in favor of the *Church of the Trinity*, in which the principal role of the Holy Spirit is clearly brought out. Due to the prominent place of the Holy Spirit in the spirituality of the Cross, the conciliar text constitutes the best introduction for marking, according to the present directives of the Magisterium, the primacy of the Holy Spirit in the life of the Church.

"When the work which the Father had given the Son to do on earth (cf. Jn 17:4) was accomplished, the Holy Spirit was sent on the day of Pentecost in order that He might forever sanctify the Church, and thus all believers would have access to the Father through Christ in the one Spirit (cf. Ep 2:18). He is the spirit of life, a fountain of water springing up to life eternal (cf. Jn 4:14; 7:38-39). Through Him the Father gives life to men who are dead from sin, till at last He revives in Christ even their mortal bodies" (cf. Rm 8:10-11).

"The Spirit dwells in the Church and in the hearts of the faithful as in a temple (cf. 1 Cor 3:16). In them He prays and bears witness to the fact that they are adopted sons (cf. Gal 4:6; Rm 8:15, 16, 26). The Spirit guides the Church into the fullness of truth (cf. Jn 16:13) and gives her a unity of fellowship and service. He furnishes and directs her with various gifts, both hierarchical and charismatic, and adorns her with the fruits of His grace (cf. Ep 4:11-12; 1 Cor 12:4; Gal 5:22). By the power of the gospel He makes the Church grow, perpetually renews her, and leads her to perfect union with her Spouse. The Spirit and the Bride both say to the Lord Jesus, 'Come'!" (cf. Rv 22:17).

"Thus, the Church shines forth as 'a people made one with the unity of the Father, the Son and the Holy Spirit'" (*Lumen Gentium*).

The Holy Spirit Dominates the Cross

If the Cross is at the center of Conchita's spiritual doctrine, the Holy Spirit is at the summit. It dominates the Cross and illumines it from above. "This Holy Spirit is He who governs the world and the Church, after I departed. After the Ascension, I sent Him. Yet if you only knew how little He is honored and how little known! There are hardly any temples in His honor. He is undervalued and little thought of. He is not given the glory He merits as a divine Person. I hide Myself within this Cross of the Apostolate in order that He reign and be adored. The Apostolate of the Cross will erect temples to Him throughout the whole world. In these churches, a cult of perfection will be rendered the Holy Spirit. Without Him this work would crumble, but with His divine breath He will communicate the Spirit of the Cross. Tell all this to your director in order that he reflect and that the first ejaculatory prayer in this Apostolate be an invocation of the Holy Spirit. He will cover with His wings this Apostolate of the Cross and His divine influence is of the greatest importance" (*Diary*, March 1894).

A Hidden and Unexploited Treasure

For many Christians the Holy Spirit is an unknown. The Lord reveals to Conchita His personal identity in the bosom of the Trinity where He is Love, and His mission on the earth is to bring souls to the hearth of Love. Hence the need of the reign of the Holy Spirit and the urgency of a renewal of His cult. The sentence recalls to us that "His mission in heaven, His Life, His Being, is Love." Here we touch on the root of all, on His proper function *ad intra*, from within. His mission *ad extra*, from without, outside the Trinitarian mystery, reflects the properties of love.

"There exists a hidden treasure, a wealth remaining unexploited and in no way appreciated at its true worth, which is nevertheless that which is the greatest in heaven and on earth: the Holy Spirit. The world of souls itself does not know Him as it should. He is the Light of intellects and the Fire which enkindles hearts. If there is indifference, coldness, weakness, and so many other evils which afflict the spiritual world and even My Church, it is because recourse is not had to the Holy Spirit.

"His mission in heaven, His Life, His Being, is Love.

"On earth, His mission consists in leading souls toward this hearth of Love which is God. With Him, there is possessed all that can be desired.

"If there is sadness, it is because recourse is not had to this divine Consoler, to Him who is perfect spiritual joy. If there is weakness, it is because there is no reliance on Him who is invincible Might. If there are errors, it is because of disregard for Him who is Light. Faith is extinguished through the absence of the Holy Spirit. In each heart and in the whole Church, there is not rendered the Holy Spirit that which is due to Him. Most of the evils that are deplored in the Church and in the field of souls comes from not according to the Holy Spirit the primacy which I have given to this Third Person of the Trinity who has taken so active a part in the Incarnation of the Word and in the founding of the Church. He is loved lukewarmly, invoked without fervor and in many hearts, even among My own, not even called to mind. All this deeply wounds My Heart.

" 'It is time that the Holy Spirit reign.' Very moved, the Lord told me this. He went on, 'and not a remote reign as something very sublime, even though it be so and there is nothing greater than He since He is God united and consubstantial with the Father and the Word. But it is necessary that He reign, here, right close, in each soul and in each heart, in all the structures of My Church. The day on which there will flow in each pastor, in each priest, like an inner blood, the Holy Spirit, then will be renewed the theological virtues, now languishing, even in the ministers of My Church, due to the absence of the Holy Spirit. Then the world will change, for all the evils deplored today have their cause in the remoteness of the Holy Spirit, the sole remedy. Let the ministers of My Church react, through the medium of the Holy Spirit, and the whole world of souls will be divinized. He is the axis around which revolve the virtues. There is no virtue without the Holy Spirit. The decisive impulse for raising up My Church from the state of prostration in which she lies, consists in reviving the cult of the Holy Spirit. Let His place be given Him, that is, the first in intellects and wills! No one will be lacking anything with this heavenly wealth. The Father and I, the Word, We desire an ardent and vitalizing renewal of His reign in the Church.' "

"Lord, yet the Holy Spirit reigns in the Church, why do You complain?"

"Woe to Her were it not so! Certainly the Holy Spirit is the soul of this so dearly loved Church! But that about which I am complaining is that there is such little consideration for this gift of heaven, and to Him there is not accorded the importance due. His devotion in hearts is routine and languishing, indifferent, secondary. This brings about countless evils not only in the Church but in all souls. That is why the Works of the Cross have just come to renew devotion to Him and to extend it throughout the earth. May the Holy Spirit reign in souls, and the Word will be known and honored, the Cross taking on a new force in the souls spiritualized by divine Love.

"To the extent the Holy Spirit will reign, sensuality, which today invades the earth, will disappear. The Cross will never take root unless beforehand the soil is made ready by the Holy Spirit. That is why He appeared to you first even before the vision of the Cross. It is because of this He is at the summit of the Cross of the Apostolate.

"One of the main fruits of the mystical incarnation is the reign of the Holy Spirit which must bring about the disappearance of materialism" (*Diary*, Feb. 19, 1911).

Action of the Holy Spirit in Souls and in The Church

The action of the Holy Spirit makes itself felt first in souls but it also extends to the whole Church.

"He is the source of divine grace and He never remains inactive. Day and night, He labors in souls who give themselves to Me, and these souls constantly advance in virtues. But when souls resist or are indifferent, then I withdraw since My graces are of too great a price to be wasted on them. The work of the Holy Spirit in souls is most delicate, and the soul who despises it is quite culpable. . . . If it does not respond to My inspirations, to what I demand of it, I withdraw. There are some souls which it is necessary to push along at each step, others which run and fly. According to the measure of their correspondence with grace, they advance constantly rising to the degree I have destined for them. Be vigilant, hear My voice. You know quite well that for hearing me it is necessary to keep your ears open. . . . A total renunciation of yourself and a constant spirit of sacrifice.

" 'Sacrifice yourself for My Church.' The Lord said this to me over and over again. On different occasions He made me understand the very close relationship which unites the Church with the Cross. He told me. 'The Church was born on the Cross.' The Holy Spirit came later to confirm her teachings and to give her life. The Holy Spirit asserted that the Church is the depositary of all His graces. He has set in Her His abode. He loves Her passionately and no one enters paradise save through Her. The Spirit imprints His seal on all her ceremonies.

"Without the divine seal nothing is done, no salvation is possible" (Letter to Msgr. Leopoldo Ruiz y Flores, June 23, 1904).

The Holy Spirit Stays Close to Souls

The Holy Spirit dwells in the very depths of souls. "He remains with you and will be within you" (Jn 14:17). The whole Trinity dwells in us. "Anyone who loves me will be true to my word, and my Father will love him; we will come to him and make our dwelling place with him" (Jn 14:23). All the baptized who possess grace, are "temples of the Holy Spirit" (1 Cor 6:19).

"Some souls think that the Holy Spirit is very far away, far, far up above. Actually, He is, we might say, the divine Person who is most closely present to the creature. He accompanies him everywhere. He penetrates him with Himself, He calls him, He protects him. He makes of him His living temple. He defends him. He helps him. He guards him from all his enemies. He is closer to him than his own soul. All the good a soul accomplishes, it carries out under His inspiration, in His light, by His grace and His help. And yet He is not invoked, He is not thanked for His direct and intimate action in each soul. If you invoke the Father, if you love Him, it is through the Holy Spirit. If you love Me ardently, if you know Me, if you serve Me, if you imitate Me, if you make yourself but one with My wishes and with My heart, it is through the Holy Spirit.

"He is considered inaccessible and He actually is but there is nothing that exists nearer, more helpful to the creature in his misery than this Being of a supreme transcendence, this most holy Spirit who reflects and who constitutes one and the same holiness with the Father and the Son. Centuries have passed and He remains ever the Principle of all things. He engraves His mark on souls and His sign on the priest. He communicates the light of faith and all the virtues. He irrigates and fertilizes the whole field of the Church. Despite this, He is not appreciated, He is not known, He is not thanked for His perpetually sanctifying action. If the world is ungrateful to Me, how much more so toward the Holy Spirit!

"Here is why I want His glory to be shown to the end of time. . . . One of the cruelest interior sufferings for My Heart was this ingratitude of all times, this worship of idols of other times, and today man's self-worship, forgetful of the Holy Spirit. In these latter days sensuality has set up its reign in the world. This sensual life obscures and extinguishes the light of faith in souls. That is why more than ever, it is necessary that the Holy Spirit come to destroy and annihilate Satan who under this form penetrates even the Church" (*Diary*, Jan. 26, 1915).

The Soul of Christ Moved by The Holy Spirit

Christ is the masterpiece of the Holy Spirit. As Word, He is with the Father, His eternal Principle. The Holy Spirit received all from the Son: His Being in its infinite perfections. He is Love in a Person who proceeds indivisibly from the Father and from the Son in the Oneness of the Trinity. But, as man, Jesus has received all from the Holy Spirit: His incarnation, His being, His life, His action on all the members of His Mystical Body.

"Every movement of My soul has been inspired and carried out under the movement of the Holy Spirit. He it is who animates My faculties, My senses, My will, holding them in His possession for the glory of the Father to whom I return everything. . . . The Holy Spirit loves My humanity with an incomparable predilection. . . . If you only know with what delicacy, with what tenderness, and with what splendor the Holy Spirit adorns My soul, My faculties, My feelings, My body and My heart! Even more than a mother He is all love. He displayed all His might, all His riches to form Me in Mary's womb, as a perfect model of all that is beautiful, pure and holy. All the riches and treasures which adorn My Heart, I owe to the Holy Spirit. I do not like devotion to My Heart, to be regarded as an end, but only as a means of being raised up to My Divinity, as a step for reaching the Holy Spirit since it is He who created, formed and enriched My human heart, who poured on it all the delights of His love as well as all the interior sufferings and the manner of undergoing universal expiation for the pardon of culpable mankind. The heart of man and his body had sinned. There was need of another heart and another body united to the power of a God to give satisfaction to this Other who is God. This plan, this action, this salvific purpose, glorifying my humanity and for the salvation of the world, are owed to the Holy Spirit" (*Diary*, Jan. 29, 1915).

The First Place in the Church

Thus opening up wide horizons, the Lord showed Conchita the unique and primordial place of the Holy Spirit in the works of God. The Holy Spirit was there before creation in the councils of the Trinity, orienting with the Father and the Son the way of the destiny of the world. The Spirit was there, preparing the coming of the Son and carrying it out at the moment of the Incarnation of the Word, ever present and acting in His Church until the end of time.

"The Holy Spirit took an extremely active part in the carrying out of the eternal plan of Redemption. Then, when the time came, He carried out the work of the Incarnation, after having made it clear to the prophets, announcing it to them before hand. During My life it was He who sustained me, He who presented to My Father My infinite expiation and touched souls, drawing them to the Truth which I am. I had promised to send Him and

I have done so, for, in each of His acts, in the sacraments and His infallible action, the Holy Spirit holds in My Church the first place" (*Diary*, Jan. 28, 1915).

Intuition—Key: From Love to Love Through Crucified Love

The greatest geniuses, often after long years of reflection, suddenly discover a central thought which takes on the form of a creative intuition, and they spend the rest of their existence probing it in order to integrate it into their lives and to derive from it a flood of practical applications in the services of other men.

The same phenomenon occurs in the lives of the saints. A Thérèse of Lisieux walked among us thus in search of an *entirely new way* of holiness. *In the Church, I will be love, and thus I will be all.*

Something similar is found in Conchita. A young widow of forty-one she turns more and more toward the Crucified. She accumulates in the rough drafts of her *Diary* for January, 1903 all *the lights of love* which Christ her Master has *dictated* to her. "All at once, while I was listening to a lecture, I became aware as a streak of light in my intellect, as His salvific effects became sensible to my heart." As Teresa of Avila whose life was radically changed when she was around forty years old, Conchita received suddenly by direct illumination from the Holy Spirit, the sovereign intuitions which will constitute the major basics of the spirituality of the Cross: At the summit: God as Love, at the center: Christ Crucified, and on her part, in her own life, a response of love in a single commitment to love.

There is in germ, the global intuition of the spiritual teachings with which the Holy Spirit and the experience of her own love for the Crucified, inspired her. This fresh view of the universe, prophetic and original, discovered for her in a most sublime perspective of wisdom, the two poles of the plan of Redemption: infinite Love and the call to unite with Love and become one with

Love through the Cross. This intuition-key might be formulated thus: from Love to Love through Christ crucified out of love.

God is Love

Our spiritual life is linked to our concept of God. If metaphysics is the moral foundation, dogma governs the mystical. The mystery of the Trinity and the Incarnation of the Word animate Christian spirituality. All the teachings of the Cross depend on the view of a God crucified out of love.

St. Augustine's God is the "Supreme Good" drawing all things to Himself. St. Thomas Aquinas' God is the God of Sinai: "I am who am." St. Thérèse of Lisieux' God is "Merciful Love." Conchita's God is "Crucified Love" which brings us to "Infinite Love." "I do not know how, I understood the essence of God who is all Love. I heard and said this a thousand times. But no, this was something supernatural, a movement which made my heart shake, a light which, like a flash of lightning, illumined the hiddenmost and innermost depths of my spirit. . . . I saw how God is Love. Not only does He possess love, but He is Love itself, eternal Love, uncreated Love, infinite Love. . . ."

Conchita's God is the God of the Gospels, such as St. John presents Him. "God is Love." Here is the supreme foundation of her spiritual doctrine. Her Crucified God is before all else a God of Love.

From this transcendant God who still is all Love, she sees, derived by way of sharing all created riches of the visible and invisible universe, all the good that exists in Him, the world of souls, every legitimate love and all the great horizons of faith: the mysteries of Creation, Incarnation, Redemption, of the death of Jesus on the Cross, of suffering itself and of the cross. I felt how all there is of good, descends from Him and how souls and all nature bear the imprint of the divine seal.

"I saw how every legitimate and holy love, filling man's heart, is a drop from this soundless Ocean, a luminous ray from this immense light! I experienced how love flares out from this infinite hearth of charity which You Yourself are and how You are pleased to set in the heart of man this insatiable thirst for loving, which neither the perishable nor the finite can quench but only the imperishable and the infinite. . . .

"I felt how souls are as it were a particle of God Himself, a gentle breeze for His divine essence, a breathing of His Holy Spirit.

"Oh! the soul is such a wonderful thing, its value is immense! Souls are born of love and must live eternally in love. That is why they are created. They are the fruit of the Most Holy Trinity, and, consequently, immortal. They are heavenly daughters, engendered by love, and inevitably tend toward the infinite, toward what is pure, holy, great and divine.

"This corporal cover was given it for struggling and for meriting, but the soul—this immortal being, what a marvel!—It cannot satiate itself with the human, even when it strives out of love of creatures to erase the image engraved in the depths of its very own being. This is impossible. Another order of things draws it, a *beyond* calls to it constantly, an inner voice cries out thousands upon thousands of times. 'Herein is not your destiny. Higher, much higher! This thirst for the divine tears its heart away from the earth, purifying its earthly affections, even the most holy, placing them in this abyss, this immensity, this bottomless endless ocean, where it was born. . . .' I feel how the love for my husband, my children, my family and for all material goods, is concentrated in one sole love . . . in God.

"I do not know what I experienced on glimpsing this eternal hearth which creation produced, redemption realized . . . founding the Church, which sustains her and setting all hearts afire. And He who is Love, who else is He but the Holy Spirit, the Term of Love? . . . He it is who inspired the creation, the redemption . . . the incarnation . . . the death on the cross . . . the reign of suffering . . . and the Apostolate of the Cross" (*Diary*).

The Cross

Let us now take up the second panel of this triptych: the Cross. Her God is a Crucified God, the central point of her intuition. She will not make a conceptual analysis of it. As all mystics, she speaks from the heart. For her, the Cross is the supreme sign of Love. She does not give a dissertation on the Cross and on Love. She lives them. There is a constant coming and going in her thinking about Love and the Cross, the one inseparable from the other. She sees souls who run away from the Cross, to their misfortune, since they run away from Love. "Show them the Cross. Show them Love." In her eyes, it is one and the same thing. She would like to go all over the world "raising up on high the standard of the Cross," for the Cross is the one and only pathway of Love. "Then comes up the magical name of *Jesus*. Love is He, and He is nailed to a Cross. At the base of her directive intuition and in the very core of her life, for her Jesus is Love Crucified.

"He who is Love wants to make us happy through the Cross, the sole means which after sin, brings us to, urges us, unites us and identifies us with Love itself.

"Why this pitiable error? Souls flee the Cross and, consequently Love, making themselves miserable.

"On my part, I became aware of the worth of a soul and, rightly, how the Heart of God breaks and suffers on seeing them irremediably lost, they who are *His own* by a thousand titles of love.

"Now I contemplate, my mind filled with light, in all created beings a vestige of Love . . . the trace of God, the outstanding proofs of His infinite Charity, which ceaselessly flows over man, vile and wretched being deserving of nothing. Oh! The immensity of the grandeur of this God, bottomless abyss of perfections! Why do we not give ourselves wholeheartedly to Him? Why do we not live absorbed in Him, one with Him?

"Love, Love, all about me cries out! . . . When I see creatures gloating over the vain things of earth, steeped in vice and their minds filled with all that is not God . . . a terrible pain pierces my soul, makes my heart tremble and cry out. 'Save them . . . Show them the Cross . . . Sacrifice yourself for them in silence and obscurity . . .' In my heart a love overflowing with zeal grows and grows. I would run and cry out, I would want my voice to be heard throughout the world and penetrate deeply consciences so that hearts would be moved. I would want to remove the blindfold from the eyes of their souls and show them Love . . . tell them that everything the soul perceives is but a spark, a flash, a ray which must return to its center and lose itself in Him to bring us happiness. I would want to raise aloft the standard of the Cross and traverse the world, announcing that here is the pathway of Love, that it is solely through thorns, blood and suffering that there we rise to be united with the Holy Spirit. He and He alone is the source which can fulfill the infinite aspirations of the soul.

"Pain, the cross! Here is the sole divine ladder by which the soul can reach the consummation of divine love . . . Detachment from the earth and nearness to heaven, to the Heart of God . . . Come, Lord, come into my arms, nail me on Yourself . . . I wish to suffer since it was Love itself that inspired Jesus to suffer in order to make me learn how much He Himself loved. Thence will come such a union between love and suffering that he who loves rejoices in suffering. Jesus loved and suffered. No longer do I wish for love without suffering since without sacrifice, love is not pure, not true, not lasting. If pain is great, love should be great, if love is immense, pain should also be immense. . . . Yes, I repeat, may there come immolation, complete annihilation, so that love may come and absorb what is still of the earth, all the dross and dregs of vices and every stain on creatures."

A Response of Love

"Love responds only to love," said St. Thérèse of Lisieux. We see in Conchita the same heroic ardor to deliver herself constantly over to Love. Her life is an endless offering to Love but to Love on the Cross. She cried out boldly. "My God, if I could take anything from Your Being, I would take away from You Love in order to love You.

"I want to live on love, but on a love which crucifies me. My soul constantly enters into the abyss of Love. My spirit feels as if absorbed in its God and Lord, living as it were in Him, aspiring and breathing in Him alone. . . . I feel as if I were deified, in an atmosphere pure and divine, with great yearnings to sacrifice myself on the altar of love by Love itself.

"Oh, what a wonderful thing love is! I would want to speak only of this Love. All around me, all creation says over and over again: Love!

"One day while riding on a trolley, all of a sudden I heard the Lord's voice. He told me: 'You will enkindle in a multitude of hearts the fire of the Holy Spirit, you will bless them with the sacred wood of the Cross. I was confused and full of shame, but I felt that the Lord would carry out all this, myself being just a poor and miserable instrument.

"God! . . . God! In these words I find abysses of love, of most pure and ardent charity. I experience and feel very strongly in my soul that the Cross springs from love!

"Love! Everything cries out to me, and an inner voice, which springs from the depths of my soul, urges me on to pain, to humiliation, to constant suffering. What a remarkable affiliation between love and suffering! I undergo, as it were, remorse for having lifted myself up to these regions of divine charity, and I seek the Cross. . . . I want to be nailed on it and to abandon myself in its loving arms. Yet, something strange happens, seized by the Cross and my own misery, I feel myself carried along with my miseries and with the Cross, and cast into this bottomless ocean of perfection.

"Lord! Lord! I have nothing but poverty, filth and misery.

Allow me to prostrate myself on the ground and cry out, from the deep abyss of my iniquities: 'Mercy!'

"Crosses are testimonials of the love which draws us to God and makes us merit.

"The sole torment of love consists in not suffering enough for the Beloved. . . . but therein is the great secret of the Cross, which is discovered only by the souls who voluntarily and lovingly sacrifice themselves, nailed on it never to come down from it. . . .

"What should I do, I, plunged in this abyss of light and of fire? How should I, poor me, correspond to this God, Charity in essence, who has overwhelmed me? My God! My God! I die on seeing my nothingness, and I love You! If I could take something from Your Being, I would take away Love in order to love You. . .

"Yes, I hunger for love, I thirst for love. I desire to love and my heart is so little a thing to hold this immensity of love which overflows within and outside of me!

"It is impossible for me to hold the Love of God in my poor soul. What I do is plunge into this boundless ocean . . . hurl myself into this fire . . . into the boundless depths of the infinite essence of God. I know no other thing than to lose myself like an imperceptible point in the immensity of the possession of God" (*Diary*).

The Two Poles

This triptych, displaying itself like an immense fresco under her contemplative gaze, is inspired by a grandiose and dramatic vision which reveals to her the plan of the Universe of the redemption set around two poles: God and man, the infinite Love of God for man and the rejection of love by a multitude of human beings called to love. Between the two poles stands the Cross to which Christ is nailed between God and men.

"The plan of Redemption unveiled itself, as it were, before my eyes. I behold it as through a magnifying glass and under a flood of light. In this field of vision, all illumined, there stands out the immense and incomparable Love of God for man and of man for God, the two poles which unite them in the abyss of its grandeur.

"I tremble upon contemplating these things, for it seems to me that God will demand of me a strict accounting if I do not profit from them by loving Him and being grateful to Him for them.

"I discover His admirabe eternal patience and the incredible hardness of the human heart. I think I am dreaming when I see men wearing themselves out running after vanities of the world, and never stopping to consider their redoubtable debt of love, of suffering and of blood. . . .

"How is what I see possible? Of what sort of insensitive nature are we formed? No, what makes the soul insensitive, is the life of the senses, this sensuality which seeks only self-satisfaction in laxity and in ease, binding the spirit and cutting off its wings.

"The absence of the Cross is the cause of all evils. Yet what do we do, we others who love? Why not go about helping our souls awakening them and inflaming them with the wood of the Cross? My God! I feel so powerless to satisfy these vehement yearnings of my heart which, on seeing that I cannot vanish nor make my voice heard by souls, as a loud cry, I feel the desire to act furiously against myself, to tear myself to pieces, to sate myself with the Cross, to compensate in myself as much as possible, although I am worthless, this need to render glory to God which consumes my poor wretched soul" (*Diary*).

"Love! I feel I am hardly at the threshold of Love and yet it carries my heart, my soul and my life toward Him.

"I see with great clarity, accompanied by rapid flashes of light, all that is vain and perishable on this earth and all that is great, divine and holy in the attributes of God, penetrating in detail all His movements which augment as it were His Bounty. What I think is going on is that the Lord deigns to let fall certain veils. And also, it is evident that I discover more light, more warmth, more fire."

The Curtain Rises

Conchita could conclude. "I feel that Jesus is behind the door of my mind. Today I feel His warmth, His radiance, His light, His splendor, and, I might say, the comprehension of His mysteries, seeing them clearly, as necessary, in natural order. My heart also felt the need for the Church, the victory won by the Work of Redemption, and all this, all at once, as when a stage curtain rises and one grasps all the details of the scene" (*Diary*, Jan. 1903).

This vision of the world, is Christ present in her intellect who revealed it to her through His Spirit of love. It is not yet complete. It lacks the priesthood of Christ, the role of Mary, the Eucharist, the mystical incarnation, the final consummation in the unity of the Trinity. It is but a rough draft and like to a creative intuition still unfinished. Conchita glimpses even now other horizons: the mystery of the Church and the definitive victory of God through the Work of the Redemption. None-the-less it was a very beautiful spectacle of God and of the universe. As at the theater the scene suddenly appears in full clarity, the Word had illumined Conchita's soul, exposing in it a flash, at the center of the world, His Redemptive Cross in the radiance of infinite Love.

Man's Destiny

"Oh Jesus, if such a distance separates us, if between this nothingness and Your Immensity there is an impassible abyss, how is union possible between these two poles?

"Jesus answered me, 'Between these two poles, God and you, I am there. I, God made man, alone can join them very closely. No one arrives at the Immensity of God, no one perceives My Divinity, without passing through Me. Likewise, without Me, no one can humble himself, nor be conscious of his nothingness. I am the center, the gateway, the road, the light which gives self-knowledge and introduces to contemplation. I am the point of encounter, the Redeemer, the Light, the Life, the Hearth of eternal perfection. Study this book, your Christ, and you will be a saint on imitating Him.'

"He explained to me how, on one side, He held one arm resting on the Cross and how He reached the opposite pole and how the union of these two extremes was accomplished in His Heart" (*Diary*, Aug. 25, 1895).

Conchita's vision of the universe, as that of mystics, does not involve a scientific knowledge of created beings, as does that of a philosopher and of a scholar, but opens up onto a spiritual itinerary which brings man to God. It is the "science of the saints." It belongs to the line of great spiritual persons such as a Teresa of Avila, a St. John of the Cross, a Thérèse of Lisieux, each respectively writing down a "road of perfection," a "path of nothing," leading souls to the summit of Mount Carmel, or a Thérèse of Lisieux, revealing "a tiny way" quite new, of confidence and love for going to God. Conchita leads souls to God through the Cross. For her, the Cross is the one and only "path of Love."

A Catherine of Sienna will say that Christ is the "point" which permits us to join God. Under different images, all profess their faith in Christ, "the one and only Mediator between God and men.", as St. Paul teaches. "How would the Crucified not be at the *center* of this doctrine of the Cross?"

After having understood that the fundamental viewpoint of this spirituality is "Jesus and Jesus Crucified," glimpsed in the superior light of the Holy Spirit, there remains for us to analyze the multiple aspects and the diverse stages of this spiritual itinerary. The sinner removes himself from evil by expiation and penitence until the death of his own "ego." He tends toward God positively by the practice of Christian virtues and the gifts of the Holy Spirit, who leads souls to the highest summit of the spiritual life: the mystical incarnation the main act and fundamental attitude of which will consist in the constant oblation of the Incarnate Word to His Father, and in the total offering of our own life through Him, with Him and in Him, for the glory of the Father and the salvation of the world. It is a new presentation of the Gospel of the Cross.

If one wants to understand this spirituality of the Cross, it is of capital importance to grasp that man, the subject of spiritual life, is a being essentially sinful. Modern thought, wholly centered on man, presents the Marxist man, the existentialist man, the businessman, the artist, the scholar, the man avid for personal freedom, the man independent of God, and master of his own destiny, in a universe constructed by and for him. An erroneous view but one spread widely throughout the globe by multiple forms of atheistic humanism. Vatican II answered this by presenting, in the light of faith, the integral vocation of man, the image of God, called to model himself on Christ, true God and true man, so much the more man as he resembles Christ, and as he enters into communion with His pascal mystery. This is the Christian view of man such as Conchita's writings now reveal to us.

Man is only explained through God. He derives his origin from the Trinity. He lives on earth imitating Christ and will fulfill his supreme destiny in "its consummation in the unity of the Trinity," a sublime view, achieving the highest aspirations of human personality.

"God created men, happy in forming him 'in His image' in order to draw him to heaven" (*Diary*, July 23, 1906).

"If man understood his divinization, he would no longer sin. He is the temple of the Holy Spirit, in his soul, an image of the Trinity. He has a divine origin (and), that is why he is immortal. He participates in God in each one of his acts and movements. He lives for Him. Consequently, how not to live out of Him? Such is precisely the disorder in the creature who endeavors by sin precisely the disorder in the creature who tries to detach Himself from God by sin, something which furthermore is impossible, since it cannot live apart from God nor erase God from its soul nor His reflection, no matter how great the stain and blackness of his sins" (*Diary*, April 23, 1913).

"God created man solely for joy but sin has thwarted this plan, for a soiled creature cannot be called to an immortal happiness. A purification is necessary, which is precisely the role of pain, to cleanse souls. Suffering, joined with the divine expiation of the Incarnate Word, has opened up heaven to us, permitting man once more to be able to possess an eternal happiness." (*Diary*, April 18, 1913).

"The soul is immortal. It bears in itself the image of the Trinity, the germ of Unity, a tendency toward the infinite and the divine. This is why, on earth, it does not find full satisfaction" (*Diary*, April 15, 1913).

"I am man. If I had not existed, man would never have existed. God loves the soul as a reflection of the Trinity and he loves the body as a reflection of Me, the perfect Man, type and model of every man" (*Diary*, July 27, 1906).

Through these texts, selected somewhat at random from Conchita's *Diary*, we find the elements of a Christian anthropology bringing us to a solution of the present problem of man. In the light of faith of his baptism, man appears to her as "an image of the Trinity." She thus has the same concept had by the greatest masters of Christian thought. St. Augustine shows the heart of man discontented until he reposes in God, for he was created to "rejoice in the Trinity." Following St. Augustine, St. Thomas states specifically, "The vision of the Trinity in Unity is the end and the fruit of our whole life" (I *Sent*. d. 2, q. 1).

As Vatican II, to understand man, the *Diary* of Conchita invites us to look on Christ. "Whoever follows after Christ the perfect man, becomes himself more of a man" (*Gaudium et Spes*, 41).

Asceticism and Penance

The Christian view of life is realistic. Faith discloses to us a sinful humanity. All the books of the Bible, from Genesis to Revelation, speak of sin, without despairing pessimism, but with consciousness that the central fact of divine Revelation is the dogma of Redemption. "Christ died for our sins" (1 Cor 15:3). Like that of the prophets of the Old Testament, the evangelical preaching of Jesus and of the Apostles is a ceaseless exhortation to repent and do penance. Due to this fact Christian spirituality is wholly penetrated by the Spirit of the Cross and is expressed by a vigorous antithesis, the basis of all Christianity and formulated by St. Paul: death and life. Christian life is a death to sin and a life in God, in communion with the paschal mystery. The more we die to sin, the more we rise with Christ, to the glory of the Father.

The struggle against sin is at the heart of the teachings of the Cross as well as those of the Gospel. The Lord reminded Conchita of this very strongly. "Penance is a great virtue and the spirit of repentance is a gratuitous gift which God grants to whom He pleases." Its influence is universal, not only for liberating man from sin, but for helping him practice all the virtues. "I have given it to you from your most tender childhood. Penance is the rampart protecting chastity. Penitence appeases God's justice and transforms it into graces. It purifies souls, extinguishes the fires of purgatory and receives in heaven a most sublime recompense. Penance pays for personal faults and those of others. Penance is the sister of mortification. Both work together hand in hand. Penance helps the soul rise above things of the earth. Penance cooperates with the Redemption of the world. Penance humbles man, it penetrates him with an inner feeling of his baseness and his wretchedness. Penance brings light to the soul. It consumes and causes to disappear all in it that is purely material. It raises him higher and higher above the earth, making him taste of delights hitherto unknown and pure. But this penance should be the daughter of reverence and exist in the soul, hidden from all humans" (*Diary*, Sept. 24, 1895).

Every master of spirituality recalls the need of a spiritual combat against self and against tendencies which remain in each of us, even after a sincere conversion. It is necessary to fight to the death, "I must strive to uproot this 'ego' which tenaciously stands up at every instant, wanting to dominate everything. With the help of grace, I feel this 'ego' growing weaker and more prone to self-surrender, but I would like to kill it and bury it deeper and deeper.

"Truly the most formidable foe of perfection is 'ego,' with

its self-love, its tastes, its seeking for ease and comfort. Once this 'ego' is conquered, the place is ours and Jesus is ours too, entirely, He does not come into a house already occupied. Then the Holy Spirit becomes everything for us. He only sets up His shelter in the solitude of a pure soul. Then the Father's eyes like to repose on a dwelling where His divine image can be reflected. Oh the delightful deprivation of everything, absolute emptiness, wholly filled with God! Oh solitude and happy quietude, total oblation of the creature to its Creator! Oh true and perfect spiritual poverty in which the soul keeps nothing for itself! It appropriates nothing of what the Lord has deposited in it. Humble and grateful, it makes everything ascend toward the eternal Master of all things!

"Blessed are the poor in spirit! This poverty possesses heaven even on earth since it possesses God Himself" (*Diary*, Sept. 5, 1897).

Two things are to be noted here. It is always in reference to the Holy Spirit and in the spirit of the Beatitudes that the teachings of the Cross are presented.

In the sinner the purification of the whole human being prepares for divine union. The Fathers of the desert formed their neophytes in total purity in order to lead them toward divine contemplation. Then it is that "perfect spiritual purity" takes on its full meaning. "It does not consist only in the absence of stain in the body and in the soul, but in an absolute separation from every affection and every act less than pure. There is the most sublime stage of this divine virtue which brings us closest to the purity of angels, that is, makes us like to God. In God purity is natural. God is as it were a crystal without a flaw and, I understand but cannot explain it. Nothing less than this divine transparency is capable of reflecting the image of the Most Holy Trinity. God is light, God is clarity. God is transparency. The Lord told me time and time again that God's essence is purity itself for purity is the essence of light, of clarity and limpidity. Where purity appears, there shines out the reflection of God, that is, His holiness. From this hearth of eternal purity, which is

God, springs light, clarity and limpidity. It is not purity which springs from light, but light which springs from purity. That is why, in pure souls, the light of the Holy Spirit is clearly seen" (*Diary*, Dec. 19, 1896).

Christian Virtues and the Gifts of the Holy Spirit

The saint advances toward God *by steps of love*, "*gressibus amoris*," St. Gregory says. When the Church wishes to place some one on the altar to be a model for all other members of the Mystical Body, she proceeds, during the process of canonization, to examine minutely into the heroicity of his virtues. The Gospel criterion is decisively confirmed: a tree is known by its fruit. The Lord Himself· reminded us of this fundamental law: "If anyone loves Me, he will keep My commandments." The books of the Old Testament never cease commending to the just the practice of all the virtues, not only faith, hope and charity but a multitude of other virtues: patience, prayer, adoration, respect for persons and for the welfare of others. Yahweh had promulgated a Decalogue as a code of the Covenant; the Sermon on the Mount, the charter of evangelical perfection animated by the Holy Spirit, speaks of precepts to observe and vices to shun. The axis of holiness revolves through the exercises of the Christian virtues and the gifts of the Holy Spirit in the spirit of the Beatitudes.

It is significant to note that the Lord was extremely concerned with *dictating* to Conchita a whole treatise on Virtues and Vices. "During these long months of Concha's illness the Lord dictated to me these virtues according to the promise He had made me some years previously.

"How many nights, while watching over my sick little child, facing the Church of the Incarnation, in the midst of spiritual communions and acts of love, the Lord made me take up my pen, to open up His heart to His poor creature" (*Aut.* 1, 146-147).

The Lord dictated to her in this way the description of ninety-three virtues and one hundred and ten vices, the Gospel Beatitudes, and, somewhat later, the gifts of the Holy Spirit. The collection constitutes a truly practical compendium, a master-piece of spirituality.

It is possible, here, to cite only a few examples, taken at random from the exposition of the theological virtues.

I Want to Speak to You about Faith

"'Today, I want to speak to you about faith.' I then felt myself flooded and enraptured by a light in my understanding, enlight-ening my mind. In this interior silence, I began to hear some divine and inexplicable things about faith. I shall try to tell in so far as I can, being so miserable, the beautiful things I heard.

"Faith is the foundation of holiness. It is a special light, com-ing from heaven by which the soul sees God in this world. It is a ray of light, illumining God's countenance and making Him visible to the soul. It is the life and force of the spirit, the sun which heats it, brightens it, ever making it increase in perfec-tion and in holiness. God so loves this virtue, a direct emanation from His own divinity, that the soul which possesses it, disposes of, it might be said, the will of God, inclining Him to grant it what it desires. It is a virtue to which He grants all His power. There is question here of the faith of a humble soul.

"Faith is a torch which illumines, with its light, the obscurity of the spirit. It is solely by this light that the soul travels safely amidst the difficulties of a life bent on perfection, so that a fully developed supernatural faith is indispensable. It constitutes the capital point of the soul which consecrates itself to the interior life. This supernatural faith attains its perfection going beyond all that is natural and supernatural in the soul, fixedly gazing on one point: God, never separating itself from Him, on any occa-sion of life or death. . . . If this faith sheds its light on souls and casts on them its divine influence, it renders them spiritual, filled with delicacy, elevating all their actions and movements higher above the earth, persisting in these obscure regions and making them acquire great merit. Faith is a light but it lives in obscurity, it is enveloped in its shadows and the soul rarely perceives it. It radiates the soul by its clarity, in its very interior, making it know and showing it the dangers and riches of the spirit. It only slightly externalizes itself. This life of obscurity which purifies souls is what makes them merit this beautiful title of martyrs of the faith, since, in truth, the life of the spirit is an existence of martyrdom, that is, a life on the Cross in the exercise of all virtues.

"Faith tears away the veil of mysteries. The soul which possesses this virtue touches, experiences and at times contemplates real presence in the Eucharist, the mystery of faith par excellence and the mystery of love. The soul sees itself miserable in the light of this mystery of faith, and if it does not as yet see the clarity of the beatific vision, face to face, none the less in truth it admires its splendor. Its ardor consumes it and, in the vivacity of this faith, it annihilates itself before the love of a God it contemplates so closely" (*Diary*, Oct. 31, 1895).

The Virtue of Hope

"The virtue of hope is one which does not linger to desire nothing or to ask nothing of the earth, neither personal prestige, riches nor honors. It has set its flight higher: it expects the possession of God Himself not due to personal merit of the soul but on account of the superabundance of My infinite merits. The soul which possesses holy hope, rejoices not for its own good which will come about for it eternally. It goes beyond its personal, legitimate and permissable good, but it rises higher, and it does not stop at its own glory but at the glory which, through it, God Himself will receive. The virtue of supernatural and perfect hope consists in yearning constantly for the possession of the Beloved, not for itself but for the glory of God, working efficaciously to obtain it, choosing and embracing the way of the Cross.

"Apropos of this, Jesus told me. 'Just as I am your hope, I am equally your way. He who follows Me never walks in darkness but the way I represent is the Cross. He who wishes to come after Me must deny himself, bear his cross and follow Me setting his feet on My bloodstained tracks. . . .' He assured me that the Cross is the dwelling place of perfection, that it contains all the mysteries, gifts and fruits of the Spirit" (*Diary*, Nov. 3, 1895).

Primacy of Love

"Love is the soul of every life of prayer and of every good work. If they are not accompanied by love, all of men's works are dead. Love is the fire which inflames everything. When a soul possesses this holy love, it revives in it faith and hope and urges it on to the practice of all the moral virtues.

"The soul which loves Me runs along the paths of perfection unconcerned about the thorns it trods on. It then comes to fly without hindrance from the thousands of obstacles it meets. It overcomes them by the interior ardor of a living faith and a holy hope. The theological virtues have their seat and their development in love. Charity communicates to them life and brings them up to heaven. The world has no idea of the grandeur of these three theological virtues which are founded on divine love.

"Some souls do not love Me. That is why they are lost. Among the souls who love Me and call themselves *Mine*, how few there are who give Me their whole heart! Almost always I receive but a part of their heart. All of it, so rarely! Nevertheless I want them to love Me '*with all their heart, with all their soul, with all their strength!*' The human heart turns partly toward creatures, toward the world, toward self. Self-love for the greatest part fills it. It lives and breathes only for that. I demand a love which surpasses everything. I have imposed this precept on them to render men happy and to save them. Despite this, how few, I repeat, are the souls who carry out My sovereign will to perfection! I wish them well and they resist. I present them with a treasure and they despise it. I give them life and they run to death. To love and to sacrifice oneself, therein is the eternal felicity in heaven.

"To overcome vices and to practice virtues, it is necessary to sacrifice oneself, but do so with love. The soul which does this, loves Me wholeheartedly and I will be its eternal recompense. Give Me a love like this, give Me souls who love Me in suffering, who find their joy on the Cross. My Heart thirsts for such a love. I want a pure love, an unselfish love, an expiatory, crucified love, a sound love such as it may be said no longer exists on earth. Yet it is the only true love, the love which saves, purifies and the love I require through My commandments. All other apparent loves do not satisfy Me; all other love is vain, artificial, often culpable, save the love which I have just shown you.

"Love Me as I have loved you, in My interior Cross, after the very first moment of My Incarnation. Love Me in suffering and in sacrifice out of love. Love Me for I am God and solely to please Me. It is toward this love I aspire, the love I desire. Happy the soul possessing it. . . . I promise that on this earth, that soul will begin to taste of the delights of heaven" (*Diary*, Sept. 11, 1900).

Divine Will and Total Self-surrender

The tableau of virtues and vices contains not only specifically distinct virtues but also presents synthetic virtues, which are as it were a harmony of many virtues. Thus, there is had *the divine will and total self-surrender.*

The Will of God

"God's will is a bouquet which is made up of all virtues practiced in an ordinary manner or in a perfect state. His will divinizes them and makes them shine with splendor in His presence. It gives to each a new value on the divine scale and, in the purified soul, it vests them with a special color pleasing to the Holy Spirit. This total and perfect submission to the most holy will of its God and Lord is the greatest of all the virtues a soul can possess. This sublime virtue implies the integral practice of all the other virtues . . . it is the culminating point.

"The Lord adds. 'I have no other food . . . from the first moment of my Incarnation than this divine will. It is through it I came into this world, through it I was raised above the earth to consummate my life in the cruelest of martyrdoms, . . . it then soothed My agony. It was My sole solace, while on earth. I would have suffered death a thousand times to fulfill it. Divine and active Love burned in My heart, had as its main motive to carry out the divine will on behalf of man. The Redemption was naught but the faithful accomplishment of this divine will. Its echo sounds constantly in the depths of My most loving heart, causing it to throb for the salvation of souls and the glorification of My Father.'

"There is a still higher stage in this divine will. It is total self-surrender interiorly to this same will of God. This self-surrender leads to the highest summit of perfection: It is the supreme stage of all virtue" (*Diary*, June 6, 1900).

One grasps the method, the fruit of a divine wisdom communicated through the experience of divine things, under the personal movement of the gifts of the Holy Spirit. She analyzes them one after the other in the same way moreover in a brief but interesting treatise on the seven gifts.

She follows the same method in the presentation of the Beatitudes.

Love is All

Not the least trace of the dolorous is found in this spirituality of the Cross where suffering is the supreme expression of love.

All begins and ends with love, through the animating and constant presence of the Holy Spirit. This lengthy treatise on the virtues and the vices, on the gifts of the Holy Spirit and on the beatitudes, concludes with the striking affirmation of the unique worth of love. It is significant and is in keeping with the purest Gospel.

When the Lord has finished His *dictations*, Conchita writes in conclusion in her *Diary* and stressing her own convictions states,

"Love is what gives life to all the virtues, to all good works. LOVE IS ALL" (*Diary*, Sept. 21, 1900).

The Mystical Incarnation

Upon stressing the unique worth of love, Conchita comes to what is most essential in the Gospel: "to love God with all her mind, all her will and all her strength . . . this is the first commandment to which all come back. . . ." Spiritual masters have described the three classical stages of this ascent to God through love. Let us hear what St. Thomas Aquinas has to say. St. Thomas is very concerned to explain things through their causes and connects these three phases to the three effects of love.

"For beginners, the primary concern is to avoid sin and imperfections, to purge away sins of the past and to be free from them in the future. The first effect of love is to fight against obstacles."

"For those making progress, love is applied above all to the practice of virtues, indispensable means for our union with God."

"For the perfect, love is based on the end, enjoyment of the Three Divine Persons, and consummation in the unity of the Trinity" (III *Sent.* 29, 8, 1).

The great mystics lingered long describing these higher states of the spiritual life. Thus did two incomparable teachers of Carmel, John of the Cross and Teresa of Avila. Under another not less genial form, St. Thérèse of Lisieux simplified it all by love. Not two doctors, but three were provided to the Church by Carmel.

There is not one sole form of transforming union, but a thousand varieties, or rather an infinity of possible realizations, according to the creative freedom of the Spirit of God and the various needs, according to the epochs, of the Mystical Body of Christ.

Conchita presents us a new type of transforming union. She also is nostalgic for God and the summits. As an adolescent, she rapidly took the first steps of the spiritual life. At the age of nineteen, after her brother Manuel's death, she resolutely lived, first as a young girl, then as a married woman, firmly without sin and in an ever and ever more heroic ascent toward God. In 1894, when she was thirty-two, after the insertion of Christ's name on her bosom, there were the spiritual betrothals (Jan. 23, 1894), and three years later in 1897, the spiritual marriage (Feb. 9, 1897), surpassed by the mystical incarnation (March 25, 1906). This *beyond* of the spiritual marriage is a higher form of *transforming union:* for there is an infinity of possible union stages between the creature and God.

Specialists of the mystical life will have to minutely examine this very point which opens up to the science of spiritual ways new horizons.

The mystical incarnation, despite its supreme rarity, is a grace of transformation in Christ received in germ from baptism and on.

In 1913, when Conchita was examined in Rome, the Lord manifested to her the profound meaning of the mystical incarnation.

The Mystical Incarnation is a Grace of Transformation Into the Crucified

"The mystical incarnation is a grace of transformation in view of an assimilation of the creature with its model Jesus, who I am. It is a transforming grace of union which is not repugnant in any way to My infinite mercies. The Incarnate Word takes possession most intimately of the heart of the creature. He takes life in it to bring about this transforming union. Nonetheless it is always He who communicates life, this life of assimilative grace, especially by way of immolation. Jesus becomes flesh, grows and lives in the soul, not in a material sense but through sanctifying grace, which is unitive and transformative. It is a most special favor. The soul which receives it feels, more or less periodically, the stages of the life of Jesus in it. These stages are ever marked by sufferings, calumnies and humiliations, in sacrifice and in expiation as it was the life of your Jesus on earth. When the Holy

Spirit takes over a soul in this way, He fashions in it, little by little, the physiognomy of Jesus, in the sense I have already indicated to you. To speak of the mystical incarnation, is then to consider the soul as entering into a phase of graces of transformation which will bring it, if it corresponds, to the identification of its will with Mine and to simplify itself in order that its union with God come to the most perfect likeness possible. Such is the purpose of the mystical incarnation which the Holy Spirit gives as a gift to certain souls.

"In the concrete, the mystical incarnation is nothing other than a most powerful grace of transformation which simplifies and unites to Jesus by purity and by immolation, rendering the being in its entirety, as much as possible, like to Him. Because of this likeness of the soul to the Incarnate Word, the eternal Father finds pleasure in it, and the role of Priest and Victim which Jesus had on earth is communicated to it, in order that it obtain graces from heaven for the whole world. That is why, the more a soul is like Me, the more the Eternal Father hears it, not due to its worth but due to its likeness and its union with Me and in virtue of My merits which constitute what counts for obtaining graces" (*Diary*, Dec. 11, 1913).

Briefly, the mystical incarnation is a grace of identification with Christ, Priest and Host, a grace which makes Him continue on in the Members of His Mystical Body, His mission of glorifier of the Father and Savior of men. It is a special grace of transformation in the priestly soul of Christ.

Such is the type of transforming union described by the *teachings of the Cross.*

The Oblation of Love

The principal act of the mystical incarnation is an offering in which is made, not in two acts but in one and the same indivisible initiative, the oblation of Christ to His Father and, in union with Him, through Him and in Him, the total oblation of our own life for the salvation of the world and for the greatest glory of the

Trinity. The principal movement consists in the oblation of the Word to His Father, accompanied by the personal and inseparable oblation of ourselves, and that without reservation, constantly renewed, bearing on our whole being, in the course of every stage of our spiritual life, in union with Christ.

The Lord clearly explained, many a time, this twofold aspect of the unique offering of Christ's love with His Church. But this offering of love, the quintessence of the spirituality of the Cross, is but an indivisible oblation of the Incarnate Word and of all the members of His Mystical Body. Christ was alone on the Cross for offering Himself to His Father in expiation for all the sins of the world. Now He offers Himself with His whole Church, conscious of the unity of this offering of love of the whole Christ. "The Word became flesh and becomes flesh again in souls only to be crucified. It is the purpose of all mystical incarnations. . . . Your Word has just become flesh mystically in your heart . . . in order to be constantly sacrificed there not on an altar of stone, but in a living temple of the Holy Spirit, by a priest and a victim who, by an inconceivable grace, received the power to participate in the love of the Father. In fact, the Father wishes that I Myself, united to your soul as victim, have you sacrifice Me and immolate Me with the same love of the Father on behalf of a world which has need of this spiritual shock and of a grace of this nature in order to be converted. Embrace the Cross and be saved" (*Diary*, Oct. 22, 1907).

The soul thus crucified is called to live, not in the narrow outlooks of its daily routine, but in union with Christ and under the vast horizons of the Redemption of the world. Its life is valued on the scale of the infinite. Although of itself it is so insignificant, it acquires an infinite value for the glorification of God and the salvation of men due to its union with the very Person of the Incarnate Word, Priest and Host. Whence comes the incalculable apostolic worth of such a life. It is the secret of the boundless fecundity of the communion of saints. The obscure and silent existence of the Mother of God, in the evening of her life, by application of the merits of Christ, for the benefit of the nascent Church, was endowed with an immense co-redemptive value incomparably superior to all the works of the apostles and to the sufferings of all the martyrs.

" 'The mystical incarnation,' the Lord has stated, 'has as its object the offering of Myself in your heart, as an expiatory victim, checking at each moment divine justice and obtaining heavenly graces' " (*Diary*, Feb. 2, 1911). The Church and Christ are but one and the same work of Redemption and glorification.

Conchita had perfectly understood it and had made of this oblation of the Word to the glory of the Father and of the constant offering of herself out of love, the whole of her life.

"This is My Body"

" I have renewed My offering to the will of God and I said to Him: 'Lord, I accept this grace of the mystical incarnation with all its consequences of joy and of sorrow, since You will it so and not because I am worthy of it.'

"Insisting on what He Himself will point out as to how this grace is to be used, He told me: 'The principal object of this grace is a transformation which unites what you will to what I will, your will to Mine, your immolation to Mine. Wholly pure and sacrificed in your body and in your soul, you must offer yourself and offer Me to the heavenly Father at each instant, at each breath, on behalf first of all of My priests and of My Church, then of the works of the Cross, of the whole world, of those who are good and those who are evil. You must transform yourself into charity, that is, into Me, who am all Love, killing the *old man*, making with Me but one single heart, and one single will.'

"*This is My Body, this is My Blood*. I say this again to the eternal Father, at each instant, on the altars. Make yourself worthy, as much as possible, to offer your body, your blood, your soul and all that you are, as I have told you, in union with this continual immolation on behalf of the world. Reproduce My life in you with the mark of sacrifice, becoming a living holocaust to His glory. Of yourself, you are worth nothing, but in union with Me you will accomplish your mission on earth saving souls in a secret holocaust known to God alone. The purpose of the mystical incarnation is the fusion of My life in you, according to its development on earth. 'Be yourself,' I told you one day, and today I tell you again: 'Let Me come to you, and be one with Me and transform yourself through the instrumentality of My divine life in your heart. Let Me possess you, simplify you in God, in Our indivisible unity through the Holy Spirit.'

"I expect all this from you for the carrying out of My most sublime designs. If you correspond to it, you will be the channel of numerous graces for the world, for this will no longer be you alone who asks and who immolates yourself but I in you, bringing gifts and charisms for souls. You must save many souls, conduct them to perfection, attract them to vocations, obtain for priests many celestial favors, but all this by the means I have given you, that is, by the Word with the Holy Spirit" (*Diary,* June 30, 1914).

This offering of love is the quintessence of the spirituality of the Cross.

"I want you to be My host and have the intention, renewed as often as possible day and night, of offering yourself with Me on all the patens on earth. I want you, transformed in Me by suffering, by love and by the practice of all the virtues, to raise heavenward this cry of your soul in union with Me: 'This is My Body, This is My Blood.' Thus by making yourself but one with the Incarnate Word out of love and suffering, with the same intentions of love, you will obtain graces for the whole world. You will offer Me Myself and yourself also, with the Holy Spirit and through Mary, to the eternal Father.

"Such is the end and essence of *My Works of the Cross:* a likeness of victims united to the great Victim, Myself, all pure, without the leaven of concupiscence. They will be marked by the reflection of My Passion, in order that there rise heavenward a unanimous cry: 'This is My Body, This is My Blood.' Transformed into priests in union with the eternal Priest, they will offer to heaven, on behalf of the Church and of priests their brothers, their crucified bodies forming but one single Body with Mine, since they are members of Him who is the Head, Christ the Redeemer.

". . . one only Host, one only Victim, one only Priest immolating Himself and immolating Me in your heart on behalf of the whole world. The Father pleased, will receive this offering presented through the Holy Spirit, and the graces of heaven will descend as rain on the earth.

"Here is the central nucleus, the center, the concrete ensemble and essence of *My Works of the Cross*. It is evident that My immolation, in itself alone, suffices and more than suffices, for appeasing God's justice. What is it, the purest Christianity, the flower of the Gospel? Is it aught else but uniting all victims in one single Victim, all suffering, all virtues, all merits in the One, that is, in Me, in order that all this be of worth and obtain graces? What does the Holy Spirit intend in My Church save to form in Me the unity of wills, of sufferings and of hearts in My Heart? What was the desire of My Heart throughout My life, but to bring about unity in Me by charity, by love? Why did the Word descend into this world save to form with His Flesh and His Blood most pure, one sole blood to expiate and to win souls? Has the Eucharist any other purpose than to unite bodies and souls with Me, transforming them and divinizing them?

"It is not only on altars of stone, but in hearts, those living temples of the Holy Spirit, that one must offer heaven this Victim like unto Him. The souls also offer themselves in hosts and in victims. . . . God will be thereby profoundly touched" (*Diary*, June 6, 1916).

In short, the offering of love is the continual exercise of the *royal priesthood* of the People of God.

"If one attentively reads over the biblical texts and the classical passages of St. Peter and St. Paul on the *Priesthood of the faithful*, one will see that this doctrine is of the very essence of Christianity.

St. Peter reminds the early Christians of their priest, for offering spiritual sacrifices, agreeable to God through Jesus Christ (1 P 2:5). "You, however, are a chosen race, a royal priesthood, a holy nation, a people He claims for His own to proclaim the glorious works of the One who called you from darkness into His marvelous light. Once you were no people, but now you are God's people." (1 P 2:9-10).

St. Paul, on his part, exhorts Christ's disciples thus: "And now, brothers, I beg you through the mercy of God to offer your bodies as a living sacrifice holy and acceptable to God" (Rm 12:1). Even better: "Be imitators of God as His dear children. Follow the way of love, even as Christ loved you. He gave Himself for us as an offering to God, a gift of pleasing fragrance" (Ep 5:1-2).

The doctrine of the *royal priesthood* of the whole People of God, was one of the peak points of Vatican II. We are struck by the sameness of certain conciliar expressions with Conchita's texts. The agreement of the wording is remarkable.

"Thus the Eucharistic Action is the very heartbeat of the congregation of the faithful over which the priest presides. So priests must instruct them to offer to God the Father the divine victim in the sacrifice of the Mass, and to join to it the offering of their own lives" (*Presb. Ord,* # 5).

One feels we are here at the heart of Christianity and that one and the same Spirit animates the faith of all.

✠

"My doctrine is ever universal.", the Lord stated some time after the mystical incarnation. Conchita had become aware of this catholicity of the teachings of the Cross. In the Prologue of her opusculum on "Perfect Virtues" (Arco-Iris) intended for the formation of contemplatives of the Cross, she noted that these pages were also addressed to all other religious since "the spirit of the Cross . . . is the Gospel." This is a judgment that Jesus Himself will ratify later, as he did for St. Thomas Aquinas at the end of his life.

"These teachings of the Cross are salvific and sanctifying . . . and of a tremendous fecundity. In them is found the germ of numerous vocations and a most sublime holiness, but they are not adequately exploited. Yet these teachings of the Cross have not been given to remain hidden and buried, but that they be spread and that they inflame and save. . . .My bounty has placed in them treasures. Was it in order that this light remain hidden under a bushel? No, these holy teachings of the Cross are My Gospel and they must sow their fertile seed. I promise you they will flourish and bring forth fruits for heaven. . . . These priceless mystical teachings, sprung from My Heart, will eliminate a great number of errors and will clear up obscure points, projecting on them full clarity" (*Diary*, Nov. 18, 1929).

So it is Christ Himself who came to stamp these teachings with the supreme seal of Truth: "The teachings of the Cross: My Gospel."

CHAPTER III.

THE VIRGIN OF THE CROSS

"Mary was the first to continue My Passion."

It was a stroke of genius, or rather a divine inspiration, that Vatican II had the mystery of Mary pass from the devotional plane to the dogmatic plane of the history of salvation, which cannot be disassociated from the mystery of Christ and of His Church. The central place of the Mother of Jesus in the Work of Redemption appears clearly on Calvary, when Christ pronounced these creative words: "Behold your Mother." All Christian generations and all peoples have acknowledged her as their mother.

Mexico, in particular, after the celebrated and miraculous apparitions of the Mother of God to the poor Indian Juan Diego, venerates her with an exceptional fervor as Mother of the Nation. One must have visited the Basilica of Our Lady to understand the filial, extraordinary devotion to the Virgin of the hill of Tepeyac: Our Lady of Guadalupe. How many pilgrims arrive there exhausted! They come from all over America. In the hardest trials of their lives every Mexican loves to hear addressed to him Mary's words to the poor Indian, her child: "Am I not here, I who am your Mother?"

Conchita, Daughter of Mexico, whose spirit was strongly marked by the characteristic Marianism of her country, shows us Our Lady of Guadalupe ever present in her life.

Often, alone or with her husband and her family, she went to the Marian sanctuary there "to empty her heart," as a child with its mother (*Diary*, March 24, 1894).

Her *Diary* shows her having constant recourse to Mary in her joys and sorrows down to the last days of her life. Filial devotion to the Mother of God is deeply rooted in the Mexican heart.

The *Works of the Cross* came to light under the maternal protection of Our Lady of Guadalupe. Her name was found in the poor chapel of the first *Oasis* of the Contemplatives of the Cross. The Missionaries of the Holy Spirit were founded in the Chapel of Roses, the site of the last apparition of the Mother of God. And the very day of the Pontifical coronation of Our Lady of Guadalupe, the symbol of the *Works of the Cross*, the Cross of the Apostolate, rose on the summit of Tepeyac, dominating, from that moment on, the whole city of Mexico.

Conchita's whole spiritual life is enveloped in her love for the Mother of God. In her *Diary* she writes her memories of her early years: "The Lord granted me feelings full of tenderness toward the Holy Virgin. During my walks along the paths, I kept silence and loved to repeat, on thinking of what I was saying, prayers to this blessed Virgin. It is a devotion my good mother taught me at her knee" (*Aut.* 30).

True devotion to Mary is a consecration and an offering. From the earliest pages of her *Diary* she wrote: "Mary, my dearest and tenderest Mother, today I consecrate myself to you in a very special way ever to serve you. . . . This devotion is above all, imitation of her virtues. Jesus told me: 'the holiest and most perfect creature that ever existed was Mary. Do you know why? Because from the first instant of her being, she corresponded with all the inspirations of the Holy Spirit. Mary is the best teacher of the spiritual life' " (*Diary*, Sept. 22, 1895).

Her Marian Horizon

Conchita's piety is essentially dogmatic. She loves to contemplate the Mother of Jesus in the eternal plan of God and in her historical development through the principal mysteries of salvation. Her outlook of faith shows her already in her eternal pre-existence in the mind of the Trinity. The Lord explained to Conchita this mystery thus: "For you, there exists but the present moment; for God all is pre-existent. Mary already existed, the joy of the whole Trinity which had formed her in Its Thought. She already constituted Its delights. Mary was already the Queen of Heaven.

"She was beautiful with the beauty of God. She was a virgin of the fertile virginity of the Trinity, a creature without the least stain and all perfect, a soul preserved already, from the time of being in the bosom of the Father, called never to be soiled nor even in the slightest way touched by the least shadow of sin. Already from this eternity, she was Daughter, Spouse and Mother, the Three Divine Persons finding Their pleasure in this perfect work which must be marveled at by heaven and earth throughout all ages. What grandeur in Mary, in the multitude of her perfections, but above all in this work of virginal incarnation of the Word, prepared for, from all eternity.

"The Trinity loved passionately this incomparable creature, and that is why the Word became flesh. He prepared her with all graces and favors of the Holy Spirit, with the prodigality of a God, coming to make of her His living temple" (*Diary*, July 23, 1906).

This mystery of the Incarnation of the Word and of the divine maternity is the center of all of Conchita's Marian reflections.

After the Incarnation, it is the mystery of Golgotha which is her major consideration. The Lord explained it very clearly to her: "It was there, at the foot of the Cross, that Mary saw My Church born, that she accepted in her heart in the person of St. John all the priests in place of Me, and further, to be the Mother of all mankind" (*Diary*, April 8, 1928).

Mary's participation in our redemption through the Cross was one of the familiar themes of Conchita's contemplation: "I have better understood the inexpressible pains felt in the purest Heart of Mary, the sole creature who read and understood the interior sorrows, the sufferings of Her Divine Son, just as she was the only one to be able to measure His pains, to grasp His purity and His innocence, to bear, too, the infinite weight of human ingratitude which crushed Him. Without being culpable, she lived an existence of suffering in union with Her most holy Jesus and obtained graces for culpable sinners. Once Mary had consented to the Incarnation of the Word, never was the divine plan erased from her spirit. Her mother's heart, broken, contemplated the Innocent and Divine Martyr.

"The life of this Virgin-Mother was, after that of Jesus, the most crucified. Her constant meditation of the future ever kept her soul torn while in her little home in Nazareth. Who could have dreamed on seeing these two pure beings living the very same kind of life, that actually they bore within them the cruelest martyrdom for the sake of mankind! Yes, Mary held an immense place in the Redemption of man. How great Mary is and how much we owe her" (*Diary*, Sept. 1, 1898).

"Mary penetrated by all the mysteries, holds an important role in the activity of the Church, imploring pardon and obtaining graces for her" (*Diary*, Oct. 6, 1927).

Conchita admires in Mary, "the creature closest to God since she is the purest that ever lived or will live on earth. . . . In Her, not the least stain coming to tarnish the supreme purity of her soul full of grace. Never did she lose a single one, ever disposed to collaborate, especially at the hour of humiliation and suffering" (*Diary*, Aug. 29, 1898).

Vatican II deemed it proper to mark out clearly Mary's place in the divine plan, within the Church but at its summit. "Because of this gift of sublime grace she far surpasses all other creatures, both in heaven and on earth" (*Lumen Gentium* # 53); "a place in the Church which is the highest after Christ and yet very close to us" (*ibid.* #54). The Lord liked to tell Conchita about His Mother's divine grandeur: "After the Trinity and with My glorious humanity, Mary is the noblest creature who exists and can exist in heaven, for God Himself, even though divine, cannot bring about anything more worthy, more perfect and more beautiful since she bears in her being the reflection of all the perfections God can communicate to the creature. That is why Mary's glory in heaven surpasses that of all the angels and of all the saints" (*Diary*, Aug. 1906).

"She belongs to the Church militant. . . . She is now the depositary of the treasures of the Church, just as She was on earth of the Incarnate Word, source of all these treasures" (*Diary*, Feb. 27, 1917).

Thus Conchita's Marian concept coincides with the horizons of Vatican II. She sees Mary in the unrolling of the divine plan. Paul VI correctly noted that never had the Church contemplated Mary in the heart of the ecclesial mystery in so vast and powerful a synthesis (Discourse at the closing, Nov. 21, 1964). This wise view sets her entire mystery on its summits. Here is the beacon that illuminates and will direct all the advances of Marian doctrine in the future.

The Virgin of the Cross

With all the saints, closeness to Mary takes on the character and form of their personal grace. Thérèse of Lisieux will say of Mary: "She is more a Mother than a Queen." Bernadette will venerate in her the Immaculate. Conchita will contemplate Mary, according to her *characteristic viewpoint*, in the mystery of her inmost association to the Cross of her Son for the glory of the Father for the salvation of the world. For Conchita, the Virgin Mary is above all the "Virgin of the Cross."

From the beginning of her *Diary* there is perceived this inclination of grace: "Preaching on the sorrows of the Most Holy Virgin has impressed me very much. . . . The Passion of Jesus was also Mary's passion. She alone was the one who understood this cry of Jesus in His abandonment. The measure of sorrow is that of love, the measure of love is that of grace, and Mary was full of grace, of love and of sorrow. Yesterday evening I was smitten with love for the Virgin of Sorrows" (*Diary*, March 17, 1894).

The central grace in Conchita's life, the mystical incarnation, revealed to her the most intimate feelings of the Mother of God: totally consecrated to the person and work of Her Son, devoted to the Mystery of the Redemption with Him and under Him, cooperating for the salvation of men in faith and with full obedience.

The Virgin of the Incarnation is the Mother of Jesus—Priest who, on coming into the world, said: "Sacrifice and offering you did not desire, but a body you have prepared for me. . . . I have come to do your will, O God!" (Heb 10:5-7). Mary's personal mission in the mystery of salvation is inseparable from that of her divine maternity as is also the redemptive role of Christ from His Incarnation.

"Mary was chosen among all women in order that in her virginal womb would be brought about the Incarnation of the Divine Word and from that moment, She, wholly pure, the Virgin-Mother, She who accepted everything with love and in the fullest submission to My Father, She did not cease to offer Me to Him as a victim; Me who came down from heaven to save the world, by sacrificing Her Motherly Heart to the divine will of this well-loved Father.

"She nourished Me to be a Victim attaining the supreme immolation of her soul when She delivered Me up to be crucified. It was one and the same sacrifice, Mine on the cross and the one which took place in her heart. . . .

"Mary ever offered me up to the Father, she ever carried out the role of the priest. She ever immolated her innocent and pure heart in union with Me to bring graces down on the Church" (*Diary*, April 6, 1928).

Her Favorite Mystery: the Presentation of Jesus in the Temple

Nothing is more revealing of the hidden interior of a spiritual person than to penetrate his experience and put yourself in his personal perspective. His peculiar grace appears clearly in his special attitude before the mysteries of the life of Christ and of Mary.

One would think at first, since the mystical incarnation is Conchita's central grace, that the mystery of the Incarnation would be the center of her Marian contemplation. But no, her favorite mystery is another: the Presentation of Jesus in the Temple.

She recognized in this privileged mystery the fundamental attitude of the mystical incarnation and of the offering of love, the quintessence of the teachings of the Cross: the oblation of the Word to His Father and the total offering of self out of love in union with Christ, but through Mary's hands.

February 3, 1907, the Lord told Conchita: "The mystery which is being celebrated today concretizes your mission: the constant offering in your heart of the Victim that it be immolated on behalf of the world. The sorrow that comes about is a holy sorrow, sublime, chosen and most pure, since the creature does not undergo it seeking itself, but suffers solely on account of My suffering. Here you have the perfection of sorrow and of love. . . ."

"I must be offered by you, at every moment, as a victim on behalf of men; and you, united with the great Victim with all His perfections. I want you to offer yourself as did Mary, with her very virtues and qualities. Imitate her and model your own heart on this so beautiful an image" (*Diary*, Feb. 2, 1907).

Throughout her *Diary*, there is mention of this mystery: "Feb. 2, 1922, the Presentation: it is my day. How often on meditating on the mysteries of the Rosary, when this mystery comes up, I have wept in sorrow and in love."

It is of interest to observe that the great liturgical reform prescribed by Vatican II, substituted the Presentation of Jesus in the Temple in place of the feast of the Purification of Mary. In full accord with traditions of the Eastern Church, the Code of Rubrics in 1960 established that this feast must be regarded as a feast of the Lord. This feast known as Candlemas is not only the feast of Light, symbolized by lighted candles in memory of Christ, *Light of nations*, but the candles also symbolize the oblation of the Incarnate Word consumed, as the candles, before God, represent the offering of Himself to His Father for His glory and for the salvation of men. Pope Paul VI wants to celebrate this rite himself. He stresses the profound and new meaning of this liturgical ceremony: the Oblation of the Word and His Mystical Body, through Mary, Mother of our Church and of all the People of God.

"Solitude" of the Mother of God

The most original aspect of Conchita, in this contemplation, was to comprehend, in the light of the Holy Spirit, the profound association of Mary to the redemptive work of Her Son during the last years of His earthly life.

Vatican II affirms that "This tradition which comes from the apostles, develops in the Church, with the help of the Holy Spirit. For there is a growth in the understanding of the realities and the words which have been handed down. This happens through the contemplation and study made by believers, who treasure these things in their hearts (cf. Lk 2:19, 51), through the intimate understanding of spiritual things they experience, and through the preaching of those who have received through episcopal succession, the sure gift of truth" (*Dei Verbum*, # 8). The mystical experience of spiritual persons is a pathway for the explanation of the faith.

The new aspect of Marian doctrine according to the spirituality of the Cross, is in imitation of the *solitude* of the Mother of God throughout the last years of her earthly existence, at the moment when her spiritual life had attained its maximum of love, which permitted her to obtain, through an interior martyrdom, up to then but little studied, the application to the Church of all the graces merited by Christ, necessary for the Church as an institution and to each of her members until the end of the world.

The word "soledad" is difficult to translate. It signifies at the same time "solitude," "isolation," and silent martyrdom in pure faith, in the apparent absence of God and of her Son now in heaven, in an incommensurable sum of offerings, to the ever increasing measure of the fullness of her immense love.

"*I Must Imitate Mary in Her Solitude*"

After 1917, throughout the last twenty years of her life, through divine inspiration, there is seen developed in Conchita a new form of Marian devotion: imitation of the *solitude* of the Mother of God in the evening of her life, at the moment when the life of love of the Mother of Jesus attained its height and its plenitude, which were of benefit to the ancient Church, to the pilgrim Church and to the Church militant, until the end of time.

"God wants me to be alone. For me at this moment, it is the hour of solitude: to be in Mary's company, to imitate Mary in her solitude during the last days of her life" (*Diary*, Feb. 14, 1917).

"*Let Mary be Your Model*"

"In my spiritual life in souls, My Mother was never separated from Me, that is, the imitation of both of our lives must be simultaneous on earth; Mary's life was modeled on Mine. Thus, just as I was the Redeemer, she was the co-redeemer. The souls who love her most and who are most like to her, are the souls who are most like to Me most perfectly. You must imitate her in the practice of virtues, I always told you, especially in her humility and her purity of heart. Observe the virtues she practiced in her solitude, in the last stage of her life, her outlook, and her soul wholly turned toward heaven, and her self effacement, glorifying Me on earth. Through her ardent desire for heaven, that is, through her passionate love, aspiring for paradise, she merited graces from heaven for the nascent Church" (*Diary*, Feb. 18, 1917).

"*A New Phase of Your Life Has Begun*"

"Each time that Mary, My most holy Mother, because of My absence, felt sad in any way, actually she always missed Me, she immediately offered it up to the Father for salvation of the world and for the nascent Church. This apostolate of suffering, which is the apostolate of the Cross in Mary during this period of solitude, was most fecund and determined heaven to shower down torrents of graces.

"And likewise for you, you have begun a new phase of life which will be a reflection of that of Mary. It will appertain to you to imitate her without losing any suffering, which united to Mine will be of worth. Under this form, supernaturalize all your sorrows of *solitude* that they may become fertile for the benefit of your other children" (*Diary*, March 21, 1917).

Solitude is participation in the inmost Passion of Christ's Cross and a consequence of the mystical incarnation.

"I have granted certain souls the grace to be assimilated to Me through the external stigmata of My wounds, but to My Mother I gave My perfect likeness in her interior, after My Passion, with all My sufferings, My wounds, and the pains My Heart underwent.

"It is in this aspect that you will imitate her: her image will be imprinted on your soul, but a sorrowful one. This is the phase the soul reaches after the mystical incarnation, and in that phase you find yourself. You will taste the bitterness of Mary, not only accompanying or keeping company with her in her solitude, but experiencing in your heart the echo of her sorrows, the reflection of her tears shed for the same redemptive and glorifying purpose: the salvation of souls" (*Diary*, June 11, 1917).

On June 29, 1917 she receives a great illumination. Mary is in the heart of the Church and she bears the entire Church in her maternal Heart. At the foot of the Cross she was constituted the spiritual Mother of mankind, and the effusion of the Holy Spirit on Pentecost produced in her a new fullness of grace in view of the accomplishment of her maternal mission: in faith, in absolute self-surrender to the divine designs, in her ardent love, in her humble obedience, impelling her to continue on the work of her Son: "In her own flesh, it fills up what is lacking in the sufferings of Christ" (Col 1:24). Mary, Mother of the Church engendered all her children for God, through the sorrows born out of her love.

But this is a secret of Mary:

"Her Heart is presented with roses, but underneath are found thorns. The roses signify graces for her children, acquired with almost infinite sorrows, with tears and with martyrdoms the weight of which I alone was capable of measuring. It is quite natural for a mother, and so much the more Mary, to keep for herself the thorns and the sorrows: it is the roses and the tenderness that she presents to her children, not the sacrifices" (*Diary*, June 30, 1917).

Mary's Last Years Were the Most Fertile

"For these last years, destined for the reign of the Holy Spirit and the final triumph of the Church, was reserved the veneration of the martyrdom of Mary's solitude, His most beloved Spouse. During this martyrdom, only the might and force of this Spirit of God could keep her alive. Mary lived, it might be said, miraculously and solely to merit the graces requisite for her maternity on behalf of mankind. She lived to give her testimony about Me in My humanity, as the Holy Spirit testified about My Divinity. She lived to be in some way the visible instrument of the Holy Spirit in the nascent Church, while the Holy Spirit acted on the divine and wholly spiritual plane. She lived to provide its first nourishment for this unique and true Church, and to merit in heaven the titles of Consoler, Advocate, Refuge of her children.

"This phase of Mary's life, constituting for her Heart a source of bitterness, the quintessence of martyrdom, the purification of her love at the same time an inexhaustible source of grace and mercy of the world, has remained unknown.

"At the foot of the Cross all her children were born. My death gave them life in the heart of My Mother. But before her death She had to manifest this maternity on earth, gaining, by the sufferings of My absence, an infinitude of graces present and future for her children. Her title of Mother of mankind, Mary won by the martyrdom of her solitude after My death. Has the world been aware of this? Does it appreciate it and is it grateful for it? The time has come when the children should show they are real children, showing their veneration for this heart broken by this subtle and most painful martyrdom, lived through for the sake of their own happiness. There, Mary gained graces for each and every man. It is time for her to be thanked" (*Diary*, June 30, 1917).

One of the sources of suffering in Mary's solitude was the absence of Jesus. This sorrow is not an egotistical one but a most pure sorrow which sprang from the ardent charity which leads to the possession of God. St. John of the Cross speaks of this love in the first stanza of *The Living Flame of Love*. If this is true in the souls of poor sinners who have been transformed by divine charity, what can we not say of the charity of the Immaculate Mother of God?

This crowning phase of Mary's life is the perfect fulfillment of her existence ever abandoned to the will of God as "the humble servant of the Lord."

The Virtues and Sufferings of Mary Have Remained Hidden

"Just as Mary's virtues remained hidden due to her humility, for example on the occasion of the Purification, since she herself did not make them known, so her sufferings remained veiled. There was neither complaint nor recrimination. She accepted them all, welcoming them all without losing a single one, loving them, adoring in them the will of God which was her life. This adherence to My adorable will which she practiced after My Ascension, was particularly inmost, throughout her life of nameless sufferings, during the martyrdom of My absence and among the crucifixions of her solitude. An adherence, a most elevated and most close union of our wills, of My wishes in her martyrdoms, a submission and a perfect conformity to My desires to immolate her, such was then the manner of Mary's life. Such was her sublime most holy and divine adherence which maintained her, absorbed in My will which led her by paths of humiliation, of suffering, of heartbreak in love itself. It is not possible to appreciate in Mary her title of Queen of Martyrs, since man remains very far from comprehending her love.

"You, as a reflection of her life and of her sufferings, you should imitate her in this adherence to My will which breaks your heart and pierces it" (*Diary*, July 2, 1917).

To the measure that Conchita progresses in this imitation of the *solitude* of Mary in her own life, she penetrates deeper and deeper into the profundity of this mystery. Mary's maternity is a committed maternity. Mary unites herself in faith and in love to the profound intent of the Word who is made flesh to glorify the Father in the salvation of men. Mary's association with the Redemption of the world is not a new privilege coming about to join her to her divine maternity, but is simply a function which this same maternity exercises in a full existential achievement.

Mary is co-redemptrix, Mother of the Redemption, since she is the Mother of Jesus, Mother of *Yahweh who saves*.

Mary's *solitude* is the most perfect association with the redemptive act of Christ. The drama of our salvation is decided at the very moment when Jesus was abandoned mysteriously by His Father, and when He Himself abandoned Himself, in response, with confidence and love, into His hands. It is the consent of a man in supreme agony.

"You had for long pondered the first solitude of Mary, that is, the exterior solitude, but you had not thought about the cruelest and the bitterest, the interior solitude which tore her to pieces and in which her spirit felt an agony on account of being abandoned.

"The martyrdom of Mary after My Ascension was not caused solely by My material absence. She suffered terrible tests of an abandonment like to that I Myself underwent on the Cross. My Father united her to Mine which gained so many graces.

"As co-redemptrix, Mary heard in her soul so wholly pure the echo of all My agonies, humiliations, outrages and tortures, felt the weight of the sins of the world which made My Heart bleed, and the moving sorrow of the abandonment of heaven which obtains graces.

"You are to be a faithful echo of this Mother of Sorrows. You must experience the pure abandonment, My own abandonment, this desertion which through purification acquires graces.

"It is evident that Mary had nothing to be purified in herself but only in mankind, that is in her children, conquering by this sorrow a new crown, that of Mother-Martyr.

"Thus it is that she suffered for her children, that she gave them the supernatural life of grace, that she obtained heaven for them" (*Diary*, June 22, 1918).

Mary is truly the Mother of men, her spiritual maternity is a committed maternity. She, the Immaculate, suffers for the sin of her children.

"The Heart of Mary obtained these graces in the martyrdom of a solitude in which she was left, not by men (she had St. John and the Apostles and many souls who fervently loved her), not by Me in My Body (she consoled herself with the Eucharist and with her living and perfect faith), but by the Trinity, which hid itself from her, leaving her in a spiritual and divine abandonment.

"Mary suffered more than all abandoned souls, since she suffered a reflection of My own abandonment on the Cross, one the worth of which cannot be estimated and which is wholly inexpressible.

"This abandonment of Mary, this vivid and palpitating martyrdom of her *solitude*, the desolating martyrdom of divine abandonment, which she suffered heroically, with loving resignation and sublime surrender to My will, is not honored.

"Imitate her in your littleness, in your poor capabilities strive with all the strength of your heart: you must do it in order to obtain graces and to purify yourself.

"It is a great honor for souls when the Father calls them to associate them with the Redemption; with the co-redemption uniting them with Me and Mary; with the apostolate of the Cross, that is, with that of innocent suffering, of sorrow full of love and pure, expiatory and salvific sorrow on behalf of the culpable world" (*Diary*, June 23, 1918).

Having arrived at the end of her existence, Conchita writes in her *Diary:* "Mother of Sorrows whom I love so much, teach me to suffer as You suffered and to love Jesus as You loved Him in your awful *solitude*" (Oct. 13, 1936). "I promise Him with all my heart to abandon Myself in the God who abandons me" (Oct. 6, 1936). "Virgin Mary, be my strength teaching me the *Perfect Joy* of the Calvary of your frightful *solitude* in every moment of life still remaining to me. Obtain for me the theological virtues more and more living and let me not die without having carried out the divine designs on earth. Only for Him, for the glory of His Beloved Father" (Oct. 20, 1936).

The imitation of *Mary's solitude* was the consummation of Conchita's spiritual life in the last years of her life.

This new aspect of Marian doctrine according to the spirituality of the Cross is of an incomparable theological depth.

The whole mystery of Mary unfolds in time. Her association with the redemptive Work of Christ is not confined solely to her presence at the foot of the Cross where "she united herself with a maternal heart to His sacrifice, and lovingly consented to the immolation of this Victim which she herself had brought forth" (*Lumen Gentium* # 58). She continued growing in the measure of her love until the end of her earthly life, coming to the consummation of the fullness of grace which brings about in Mary, in conformity with God's design, her glorification and especially her Assumption into heaven.

The *solitude* of the Mother of God is the supreme configuration to Christ Crucified. Her spiritual maternity is amplified therein by the salvific suffering which springs from love and charity reaching their peak. Thence comes the perfect joy which flows from the Cross of Christ, and which is the fruit of the Holy Spirit.

The Pastoral Riches of This New Devotion

Let us point out three main aspects: 1) The *solitude* of the Mother of God sheds much light on the participation of the Church in the mystery of Christ's Cross.

Two diverse aspects must be distinguished in Mary's association with Christ in the work of our salvation: the phase of acquisition and the phase of application.

The first appears at the moment of Christ's virginal conception and reaches its summit at the foot of the cross where she stood in keeping with the divine plan (*Lumen Gentium* # 58; cf. Jn 19:25).

This aspect is *proper, unique, personal* to Mary, for it is founded on her divine Maternity and her spiritual Maternity for all men.

The glorification of Christ inaugurates the phase of *application.* The effusion of the Holy Spirit on the day of the Pentecost brings about in Mary a new fullness of love in view of her mission as *Mother of the Church.* Mary already symbolizes the Church in the mysterious Woman of Revelation "because she was with child, she wailed aloud in pain as she labored to give birth" (Rv 12:2).

The profound reason for the existence of the Church, throughout its pilgrimage on earth, is to continue the Work of Redemption which Christ achieved, once for all, on the Cross. In imitation of Mary, the Church will continue the passion of its divine Master in its martyrs, saints, in all its members, even the most imperfect, provided they truly love Christ.

Co-redemption is of capital importance in Christian life. One cannot truly love Christ without feeling the desire to participate with Him for the salvation of the world.

2) The *solitude* of the Mother of God helps understand the value of human suffering for the salvation of the world, when it is joined to Christ's suffering.

Sorrow of itself has no value. It is a consequence and a fruit of sin. But love has the prodigious power to convert it into the price of redemption. The most fertile apostolate is *the apostolate of the Cross.*

Further, participation in the Cross of Christ is not only personal purification and expiation. It is, above all, a call to collaborate in the salvation of the world. The more suffering is innocent and pure, the more it is capable of saving men and of glorifying God.

Only the saints who have undergone *dark nights* of purification and who have arrived at *transforming union* fully participate as Mary in her co-redemptive and apostolic *solitude,* in the mystery of the Cross.

3) Mary in her *solitude* is a model for outwardly useless lives. They will find, on imitating her, the fullness of their Christian achievement.

At a period when old age poses for the Church a new problem of pastoral ministry, this new form of devotion to Mary brings a solution to the apparent uselessness and to the discouragement of these human lives about which younger or fully mature persons are unconcerned. It will give courage and spirit to so many valiant Christians, whose last days must bring them ever closer to God than to men.

There is also an analogous problem for all men and women in that their living conditions do not have an *appearance* of external apostolic activity. For all such as they, the life of *solitude* of the Mother of God sheds light on the profound law of the communion of saints.

Pure love is of far greater apostolic fecundity than the most outstanding works accomplished with less than love. It is at the eve of life, in silence and isolation, in prayer and in sacrifice, that God's Mother attains her maximum of love and her fullness of apostolic fecundity in the service of the Church of Christ, just as Christ Himself did not save the world in the luster of His Word and of His miracles, but on the Cross.

The Lord said to Conchita, "I do not believe that to know Mary's *solitude,* her sufferings because of My absence and her bitter sorrows as a Mother, will bring sadness to man. What is expressed by roses, and the fruits of her tears, will remain. But gratitude will be aroused, when it is recalled that from so many sufferings the crowns worn by their children in heaven have been purchased" (*Diary*, July 4, 1917).

Devotion to Mary's *solitude* is then devotion to the Virgin of Pentecost, *to Mary, Mother of the Church.*

CHAPTER IV.

THE MYSTERY OF THE CHURCH.

The Church, the universal sacrament of salvation, is the fulfillment of the salvific design of the Father's love. The Father has willed to bring together all men in His Son by virtue of His sacrifice carried out once for all. Christ loved His Church and delivered Himself up for Her to give us His Spirit.

Conchita's spiritual doctrine on the Church reflects a progress made which finds its climax in her message of holiness for the renewal of the entire People of God, thanks to a *new Pentecost*.

In a period when piety had an eminently individualistic character, and which did not seem to be aware of the dimension of the *Church*, it is admirable to record how God manifested to Conchita this essential and constituent aspect of the ecclesial mystery and how from the beginning of her spiritual life this thought opened up to her boundless horizons.

Mission to Save Souls

"The first spiritual exercises I made were given by Father Antonio Plancarte, in 1889.

"I took part in them only during the day for I could not leave my children alone.

"One day, as if come down from heaven, when I was readying myself with all my soul for all the Lord would wish from me, I heard clearly in the depths of my soul, without any possible doubt: 'Your mission will be to save souls' " (*Aut.*, 1, 51).

These first words of the Lord give us the key for understanding the meaning of Conchita's life: she will be wholly consecrated to the Church.

Jesus, Savior of Men

There are some decisive moments which definitively transform a life. The initials which Conchita engraved on her bosom on January 14, 1894 oriented her toward the salvation of the world through the Cross. The importance of this fact is not only found in the heroic act a woman carried out as an expression of her love for Christ, but in what God operated in her as a response: an interchange of love which communicated to her a New Love, the sharing in His own salvific love which thus presented the seed of the Works of the Cross.

She wrote: "A supernatural force tossed me to the ground. Forgetting the joy which possessed me, I thought only of the salvation of men. My soul burned with zeal for the salvation of souls, and with a fire which was not my own, I repeated: "Jesus, Savior of men, save them, save them!" (*Aut.*, 2, 33; *Letters*, 10, 18, 56).

The entire Work and the whole doctrine of the Cross are born of this vital experience of the innermost and most substantial reality of the mystery of the Church: the association with the Redemption of men brought about by Christ.

Global Perspective

Conchita learned about the Church through the Cross. "While I was saying various prayers, the Lord gave me the grace to understand the innermost relationships that exist between the Church and the Cross, though without the Cross, there would be no Church. He told me that the Church was born of the Cross. The Holy Spirit came afterwards to confirm its teachings and give it life" (*Diary*, May 28, 1898).

The first revelation of the mystery of the Church, is that it is the Church of the Crucified, and this entails a call to a commitment.

"The Lord told me many a time: 'Sacrifice yourself for the Church. My Church is what I love most and she it is who caused Me to suffer most. In truth, I live crucified in her.' (I realized He was alluding to evil priests and to ministers who do not seek the interests of Jesus Christ, but their own interests, coupled with numerous laxities and culpable behavior). 'I want you to be a victim on behalf of the Church. You do not know the value of that. Do not resist. It is a gift I want to give you. Souls sacrificing themselves as victims for the Church, receive a special recompense' " (*Diary*, May 28, 1898).

"Souls who are victims for the Church must unite themselves to My Heart, the supreme Victim, to offer themselves to the eternal Father on behalf of this so beloved Church, in order to expiate sins. I love My Church so much that in union with My Heart I seek victims who immolate themselves in order that the just wrath which menaces her be assuaged and changed into a shower of graces.

"I want, more than external martyrdom, interior martyrdom of the heart. That is why I want them to unite themselves to My Heart which is broken more than any other. I want to obtain this glory for My Father, and the Holy Spirit will ever bless the victim souls who united themselves to Me" (*Diary*, June 14, 1898).

The expressions *victim* and *victim souls*, in Conchita's usage, is found wholly without any doleful sense, without a certain emotional egocentric emphasis which might be counter to its import and lead to a pitiable caricature, to a psychological complex of a masochistic tone.

The doctrine of the Cross is solidly founded on a spirituality of giving which springs from its very self, imitation of and conformity with Christ who came "to give His own life as a ransom for the many" (Mt 20:28). It is ruled by the demands of the Redemption. Whence the Trinitarian perspective which appears all of a sudden and unexpectedly.

The Church of the Trinity

"The Church is the deposit of all the graces of the Holy Spirit. In her, He has set up His dwelling place. He loves her with an unbelievable love. No one enters heaven save through the Church. The Holy Spirit imprints His mark on all her ceremonies. . . . Apart from this divine stamp, there is neither any attainment of nor even possibility of salvation. From out of the Church there rises constant praise to the Most Holy Trinity. The eternal Father fixes His gaze entirely on her while the Son is there with His holy humanity united to His divinity and perpetuates within her His sacrifice through the Eucharist.

"How beautiful is this harmonious unity, this blessed Trinity in its divine communications with the Church! Therein I see, now, the immense love shown by God toward His creature in so admirable a way! I admit it, I had never understood it so clearly; nor had I ever thanked God for this uninterrupted chain of benefits which from baptism to our burial, this holy Church distributes to us. What account will I have to render to the Lord for so many graces and so many means of sanctification which His eternal bounty has set aside for us in His Church" (*Diary*, May 28, 1898).

This Trinitarian perspective is then far from a horizontal view of the Church in her structures and in her multiple activities among men. It is a perspective from above, a very sublime and wise view of the Church in the light of the Trinity. Furthermore, it opens up with a prime global synthesis. The Church is at one and the same time the Church of the Cross, the Church of the Trinity.

The Church of the Incarnate Word

"The Church sprang from My Heart on the Cross. There it is that the Church so pure and beautiful was born from My side as Eve from Adam's side, in order to be the Mother of all Christians, of all souls, to save them through the infinite merits I deposited in her immaculate soul" (*Diary*, March 14, 1928).

This classic and basic theme of ecclesiology is contemplated by Conchita in the characteristic viewpoint of her own personal grace. The expression *Cross* has an eminently personalist resonance. The Cross signifies, above all, Christ crucified, Christ Priest and Victim who out of love offers Himself to the Father for our salvation. The Cross designates also the Christian who wants to be like Christ by identifying his innermost feelings with His, and frequently Conchita will affirm that the genuine Christian must be a *living cross*.

Even more, the Cross which gave birth to the Church is not only the external and visible cross which was raised on the summit of Calvary, but the interior, inmost core of the Heart of Christ, which began with His Incarnation and was consummated when He delivered His spirit into His Father's hands.

"Through the external cross which all can see, I was a victim acceptable to the Father by shedding My blood, but it was above all through the interior cross that Redemption was accomplished" (*Diary*, Sept. 7, 1896).

We have already seen that the *inmost cross* is a central theme of the teachings of the Cross which lead us to the heart and to the essential of the mystery of salvation.

The interior cross is the purest sorrow, born and vivified solely through love. "I loved My Father and I wanted to glorify Him by paying off the debt of sinful man. I loved men with an infinite and human love and I wanted to make them happy and save them" (*Diary*, Jan. 23, 1928).

Both these loves, founded on one single love, on the Holy Spirit, form the heart of the Redemption.

The Cross is Perpetuated in the Eucharist

Conchita asked the Lord: "If the Redemption satisfied Your justice to efface sin, if by it the distance between man and the divinity was overcome, why did You perpetuate this same sacrifice of the Cross on the altars?"

The Lord answered her: "Solely out of love, solely out of

charity, I remain on the altars because burning thirst consumes the Word made flesh who rejoices in His immolation for the sake of man.

"I have stayed on the altars to perfect in their souls by My life as a victim what is wanting of sacrifice in them.

"I have stayed thereon to continue expiation for man's ingratitude through a perpetual sacrifice.

"I have stayed thereon since I am the only pure victim.

"Without Me every immolation would be futile, by My perpetuating My sacrifices, forgiveness is likewise perpetuated, giving their value to the sacrifices of men when they are offered in union with Mine.

"I have stayed thereon to bring souls, through My example, to become lovers of pain under all its forms.

"I have stayed thereon due to the pleasure the Incarnate Word feels from the proximity of His creature" (*Diary*, July, 1906).

"In the Mass is perpetuated the same immolation of the same Victim, Me, on Calvary. It is not a prolongation or a repetition of My sacrifice, but the same sacrifice though unbloody, the same living crucifixion with the same and only loving will of the Father to give His own Son, His only Son, for the salvation of the world" (*Diary*, Aug. 2, 1933).

The Whole Church is Priestly

Christ, the Sole Priest, has raised up a Church, an entire priestly people, as a sacrament for the salvation of the world.

She is a chosen nation, a royal palace, a priestly community, a holy nation, a people whom God has acquired for Himself (cf. 1 P 2:9).

The view of a wholly priestly Church is an essential aspect of Conchita's spiritual doctrine, fifty years before Vatican II.

"There are souls who have been consecrated through priestly unction, but there are likewise, in the world, priestly souls, who, although they have neither the dignity nor are consecrated as priests, have a priestly mission, and they offer themselves to the Father in union with Me, to immolate themselves as He desires. These souls mightily aid the Church on the spiritual plane.

"As for priests, they should be victims, transforming themselves into gifts, renouncing themselves and offering themselves to My Father in union with Me for the salvation of souls, as I do" (*Diary*, Jan. 8, 1928).

Spiritual Priesthood

There is but one priesthood, that of Christ, but everyone can participate in it for the spiritual priesthood is at the same time the characteristic and charism of the ecclesial community.

The ministerial Priesthood perpetuates Christ's oblation in bringing about the Eucharist *in persona Christi*, rendering possible for the whole Church the exercise of the spiritual priesthood, the offering of Christ really present among His people who offer themselves in union with Him.

"When I pronounced these words: 'Do this in memory of Me,' I was not addressing Myself only to priests. Of course, they alone have the power to change the substance of bread into My most holy Body and the substance of wine into My Blood. But the power to unite in one single oblation all oblations belongs to all Christians. It belongs to all Christians, members of one single Body, to become one with the Victim on the altar by faith and works, offering Me as Host in propriation to My eternal Father" (*Diary*, June 7, 1916).

This twofold participation in Christ's Priesthood constitutes the *structure of the Church of the Cross*, of the Church of Christ Priest and Victim.

"I cannot separate Myself from this sacred heavenly bond, for it is through it I came into the world. My universal Priesthood is naught else but My infinite charity to save man. The Father, I might say, found no other adequate way to save the world than the priesthood, which forms the body of the Church and of which the center or the heart is the Trinity itself. That is why the Word was made flesh, most particularly to be a priest and to spread His Priesthood in souls.

"For thence proceeds the spiritual and mystical priesthood. Religious and laity in the world form part of the mystical Priesthood to the measure of their more or less close union with Me" (*Diary*, Nov. 29, 1928).

The ministerial Priesthood represents Christ as Head of the Church. "From time immemorial I behold My Priests in the light of a love which chooses them and embraces them from all eternity, including in this embrace not only their beloved souls but also thousands of souls, for each priest is the head of many other souls."

"Upon eternally considering the priest, I contemplate in him a multitude of souls engendered by him through the Father's generosity, ransomed by him in union with My merits, formed by him, sanctified and saved by him, souls which will render Me glory eternally."

"Do not think the life of a priest is unique or isolated. No, in the life of a priest I contemplate many lives in the spiritual and holy sense, many hearts which will give Me glory eternally" (*Diary*, Nov. 14, 1927).

The Priest Is Another Christ

In the present crisis, when priestly identity seems to be lost, Conchita's message is strikingly pertinent.

"When I took on human nature, I brought love to man. Having the same blood, the brotherly bond uniting both natures, the divine and the human, I divinized man, putting him in contact with the Word, raising him above the things of the earth that he aspire for heaven.

"But among all men, I singled out some who should be Mine, *other Christs*, those who would continue on with the mission which drew Me to earth, that of bringing to My Father what had sprung from Him, souls who would glorify Him eternally" (*Diary* Jan. 11, 1928).

"I would never finish saying all that priests are for Me: My hands, My works, My Heart and the center of innumerable souls.

"In the priest I contemplate My Father's reflection. I see Myself and the Holy Spirit. In the priest I contemplate mysteries, that of the unity of his inmost being with the Most Holy Trinity; the mystery of the Incarnation which the priest makes present at each Mass; that of the Eucharist which would not come about without his concourse; finally, that of the Sacraments and My beloved Church and thousands upon thousands of souls engendered in his souls for the glory of God. At every moment in My priests I contemplate Myself but Myself as I am in them, Saint among saints and not disfigured by their sins" (*Diary*, Nov. 20, 1929).

The Church Must Continue The Passion

"I am the Head of the Church, and all who are Mine are the members of this same Body and must continue in union with Me, expiation and sacrifice till the end of time.

"My Passion was consummated on Calvary, but those who form My Church must continue the passion in themselves, offering themselves in reparation for themselves and for others to the Trinity in union with Me, victims with the Victim, and having the same qualities of victims.

"This is the law of love, the law which governs My Church: ever love, expiation and union" (*Diary*, July 24, 1906).

"I have no need of anyone to save the world, but all Christians must suffer with Me, cooperating in this same Redemption for the glory of God and their own glorification" (*Diary*, May 16, 1907).

A prayer of the *Liturgy of the Hours* expresses this same spirituality: "God our Father, You brought salvation to all mankind through the sufferings of Christ Your Son. May Your people strive to offer themselves to You as a living sacrifice and be filled with the abundance of Your love" (Vespers IV).

Mary, Mother of the Church

The priestly Church of the Incarnate Word has as her Mother Mary, Mother of the eternal Priest.

"Mary was chosen among all women that in Her virginal womb the Incarnation of the Divine Word be brought about and from that very moment She, wholly pure, the Virgin Mother, She who consented to it with love in most total submission to My Father's will, has never ceased offering Me to Him. The victim came from heaven to save the world, but She sacrificed Her maternal heart to the divine will of the Beloved Father.

"She reared Me to be a Victim, attaining the supreme oblation of Her soul when She delivered Me up to be crucified. One sole sacrifice was there, that which I offered on the Cross and which took place in Her heart. She continued this sacrifice by Her martyrdom of solitude, offering up Her sufferings to the eternal Father in union with Me.

"When I left the world, when I parted from My disciples, I left them Mary, to represent Me by Her virtues, in Her maternal tenderness, in Her Heart; perfectly faithful to Mine. I left Her to be a necessary factor for the foundation of My Church, as well as sustenance for My Apostles and My first disciples.

"The nascent Church relied on Mary, who sustained Her by Her sufferings and Her virtues, Her prayers and Her love.

"That is why, when I sent the Holy Spirit to My Apostles, I did not take Mary away, although She was even now full of grace and filled with the Holy Spirit. This was in order that the Church see in Her, her Queen, that priests judge Her indispensable, and that neither they nor the faithful suffer from the absence of their Mother's love and sacrifice" (Diary, April 6, 1928).

The Church of the Holy Spirit

The Incarnate Word, by His death and resurrection, brought men together and, on communicating to them His Spirit; He made them members of His Mystical Body. The Holy Spirit is the same in the Head and in the members. He vivifies the whole Body, He unites it and moves it in such a way that He becomes its vital principle. He is the Soul of the Mystical Body" (Cf. *Lumen Gentium:* # 7-8).

"After My Ascension I sent the Holy Spirit and it is He who directs the world and My Church" (*Diary*, March 1894).

"The Holy Spirit brought about the Incarnation, and the fruit of the Incarnation must belong to Him, that is, My Church. It is His function by right to illumine her, to give her meaning, to inflame her, to fortify her and give her life and grace" (*Diary*, Jan. 29, 1915).

From Conchita's doctrinal riches about the Church and the Holy Spirit we shall extract only three aspects:

a) The Holy Spirit is the *soul* of the structures.

b) He brings about the *holiness* of the Church.

c) He is the principle of *unity* and leads the Church to her consummation in the Unity of the Trinity.

"My Church is Founded on Love"

When, in the present day crisis, it is asserted there is opposition between the hierarchical Church and the pneumatic Church, the Church of Authority and the Church of Charity, Conchita reminds us of the principle which brings out how false is the problem. There can be no opposition between structures and charisms since the Church of the Incarnation and the Church of the Spirit is one and the same.

The Spirit is the principle which animates and vivifies the *structures.*

"Only one thing was necessary for Me to establish My Church on earth on an indestructible foundation: love, love alone. My

Church must be founded, grow, develop in love, for love is her heart and soul and life. The Holy Spirit is all love. That is why I posed those admirable questions which will be remembered throughout all ages to him who was to be the Supreme Head of My Beloved Church, questions which still have their repercussions in the hearts of all Popes: 'Do you love Me more than these?' And, My Heart of a God-Man once assured of this love, I delivered souls to the supreme Shepherd who represents Me on earth. I handed over to love My loves, that is, souls. The Pope had need of only this, and it is the only thing I ask of him, for love makes him a Father, and a Father knows only how to love, since, even in his strictest demands, he is all love, naught but love.

"Contemplate the tenderness of My Heart toward all souls, but ponder deeply how this so touching a question asked of Peter, for entrusting to him the redeemed world, was not only directed to the first Head of the Church, but particularly to all My priests. I turned over to him the Church along with Myself, and in Me all priests who form her from the first to the last. The Pope communicates his powers wrapped in his paternal love to his favored and beloved sheep, to his priests, who form with Me and with him, one only Jesus, Savior of souls. The Pope is the first to transform himself into Me, in the unity of the Trinity. My Father communicated to him the best fruits of His fecundity, the Word, Me, and I delivered Myself up to him to represent Me in the Church by perfect transformation into Me. The Holy Spirit protects him, penetrates, impregnates, transforms him, enlightens, sustains him, communicates to him His gifts and assists him in his decisions, marking his words with the most holy seal of infallible Truth which cannot be deceived.

"Yet all this demands but one condition: love, love, love! Thrice I assured Myself of this love for only a loving soul is worthy to represent Me, to communicate the Father's fecundity, the Father who is Love, and the likeness and personality of the Incarnate Word who is Love, and My Spirit who is Love. This entire ensemble of love, in the unity of the Trinity, is joined infallibly to the head of the Church and in him to all his brethren.

All of them are in Me, in diverse degrees and hierarchies. For My Father sees Me in the Pope, in the unity of the Church, and in all priests sees them in Me, one sole Jesus, one sole Shepherd, one sole Priest, one sole Savior.

"How truly beautiful and divine is this inmost and unique link with My beloved Church in the world! Due to what is divine in her, nothing and no one is capable of shaking her, of making her vacillate, of destroying her structures, of rupturing her unity. Her origin is divine and divine is her fecundity. The God-Man who dwells in her, defends her, protects her, sustains her and glorifies her. So long as love sustains the Church in her Head and in her members, so long as her Shepherd is love (and it will always be so through the innermost assistance of the Holy Spirit), she will undergo storm and strife, treason and schism and conflicts, and She will sail on without being overturned, without being sunk.

"I am her Pilot and that is why centuries will pass and My Church will reach the shores of heaven as pure, as holy, as maternal, as filled with love and charity as when She came from My hands. What matter betrayals and persecutions, even on the part of her own (the most painful), She will majestically sail on through the myriads of tempests which served, serve and will serve but to render her more wondrous and glorious.

"Who can prevail against God? Generations pass, persecutions cease, schisms are mended, only My Church goes on as beautiful and pure, holy and immutable as when She came from My hands, borne by love which does not change for it is divine, thanks to the unity She possesses in herself, impregnated by love and diffusing only love.

"Yet the time has come to exalt the Holy Spirit in the world. He is the soul of this Beloved Church. This divine Person diffuses Himself prodigally in every act of the Church. I desire that this last epoch be consecrated in a very special way to this Holy Spirit who ever operates out of love. He guided the Church from her very beginnings, by the three acts of humble love in Peter. I desire that in these latter days this holy love inflame all hearts but most of all the hearts of the Pope and My priests. It is His turn, it is His epoch, it is the triumph of love in My Church, in the whole universe. To obtain this, I again ask that the world be consecrated in a very special way to the Holy Spirit, beginning with all the members of the Church, to this Third Person of the Trinity. Since the Spirit binds and unites the Trinity itself and makes God God (for God is love), and the Holy Spirit is the Person of love (Love itself). . . . That is why the Holy Spirit is the soul, the great divine force, the energy, the heart, the heartbeat of the Church of God" (*Diary*, March 2, 1928).

The Church is Holy

The Church is indefectibly holy. As Vatican II says: "Faith teaches that the Church is holy in a way which can never fail. For Christ, the Son of God, who with the Father and the Holy Spirit is praised as being "alone holy," loved the Church as His Bride, delivering Himself up for her (cf. Ep 5:25-26). He unites her to Himself as His own Body and crowns her with the gift of the Holy Spirit, for God's glory" (*Lumen Gentium* # 39).

The whole Church is ordered to holiness, for she is the end and object of the Father's salvific design. The Apostolic Church, One and Catholic must be the Holy Church.

One of the jewels of Vatican II is Chapter V of *Lumen Gentium* which calls to mind our universal vocation to holiness: *The Call of the Whole Church to Holiness* (#39-42).

Conchita wrote on February 24, 1911: "All men were born to be holy. If souls had an interior life, if they gave themselves up to the Holy Spirit, how much would the mystical life increase, how many means of grace there would be!

"May souls give themselves up to the Holy Spirit and He will possess them and My saints will be multiplied. The Church will have chosen instruments and the world will change" (*Diary*).

Thus the destiny of the People of God depends above all else on the holiness of its Shepherds. "God, who alone is holy and bestows holiness, willed to raise up for Himself as companions and helpers men who would humbly dedicate themselves to the work of sanctification" (*Presb. Ord. # 5*).

"Inasmuch as it is connected with the episcopal order, the priestly office shares in the authority by which Christ Himself builds up, sanctifies and rules His Body" (*ibid. #2*). Christ even built His Church on her ministers.

Conchita, a simple laywoman, was chosen by God to communicate to the Church an important message. It is a call to *priestly holiness*, the sole solution to the present crisis of the Church.

More than a thousand pages of her *Diary* are filled with what the Lord confided, pages which at once reveal the grandeur and the weakness of priests. Therein are found pages without precedent in the history of Christian literature. This urgent appeal for priestly holiness, written thirty years before the Council, is the culminating point of Conchita's *prophetic mission* in the Church.

Vatican II reminds us that every Christian shares in the prophetic, priestly and royal mission of Christ. It is a constant law in the history of Salvation. God gratuitously chose what was smallest, humblest, to carry out His wondrous works. Conchita is a *word of God for the Church of today*.

It's the Priests' Fault

"If souls lag along the road and their interior life is extinguished, it's the priests' fault. The gates of divine communication opened up for the mystical life, are closed. Why? Through apathy in My service, through dissipation of their lives, through their lack of mortification, through their neglect of study in this domain, through absence of close and consciencious rapport with souls, through want of the spirit of sacrifice, because they do not love enough. Here are the motives, here the cause or rather the many causes which bring about and maintain these results: lack

of prayer, of the interior life, of purity of soul, of intimate relations with Me; absence of love and devotion to the Holy Spirit,
of union with God.

"The world opens at this moment a large breach in the hearts
of priests and you know the number of vices which accompany
this redoubtable enemy: an excessive contact with creatures chills
their fervor, the neglect of external and interior recollection
brings tepidity. Thence, where the world enters, thence the Holy
Spirit departs. When the Holy Spirit leaves the heart of a priest,
he is ruined, for if anyone has not only the need but the most
imperious obligation to live and breathe in the Holy Spirit, it is
the priest. To the measure he departs, materialism penetrates.
Woe to the priest who founders himself in matter, he can consider himself lost. This is so easy in a dissipated soul, in a heart
which does not pray and is not mortified. Out of his infernal
hatred for My Church, in a matter of such capital importance
for so many souls and for the priest himself, Satan aims at her,
his most poisonous arrows. He makes every effort to find the
opening through which the world will enter into the priest's
heart under any form whatsoever. After that, this unfortunate
soul smoothly glides down the slopes toward sin" (*Diary*, Feb.
14, 1907).

Priests Are Asleep

"I will tell you a very deep secret. Graces accumulate upon
My Church as well as the treasures, the riches, the most fertile
sources of the merits of the Incarnate Word, but each day, men,
even those who are called *Mine*, close the doors to the Holy
Spirit. Satan undermines the Church through the weakness and
dissipation of those who should be the guardians of the sanctuary.
Souls languish through want of directors possessed by the Holy
Spirit. My Church, so beautiful and rich, must leave her treasures
locked up for she does not know to whom to distribute them.
The saddest thing is that these infinite treasures of grace I bought
at the price of My Blood, remain inactive in My Church, due to

want of laborers who are holy. They understand in their own way the spiritual life and, due to lack of profound studies in this matter, due to ignorance and negligence they leave unachieved the designs of God on a great number of souls.

"My Heart is saddened because My ministers are sleeping. On many occasions, they are the first to conform themselves to superficial piety. They do not make the Cross enter souls, and still less do they reveal to them the Holy Spirit. I tell you again in greatest confidence that routine has deeply penetrated the sanctuary. This devotion *in spirit and in truth* is completely extinguished in numerous communities. May My ministers react through the Holy Spirit, may they appreciate to the full the interior life! May they possess it themselves and communicate it through the Holy Spirit! Then the Church will reflourish in her prime vigor. There is lacking in My Church the stamina of the Holy Spirit, it is wanting in seminarians and in members of the clergy. Consequently it is wanting in souls who live and are nourished by this vital essential, called to communicate to them the life of grace.

Conchita says: "Lord of my soul, my divine Jesus, what should I do? My God! may then this Holy Spirit come as soon as possible to set hearts aflame! I would like to be a missionary, My Jesus, and be able to carry out the task of thousands and hundreds of thousands. I would like to be able to travel over the entire world and give my blood on every occasion in the cause of the Church I love each day with a more ardent love burning with a flame I knew not of up to now: Oh Jesus! Jesus! Jesus!" (*Diary*, Feb. 21, 1911).

Call to Holiness

"I want love in My priests. I want interior life. I want these consecrated souls to live most closely to Me.

"I want to banish apathy from their hearts and make them burn with zeal for My glory. I want to activate the divine life of so many souls who belong to Me and who are failing. I want to destroy the indifference which paralyzes God's action and which deprives priests of My graces.

"The fire must be rekindled and this will be done only by the Holy Spirit, by the divine medium of the Word, offering Him to the Father and asking for mercy" (*Diary*, Sept. 23, 1927).

The Holy Spirit Alone Sanctifies

"I want a living, palpitating, clear and powerful reaction of the clergy through the Holy Spirit.

"A priest no longer belongs to himself. He is another Me and he must be all to all, but first of all by sanctifying himself, for no one can give what he does not have and only the Sanctifier can sanctify. So then, if he wants to be holy—as it is imperious he must—he must be possessed, impregnated by the Holy Spirit, since if the Holy Spirit is indispensable for the life of any soul whatsoever, for the soul of priests He must be their breath and very life.

"If priests are Jesus, should they not have the Spirit of Jesus? And this Spirit, is He not the Holy Spirit?" (*Diary*, Oct. 9, 1927).

Pressing Actuality

"I hasten ever on time and most opportunely, no matter what epoch of the world, to the assistance of My Church Militant. In these difficult times My priests have need of this divine reaction for resisting the assaults of the enemy, for repelling the world which has invaded even the Sanctuary, preventing for future evils; for consoling My Heart and for glorifying My Father, purifying and sanctifying more and more the members of My beloved Church.

"As I have told you, there will come even worse times for My Church and She needs holy priests and ministers who will make her triumph over her enemies, with the Gospel of peace, of forgiveness and charity; with My teaching of love which will overcome the world.

"But I have need of an army of holy priests transformed into

Myself, who exhale virtues and attract souls with the good aroma of Jesus Christ. I have need of other Christs on the earth, forming one sole Christ in My Church through unity of objectives, intentions and ideals, forming one only Mystical Body with Me, one only will with the will of My Father, one only Soul with the Holy Spirit, one unity in the Trinity, out of duty, out of justice, out of love" (*Diary*, Dec. 29, 1927).

Transformation into Christ-Priest

This call to priestly holiness has as its object the realization of their personal vocation: the transformation into Christ-Priest.

"My object for priests is to realize their transformation into Me, removing impediments to it, and unifying them in the unity of the Trinity for which they were engendered in the bosom of the Father, created and ordained for My service with the unction and divine action of the Holy Spirit" (*Diary*, Dec. 29, 1927).

"I ask for this spiritual reaction from My priests, since souls cannot have it, if, before, they do not have My very Spirit, they do not transform themselves into Me" (*Diary*, Feb. 13, 1928).

There is no question here of copying some of Christ's traits or of imitating some of His virtues. The transformation to priestly holiness brings about full identity with Christ-Priest.

"The transformation of the priest in Me which takes place in the Mass, he must continue in his ordinary life, in order that this life be interior, spiritual and divine.

"When a priest is not transformed into Me, or on the way to such transformation by constant effort to be so, he will be in the Church, but, in a certain sense, separated from the intimacy of the Church, separated from her Spirit, from the transforming nucleus of My Church.

"Yet how many priests there are who do not think about this, who do not seek it, who make no effort to acquire it! They take on the incomparable dignity of the priesthood as if it were just an ordinary secular profession. Such is not the sublime and holy purpose of the priesthood, which consists in perfect transformation into Me through love and through virtues.

"My Father wants to see the priest transformed into Me, not only during the time of Mass, but at all times. He wants to see him transformed in such a way that no matter where or when the priest can truly say, in the interior of his soul, these blessed words, constantly fulfilled in him by his transformation into Me: *This is My Body; this is My Blood* (*Diary*, Dec. 31, 1927).

Transformation into Christ-Victim

"What is wanting to many of My priests is the spirit of mortification, love of the Cross, knowledge of the riches found in suffering.

"Many preach the Cross but do not practice it. They advise abnegation and self-renunciation and they do not even dream of practicing these virtues so necessary for priests, for sacrifice is one of the culminating points and is the base for transformation into Me who was a Victim from the very moment of My Incarnation on to My death.

"To be acceptable to My Father, a victim must be pure and sacrificed. My entire life is reduced to this beautiful work which synthesizes the essence of the Christian and even more that of the priest: immolation! I was voluntarily immolated on earth and I continue this life of immolation on the altars.

"I came into the world to sanctify suffering and to take away its bitterness. I came to bring about love of the cross, and the most perfect transformation into Me must be brought about by loving suffering, by painful love.

"Thus then, a priest who wants to assimilate himself to Me as is his obligation, must love sacrifice, must aspire to voluntary immolation, by devoting himself, by renouncing his own self and sacrificing himself constantly on behalf of souls.

"Priest means one who offers himself and offers, who immolates himself and immolates.

"Priests must love the cross and be in love with Me crucified. I am their model" (*Diary*, Jan. 1, 1928).

This life of immolation as the ministry demands, is the service of souls. The priest is as Jesus, the Good Shepherd who must give his life for his sheep.

"The love with which I love My priests is infinite. I ask them to correspond to My love, and since their vocation in My Church is to save souls, they must love Me, they must possess My Spirit, be impregnated by My Spirit, live out of My Spirit, that is, live out of love.

"But my love does not consist only in making some acts of love, but in self-surrender to love unconditionally, by all the immolations the love of God and the love of souls demands.

"I am not deceived. Transformation commits to suffering, to overcoming self, to self-sacrifice, to death. But love is stronger than death, than this death which gives life. The Holy Spirit gave Me the inclination to the Cross. After I had voluntarily embraced it, the Cross changed into love" (*Diary*, March 4, 1928).

"The Holy Spirit inspired My death on the Cross. This death was a work of infinite love toward My Father and toward souls, but with so noble a purpose as to associate very specially to My Cross, to a life of sacrifice, all My future priests, who on being other Christs, making themselves one with Me would have to perpetuate My Sacrifice in themselves and on the altars to honor My Father, offering themselves and Me as one sole Victim pure and holy who would glorify Him" (*Diary*, Dec. 12, 1931).

Transformation into Christ demands being with Him at the same time as priest and victim. The grandeur of the priest is essentially a eucharistic grandeur.

A prayer in the Roman Missal expresses this spirituality admirably: "Receive, Lord, these gifts we offer You, and considering Your Christ, Priest and Victim, grant me, who shares His Priesthood, the grace to offer myself each day as an acceptable victim in Your presence" (*Offertory prayer of Mass for the priest*).

The Holy Spirit Alone Transforms Into Christ

"The Holy Spirit alone sanctifies priests. This divine Spirit alone raises them from the terrestrial to the divine. He alone is capable of urging on, by His breath, priestly souls toward heroism, toward the sublimity of their vocation. He is the delicate and most pure link which eternally unites the Trinity. He is also the link, the sweet and loving chain, which must sweetly unite as all that is His, priests with Me, to carry out the desire of My Father, Unity in Trinity, by the Holy Spirit.

"How much I desire the perfect reign of the Holy Spirit in the hearts of those who are Mine! This interior reign in the soul of My priests, must be His throne and nest. If they are other Christs, My priests must have My same Spirit, the Holy Spirit" (*Diary*, Jan. 12, 1928).

In the Unity of the Holy Spirit

The Father's salvific intent on sending His Son, was to unite all His dispersed children (cf. Jn 11:52), and to establish a Kingdom of Priests from men of all races, of all tongues and of all nations (cf. Rv 5:9).

"I came into the world with the sole purpose of uniting all men in the Unity of the Holy Trinity, by the Holy Spirit, that is, by Love" (*Diary*, Dec. 28, 1927).

"On founding the Church, the Father had but one purpose, unity, for neither in Himself, nor in His eternal thoughts, nor in His creation, nor in His desires, nor in His works, can He have other thoughts or intentions than unity. Consequently, when He founded the Church, His idea was not to make priests who departed from this unity, but one sole Priest in Me, one sole Saint in Me, by the Holy Spirit" (*Diary*, Feb. 13, 1928).

In a text of extraordinary doctrinal density, St. Paul stresses the unity of the Church. "There is but one body and one Spirit, just as there is but one hope given all of you by your call. There is one Lord, one faith, one baptism; one God and Father of all, who is over all and works through all, and is in all" (Ep 4:4-6).

Unity is the most divine characteristic of the Church. So there is no reason for being surprised if the spirit of evil strives to destroy her.

"The devil encourages disunity and in this way he weakens strength. The Holy Spirit seeks to unite, to relink paternal, filial and fraternal bonds, the breaking of which brings about so many evils in the Church. If I am in the Unity of the Trinity, why do not My priests and My shepherds have one only soul, one only will for My glory, one only heart in My Heart?

"I offered Myself up as a victim most especially for them, and I only asked them to persevere in love, My love which unites. If I desire men to love one another, with far greater reason I want My priests to love each other, and in this group of the elite, particularly chosen, I do not want to regret hatred, discord, separations, dissidence of wills and affections, all those miseries which make cold, tepid and separate hearts.

"This division in My Church is a terrible evil in itself which can bring about a schism. What is most painful for My Heart, what I regret most, is rejecting My commandment—love one another—they forget that I pronounced these words in particular for My priests, who are human and consequently subject to human passions.

"If I said that it would come about that they are Mine because they love each other, that means that when souls will see this coldness among them, this lack of love, the world will be scandalized and will not recognize them as My disciples.

"I insist, and I will always insist, on this unity of the Trinity and on this unity of charity, which is love, which is union through the action of the Holy Spirit.

"What I complain about is very human, this division among the members of the Church, which opens up great and profound evils which I alone can measure. It is a descent toward the world. But My priests are not of the world, they must not be of the world, they cannot follow the maxims of the world. There are so many materialistic things, vices, passions in the world from which My priests must keep themselves apart!

"Divisions, human respect, envy, self-seeking, and estrangement of hearts, all this comes from the world.

"The Pope, the cardinals, the bishops and priests, the whole ecclesiastical hierarchy, form but one single divine block, a rock in Peter, a rock against which the waves of the world and My enemies crash. But the block must be one, it must not be divided, thence derives the whole divine force against Hell. This is so since it is protected by the unity of the Whole, by the unity of the Trinity" (*Diary*, April 22, 1928).

"I insist on this unity of wills and minds in Me. Of course, rivers flow to the sea by different routes, and spring from different sources, but I want these rivers, in My Church, to be one in the union of Charity, that is, that My bishops and My priests form but one sole river which flows into one sea, Me. I want My Church in its tributaries to converge in wills and in love.

"Unity, unity of judgment, of wills in Mine is what gives peace to My Church and to hearts.

"How many bishops lament the lack of unity of their clergy, not only with those around them but among them, for their disagreements provoke uncharitableness and criticisms which wound My Heart, which is wholly obedience and charity.

"If the priesthood has so sublime an origin, which is found in the loving bosom of the Trinity, it has the unavoidable obligation to assimilate itself to the Trinity, and this above all in its unity. As the Church was created by the Trinity, she must live and breathe unity in It, in simplicity obeying My will manifested by superiors, that is by the Pope and the bishops on whom the priests depend.

"This unity is lacking in the world, and from this lack flow so many evils which crush the world. Souls are diverted from their center, and thence come the tragedies which oppress fallen mankind. Here is the central and capital point of its ruination, living apart from unity, following erroneous doctrines, in self-opinionated pride, in a multitude of sects, in the mist and obscurity of confusions. The day the world will return to its center, the *unity of the Trinity* in its Church, that day the world will be saved.

"But what is most sorrowful, and what causes Me most pain, is that even among Mine there exists this disunity which separates them from the center, from the most simple and luminous Trinity, the most holy and most perfect union, in the three Divine Persons" (*Diary*, Nov. 28, 1927).

Unity cannot be brought about solely by human endeavor. It is a gift which comes from heaven, and that is why Christ at the culminating moment of His life sent up a prayer to His Father asking unity for His Church.

"In this most tender plea to My Father, there rose at the Last Supper, a prayer which came from the innermost depths of My soul, by which I wanted to express to My Apostles, and in them, to My priests of all times, all My sublime tenderness and the quintessence of My soul for them. I asked My Father for what was the greatest, the most beautiful, *that we be one*, consummated in the unity of the Trinity.

"This request for the consummation of unity in My Father and in Me, has not remained sterile, for from it many graces have poured out on the earth, and in particular on My priests who have thus been able to become other Christs. For this reason, for this reason alone, I have given them My own Spouse, the Church, but with the same duties of fidelity to and of purest love for Her; with the obligation to serve her, to console her, to give her spiritual and holy sons, to extend her kingdom, to respect the hierarchy, to bring about among them on earth this unity, echo of this holy, fecund and most pure unity, that of priests in Me, coming from unity in the Trinity.

"All that rejects this unity is diabolical; all that does not lead to this unity is false; all that separates itself from this unity will be of no worth in heaven" (*Diary*, March 14, 1928).

Conchita will ever show toward priests a profound respect and a love of predilection. She does not criticize them, she offers her life in expiation for their weaknesses and to obtain for them the grace of an eminent holiness. She sees, feels, is silent. But she constantly immolates herself, as a victim for the Church, and above all for priests.

"*Offer* yourself as a victim with Me for the Church.

"Offer yourself up in oblation for My priests. Unite yourself to My sacrifice to obtain graces. It is necessary that in union with the eternal Priest, you carry out your role as priest, offering Me to the Father to obtain graces and mercy for the Church and for her members. You remember how many times I asked you to offer up yourself as a victim for My beloved Church? Don't you see you are all hers since you are Mine and you are Mine because you are all hers? Precisely on account of this special union which links you to My Church, you have the right to participate in her anguish and the sacred obligation to console her by sacrificing yourself for her priests" (*Diary*, Sept. 24, 1927).

Only the Spirit Unifies

"To bring about this ideal of unity of My beloved Father, that which He has for my priests, the indispensable and all-mighty motive force is the Holy Spirit. He alone, and only He, can renew the face of the earth, and unite hearts with the Word, for He is the bond of ineffable love between the Father and the Son. It is He who unifies the Church since He unifies the Trinity in Love. It is He who makes it one since He is Love.

"Love alone unites, simplifies, sanctifies. Love alone reconciles, embraces, tightens bonds and brings hearts together.

"Love is the motive power of the Church and of the sacraments. It is love which engendered priests in the Father, for the whole Trinity is alone the essence and will, without beginning. Love, fashioning priests, who, if they were engendered from all eternity in the mind of the Father, will be born under the impulse of the loving and sorrowful beating of My Heart on the Cross, and consumed from beginning to end by love.

"If you see unity in one only essence of the Trinity, then you will see how the Church is a reflection of the Trinity itself, and how all her activity on earth is summed up in bringing about the unity of one flock under one Shepherd.

"Unity is what is most beautiful for God, for unity describes Him since He is the Supreme Unity. God is most simple in His Being and His greatest joy, His only joy is to love Himself, to be Three Persons in one sole substance and essence of love, even though Love be personified in the Holy Spirit; to rejoice in one sole infinite point, which fills Him wholly, which absorbs all, which produces all: souls, worlds, products of love, of a most pure love which makes the heavens marvel and makes created beings cry out: 'Holy, Holy, Holy!', in ecstasy before these infinite perfections which surprise, amaze, divinize and unify in God all things.

"Why have I spoken to you about this most holy, most sublime, most perfect unity, which enraptures God Himself who is eternal and infinite in His perfections?

"Because this unity, produced by love, reflected by My Church which must be *one* consonant with the unity of the Holy Spirit, does not exist in the case of many of My bishops and priests.... I wanted to show you this pain which afflicts My God-Man's Heart; the painful picture of the disunion of will of so many members of My Church.

"What is the use if externally wills are united by human respect, if interiorly there is discord, criticism, intrigues which I alone clearly see, but which at times provoke scandals? This hurts Me, this lack of fraternal, filial and even paternal union. This harms Me for from it come so many evils which sadden Me, and which are felt in My Church, harming her in many ways.

"They should carry on their work united, united in thought and attitudes. But this must be really so, not feigned or by participation! The Trinity should be imitated, by striving to bring about unity so that the whole Episcopate has but one single heart and soul, forming only but one family in Me by My Spirit. I repeat: My concern is for what is interior.

"Priests on their part must bring their wills into accord with that of the bishop, respecting his decisions, without dissension.

As for the bishop, he should avoid more than anyone else being uncharitable in this point which is more important than it seems.

"I insist that for this it is necessary to go to the Holy Spirit, the Conciliator who unifies minds and wills. He reflects unity in souls, since He is an intrinsic part of unity by essence. The Holy Spirit, the soul of the Church, is the standard bearer of unity, its principle, its center and its object, for He is Love.

"May bishops and priests have recourse assiduously and with ever growing love to the Holy Spirit, and He will be their light, their director, their guide, to bring them to unity.

"I want but one only apostolate in My Church, one only faith, one only truth, one only objective. One martyrdom, if all bear witness; one joy, if all rejoice; one triumph, if all succeed; one Calvary, if all suffer; that is, a bond of charity which unites, the very link which forms unity by love, the Holy Spirit. There must be one son, Jesus, God-Man, who warns them, and one goal, My Father, since all goes to Him through the Holy Spirit and through Mary" (*Diary*, Nov. 27, 1927).

Consummation in the Unity of the Trinity

"Consummation in Unity" comes about when the Christian and particularly the priest, *loves with the Holy Spirit*, that is, when his charity is not practiced in a human manner under the influence of infused prudence, but supernaturally under the *inspiration* of the Holy Spirit. *Charity perfected by gifts* loves with the Holy Spirit.

"The Church is love, she is charity, since her origin and her being and her life proceed from the Father's fecund love. That is why Christians must be love, all love, raised to the summit of unity by love. What is Love if it is not the Holy Spirit? This Spirit was My Spirit, and through Him, I loved the Father. Likewise I want My priests and all Christians to love the Father as I love Him, with the same Holy Spirit. Such is the perfection of love.

"It is a love which unites you with the Trinity, which simplifies in holiness, which unites you, which engenders what My love desires, what My Father desires, that all priests be one only priest in Me, one only Christ on whom rests His loving gaze and on whom He finds pleasure.

"Do you understand that on founding the Church, such was My ideal? I in the Pope, as head and all priests forming in Me but one only Body and one only will with that of My beloved Father. After priests, My chosen souls, all Christians must unite in Me, consummated in Unity" (*Diary*, July 5, 1930).

A New Pentecost

"On sending to the world a new Pentecost, I want it inflamed, purified, illumined, inflamed and purified by the light and fire of the Holy Spirit. The last stage of the world must be marked very specially by the effusion of the Holy Spirit. He must reign in hearts and in the entire world, not so much for the glory of His Person as for making the Father loved and bearing testimony of Me, although His glory is that of the whole Trinity" (*Diary*, Jan. 26, 1916).

"Tell the Pope that it is My will that in the whole Christian world the Holy Spirit be implored to bring peace and His reign into hearts. Only this Holy Spirit will be able to renew the face of the earth. He will bring light, union and charity to hearts.

"The world is foundering because it rejects the Holy Spirit, and all the evils which afflict it have therein their origin. The remedy is found in Him. He is the Consoler, the author of all grace, the bond of union between the Father and the Son and the supreme conciliator since He is charity, uncreated and eternal Love.

"May the whole world have recourse to this Holy Spirit since the day of His reign has arrived. This last stage of the world belongs very specially to Him that He be honored and exalted.

"May the Church preach Him, may souls love Him, may the

whole world be consecrated to Him, and peace will come along with a moral and spiritual reaction, greater than the evil by which the world is tormented.

"May all at once this Holy Spirit begin to be called on with prayers, penances and tears, with the ardent desire of His coming. He will come, I will send Him again clearly manifest in His effects, which will astonish the world and impel the Church to holiness" (*Diary*, Sept. 27, 1918).

"Ask for this renewal, this new Pentecost, for My Church has need of priests sanctified by the Holy Spirit. The world is foundering in the abyss since it lacks priests who will help it from falling in; priests who bear the light to shine on the paths of good; pure priests to pull out of the mud so many hearts; priests afire who will fill the entire universe with divine love.

"Ask, supplicate heaven, that all may be restored in Me by the Holy Spirit" (*Diary*, Nov. 1, 1927).

"I want to return to the world in My priests. I want to renew the world of souls by making Myself seen in My priests. I want to give a mighty impulse to My Church infusing in her, as it were, a new Pentecost, the Holy Spirit, in My priests (*Diary*, Jan. 5, 1928).

"To obtain what I ask, every priest must make a consecration to the Holy Spirit, asking Him, through Mary's intercession, to come to them as it were in a new Pentecost, to purify them, to fill them with love, possess them, unify them, sanctify them and transform them into Me" (*Diary*, Jan. 25, 1928).

"One day not too far away, at the center of My Church, at Saint Peter's there will take place the consecration of the world to the Holy Spirit, and the graces of this Divine Spirit, will be showered on the blessed Pope who will make it.

"It is My desire that the universe be consecrated to the Divine Spirit that He may spread Himself over the earth in a new Pentecost. (*Diary*, March 11, 1928).

CHAPTER V.

THE ABYSSES OF THE TRINITY

"In the clarity of these lights I contemplate the abysses of the Trinity."

The Trinitarian character of Conchita's whole life and of all her teachings is one of the most admirable and profound aspects of her spirituality.

The blossoming in her of baptism, and the progressive development of personal grace under the action of the Holy Spirit, impel her to identification with, transformation into Christ-Priest and Victim for continuing her oblation of love to the glory of the Father on behalf of men. Conchita's entire spiritual life expanded under the sign of the Trinity.

From the very first pages of her *Diary* there stands out a call of grace which carries her on toward the profundities of the inmost life of God. To the measure she advances in the spiritual life, she receives special lights, and comes to the full life of union, the action of the gifts of intelligence and wisdom, she immerses herself in the abysses of the Trinity.

The pages Conchita wrote on the Trinity are the most sublime of her *Diary*, they would fill a whole book. We have been obliged, regretfully, to extract only part of the text of the treasure of her teachings.

Great Devotion to the Most Holy Trinity

Her vital relationship with the divine Persons follows a constantly ascending course.

From the very beginnings of her spiritual life, the Lord led her in a very conscious and practical way to orient her life to the glory of the Holy Trinity. He told her: "Fill your life, hour by hour, without thinking of what comes later, as if it were your last hour; fill it, abandoning yourself to My will, seeking only to please Me. Repeat this: May Your will be done, oh Father, Son and Holy Spirit. Glory to You Most Holy Trinity" (*Diary*, 1893).

The vision of the Cross of the Apostolate—symbol of the spirituality and of the teachings of the Cross—is wholly enveloped in a profound Trinitarian sense. Conchita glimpses this, and, turning to Jesus, writes: "... the Father by His approval, You fastened to the Cross, and the Holy Spirit as Protector ... the whole Trinity is going to direct this Work" (*Diary*, March 1894).

The result of this sanctifying action of God is shown in Conchita who wrote a short time later:

"Here I am wholly immersed in God. I have a great devotion to the Most Holy Trinity. I have consecrated these three days to Him with all my soul. Yesterday, the Father ... today Jesus ... and tomorrow the Holy Spirit, whom I love so much. I have often felt Him inclined over me with His rays of light, making me experience an ineffable sensation which lulls me, enchants me and fills me with an unction which transports me" (*Diary*, May 19, 1894).

"The Whole Trinity is Love."

From the central perspective of her personal grace, the mystery of the Cross, Conchita contemplates, in the light of the Holy Spirit, the mystery of this God who turns toward us. It is a capital text, for from the beginning, it gives us the key to the interpretation of the whole doctrine of the Cross:

"The substance of the Father is Love and so great is His love for man that He gave His own Son to redeem the world. The substance of the Son is Love and a love so great, for the Father and for men, that He gave Himself up to suffering to save them, for the honor of the Father. As for Me, the third Person, My substance is Love, in concordance with the Father and the Son for the glory of the Trinity, taking part in the mystery of the Incarnation, accompanying Jesus throughout His life, attesting to His divinity and sealing the work of Redemption, protecting the Church, My immaculate Spouse.

"The substance of the Father is Love and might. My substance is Love and life, the substance of the Son is Love and suffering. The substance of the Three divine Persons is Charity, that is, the purest Love which communicates itself. This is why It is called Charity, because of this giving of self. It is the most perfect love.

"Suffering, or the Cross divinized by the Son, is the one and only ladder for reaching to the love of charity. Now do you understand the value of the Cross? Those who are most crucified are those who love the most, since suffering, the emblem of Jesus, draws to it the Three Divine Persons. We dwell in this soul and there I set up my dwelling" (*Diary*, July 9, 1895).

Trinity and Incarnation

"I am the way, and the truth, and the life; no one comes to the Father but through Me" (Jn 14:6).

The mystery of the Incarnation led Conchita toward the profundities of God.

"The Lord then raised my spirit up to the contemplation of the Incarnation of the Word. He made me understand very profound things concerning the Most Holy Trinity, of which He is the Second Person.

"From all eternity the Father existed. He produced from His own depths, from His own substance, from His very essence His Word. From all eternity, too, from the beginning the Word was God, as the Father was God, the two Persons constituting but one divine substance. But never at any moment did these divine Persons, the Father and the Son, exist alone, never were they but two. In this same eternity, though proceeding from the

Father and the Son, the Holy Spirit existed, the reflection, substance, essence of the Father and the Son and, equally, Person. The Holy Spirit is a divine reflection on the bosom of Love Itself. He is the reflection of light at the heart of light itself, the reflection of life in the innermost of Life itself, and so of all infinite perfection within the inmost core of eternal perfection.

"This communication of the same substance, of the same essence, of the same life and of the same perfections which form and which are actually one and the same essence, substance, life and perfection, constitute the eternal felicity of one sole God and the endless complacency of the Persons of the august Trinity.

"Oh how great, immensely great, God is! What abysses in Him, incomprehensible for man and even for angels! Before this grandeur, I feel like the tiniest atom. Yet my infinite soul, on feeling capable of receiving a feeble reflection of this same grandeur, expands, fully joyous on contemplating the felicity, the eternity, the incomprehensible immensity of its God.

" And is the Word there? I ask myself, wholly moved, whether it is from this throne He will descend to the vile atom of the earth? Oh my eternal God, how can I accept such condescension?

"Jesus went on: 'The Word, the Second Person of the Most Holy Trinity descended into the most pure womb of Mary and, by operation of the Holy Spirit who made her pregnant, the Word became incarnate and was made man! So profound an abasement as only the love of a God could bring about!'

"I heard about this marvelous and so sublime mystery some things so profound that they are only for my soul, for I cannot explain them to others, for lack of words." (*Diary*, Feb. 25, 1897).

It must be emphasized that the lights she receives do not result in Conchita having a purely abstract knowledge. There is not question of a speculation about God, but of an experience of love which perceives in the profundity of the inmost life of God the *raison d'etre* of a love for men extended even to the *folly of the Cross.*

Her Early Experiences

The life of grace is a ceaseless progress and so it was that Conchita's characteristic and personal aspect in her relations with the divine Persons does not clearly appear at the beginning. Here is how she describes her early experiences:

" I had in some prayers some inexplicable points of knowledge of God (I do not know how to say it) in the Most Holy Trinity . . . To experience (I do not say to understand) what He is . . . A sort of rough draft of His so pure essence . . . in His Whole-Unity . . . in His eternal generation . . . in His attributes . . . immensity . . . bounty . . . justice . . . but all this, as it were, in a point, a point of interior light of an inexplicable sweetness, a sweetness not like that which comes from other prayers, but much more sublime and pure which brings out the soul or suspends it but with a clear knowledge of God who envelopes it, forgetting everything, even one's self.

"I suffer when I see certain paintings or representations of the Most Holy Trinity. Oh, that is not what I feel! God is light, purity, divine perfume, an array of beauty, the hearth of all perfection, peace and candor. He is love, love, love, incomprehensible, eternity apart from time, a point which enkindles and absorbs all, dazzling, majestic, and exceedingly sweet, which attracts everything and ever communicates itself . . . without ever diminishing its plentitude!

"Oh, how this eternity apart from time is deeply imprinted on my heart! This God, God thrice holy, holy, holy, whom I do not understand but whom I experience, who will be able to say what He is, if even in heaven there is no language to explain it?

" To feel, that makes me fear. But all at once, I feel myself immersed in this ocean of ravishing perfections, in this eternity of beauty and personal happiness! I see the three divine Persons communicate to each other this eternal complacency which is ever produced (I would say this in explanation) and at each instant on contemplating themselves . . . I feel or I see with my soul (I do not know how to express it) an eternal abyss of eternal perfections, ever new, in which the three divine Persons rejoice. All Three have, the Lord tells me, the most pure joy of communication. They are three Persons but with one only divine substance, equal in might, wisdom, goodness and all other attributes! Oh, how immense God is: How good, how holy, how pure! He is Love, to that everything I can say comes back" (*Diary*, May 14, 1898).

Toward Union

As an immediate preparation for the full life of union, Conchita receives some remarkable lights about the Trinity.

"There does not exist two nor three but one Only God in Three divine Persons. I understood this most clearly. I saw that it must be so, and that there was a marvelous reason for this. (I do not know whether I explain well what I would like to say).

"The Lord continued: 'There are not three lights, but one only light, eternal and equal in three divine Persons. The formula *God from God*, means there is equality. At the same time it also is intended to indicate the same Being communicated to the Word. In a reflection of this eternal hearth of grandeur, of light and of infinite perfections, the Holy Spirit is produced, the term and, so to say, conclusion of this divine mystery, but not less than the Father and the Son. Nothing, absolutely nothing is lacking to Him, but the Three Persons, equal, in one and the same essence, form but one hearth, one only Being without beginning and end. None of the Persons is anterior or superior to the other, but the eternal Three from the beginning, yes, are eternal and in a truly sublime, admirable communication, which constitutes the felicity of the only God.'

"I explain this in poor human words because there is not—and I think there cannot be—any created language which would be able to express the inexpressible" (*Diary*, Feb. 2, 1897).

The Infinite Purity of the Trinity

"Today, in church, the Lord has not let me pray nor open my book. As soon as I have received holy communion, He puts me in a state of great recollection, raising my soul up to another atmosphere, far from the earth.

"I have understood, I do not know how, something about God's infinite purity and how, in the eternal generation of the Word, the eternal Father communicates to Him His own substance and essence, the essence of the Father being purity itself. But by this word 'PURITY,' meaning divine transparence, I designate a clarity, a whiteness, a light for which I find no word to express, for all light is darkness in comparison with this divine clarity: white seems black and the sun itself is like an inkblot. Oh my God! Oh eternal splendor! How do I explain the inexplicable in human language? Stainless beauty ever ancient and ever new, ineffable splendor one brilliance of which human eyes cannot endure. And I, I saw, or I sensed all this, but in the depths of my soul.

"I saw God the Father (rejoicing eternally in Himself in His infinite perfections, in an ineffable complacence) reproduce Himself with all the ardor of His purity in the Second divine Person, who is the Word.

"I saw this Word as a perfect and full reflection of the Father, in the eternal transport of this most holy divine Love which exists between the Father and the Son. I saw their bond of light and of love, the Holy Spirit, inseparable from the Father and from the Son, although constituting one distinct person. He followed His orbit, rendering thereby the three divine Persons perfectly happy. I do not know how to explain this. I grasped everything in an instant, unmeasured in time and indivisible, and yet as three distinctive divine Persons of the adorable and most Holy Trinity.

"Oh blessed Trinity! Who then will be able to comprehend You, if by one single ray emanating from Your transparence the soul is now wholly absorbed? What then is, yes, what is then Your nature?" (*Diary*, April 28, 1898).

Intimacy with the living God, with the Father, the Son and the Holy Spirit is characteristic of the life of union. Conchita received eminent graces of this order. That is what the Most Holy Trinity constitutes, the center of her life.

"The Trinity: Center of My Life"

"In the abyss of my misery and counter to my will, my spirit breaks the ties which fix it to the soil of my nothingness, and flees. It rushes toward the divine throne of the most Holy Trinity as if there was its center and its life, there, within Life itself. If my spirit cannot find its satisfaction in the little pools of water I present it, I seek the boundless Ocean without shores, its God and Lord. I enclose my spirit in the narrow well of self-knowledge, but it takes flight out of it and rushes off into this immensity of its God, the only place where it can find satiety and breathe.

"Why are there in me, who am so weak, so small, so corrupt, why are there in my so miserable soul, these feelings: this thirst and this suffocating sensation in all that lacks grandeur and in all that is not God? If I am not capable of holding a tiny drop of water, why this desire to swallow the ocean? If I am but a dot in space, how is it possible, how does it come to my mind, to embrace eternal immensity?

"What is happening, oh my God—I understand—is that this drop of water is lost in the ocean and the nothingness in the infinite. That is, it is not only God who enters into me, even when He penetrates and takes possession of my soul, it is also I who enter into Him. Rather, I am not worthy to enter and I stop at the door, but He takes me in His arms and brings me into these regions unknown to the material world. How rapidly my soul covers these distances! It knows, it sees, it hears, without seeing nor hearing. It finds itself brought together in one point, but an infinite and eternal point, a point of uncreated love. There only it breathes life, is fulfilled and happy, outside of time" (*Diary*, May 31, 1890).

Trinity and Mystical Incarnation

The doctrine of spiritual persons is strictly related to their lives and their experience of God is carrying out the mission the Holy Spirit assigns them.

If Conchita receives such sublime lights, it is not directly in view of an instruction to impart or of a teaching assignment, but in order that she may above all live profoundly her personal grace and arrive at the holiness to which God calls her for the spiritual benefit of many a soul.

The eminent grace of the mystical incarnation will bring with it its nuances for her life of intimacy with the divine Persons. This grace, we have already said, is a grace of transformation into the Incarnate Word who glorifies the Father and ransoms men, in Christ Priest and Victim. It is found at the base of Christian existence, since the Father "has predestined us to share the image of His Son" (Rm 8:29), and consequently "to offer your bodies as a living sacrifice holy and acceptable to God, through spiritual worship" (Rm 12:1). Under the sign of the Son, the whole Church enters into communion with the inmost life of the Trinity.

Conchita's central grace, by its nature, supposes personal relations with each of the divine Persons. There is here an eminently Trinitarian grace.

"Do not think that in the mystical incarnations of the Word it is I who act, but the Trinity of the divine Persons do so, each one of them operating according to His attributes, the Father, as Father, engendering: the Word as Son, being born; the Holy Spirit making fertile this divine action in the soul" (*Diary*, Sept. 22, 1927).

From this action of the Trinity which brings about configuration to Christ Priest and Host flows the necessity of living in perfect identity the most intimate sentiments of His Heart, in a constant oblation of love. To offer Christ and to offer one's self in union with Him to the Father under the movement of the Holy Spirit for the salvation of men, such is the proper and characteristic act of the mystical incarnation.

That Conchita could live consciously and fully her central grace, the Lord showed her the concrete and practical way of living in the intimacy of the divine Persons.

The Chain of Love

"I, from the moment of My Incarnation in Mary's most pure womb, acquired graces. I want you, transformed into Me, living out of My own life, not to do from now on anything else. You must forget yourself, and day and night offer up everything for the salvation and perfection of souls.

"Listen, you are going to make a chain. Each hour of your life will be one of its golden links, if you offer it for this intention, and I want you to stop only on your death.

"This chain begun in Me, the chain of expiation on earth, will be changed into graces. I began this chain with My Incarnation, and as its reflection in your heart, I have wished to associate you with it out of pure bounty.

"The Chain is to live 'in Christ-Jesus' with His same salvific intentions.

"All virtues not enwrapped in love will not be part of this chain which binds Me, the Word, to earth, and so much ingratitude has not been able to break. Who, then, do you think sent it to earth? The Holy Spirit, [on] the day of the Incarnation in Mary" (*Diary*, June 4, 1906).

"You are altar and priest at the same time for you possess the most holy Victim of Calvary and of the Eucharist, which you can constantly offer to the eternal Father for the salvation of the world" (*Diary*, June 21, 1906).

To Christ's oblation she must join her own oblation.

"You must perform the function of priest but by sacrificing yourself at the same time. There is the true priesthood: being victim with the Victim" (*Diary*, July 17, 1906).

The Chain of love begins with insertion into the inmost life of God in baptism. This grace of filial adoption becomes personal and conscious and it normally demands a progressive identification with Christ the Priest, the center of every salvific design of the Father. When we view the spirituality and the doctrine of the Cross from the standpoint of a theologian, what strikes us most is the fact that it springs from the very essence of Christianity.

The inmost life of God is Father, Son and Holy Spirit and is manifested in His attitude toward us. God is Love which is spread and overflows liberally and freely to save what has been lost, overcoming the obstacle license had erected against the expansion of divine Good.

The Father out of love gives us His Son. The Son out of love gives us His life. The Holy Spirit is at the same time the beginning in God and the fruit in us of the salvific design. The glorious Cross is the supreme epiphany of the mystery of the living God.

This revelation is a Word addressed to man which by nature is a summons, a call, a loving demand for a response. When man under divine initiative opens himself up to His action, then vital relations of dialogue rise up in him, which correspond to the movement of descending Love.

"The love of God has been poured out in our hearts through the Holy Spirit which has been given to us" (Rm 5:5). This love impells us to identify ourselves with Christ in His attitude of self-giving and oblation on behalf of men for glorifying the Father from whom all good proceeds. In this way there is reestablished the flow and reflow of the divine good communicated to man. It is a chain which ties up to God, not a chain of servitude or of simple dependence as a creature, but a "Chain of Love."

It is a synthesis of the fundamental experience of saved existence which members of the Mystical Body of Christ lead, a lived experience of the mystical incarnation which finds its consummation in the Unity of the Trinity.

The Chain of Love is also the exercise of spiritual priesthood by which "all their works, prayers, and apostolic endeavors, their ordinary married and family life, their daily labor, their mental and physical relaxation, carried out in the Spirit, and even the hardships of life, if patiently borne—all of these become spiritual sacrifices acceptable to God through Jesus Christ" (cf. 1 P 2:5), (*Lumen Gentium* # 34).

This spiritual priesthood culminates in the celebration of Eucharist: "Taking part in the Eucharistic Sacrifice, which is the font and apex of the whole Christian life, they offer the divine Victim to God, and offer themselves along with it" (*Lumen Gentium* # 11).

It is evident that to the extent that Christian life becomes more intense, spiritual priesthood is carried out with a quality and greater perfection and comes to be a living and continual contact with the divine Persons.

"You Must Live in Continual Contact with the Trinity"

"You must live in continual contact with the Trinity, united to the three divine Persons by the grace of the mystical incarnation: with the Father offering Him His Word, with the Son, giving delights to the Father, with the Holy Spirit accepting Him for your spirit, the inspirer of your feelings and of all that you are, transforming you since you are possessed by Him.

"You must live, breathe, labor, in the bosom of these three divine Persons. They must constitute your atmosphere, your breathing, your existence. Thus, you will sanctify your life and what you are, divinizing your whole being and each of your steps to heaven.

"From today on, you must live more and more in this intimacy with the Trinity, drawing from It light, the way you conduct yourself, force, grace and all the helps needed to carry out your mission on earth. You should not leave on high, as on a throne and far away this Trinity of Persons, but live, breathe and dwell in its bosom, under its fecund influence, in the radiance of Its divinity, in the shadow of Its grace. If you are possessed of the Holy Spirit, if you truly possess Him, you will not be able to separate yourself from Him, but on the contrary, you will remain most intimately united with the Father and the Word.

"If in your soul there is operated the mystical incarnation, there attracted by the Word, will be found the Father and the Holy Spirit. If, the Holy Spirit and the Word divinize you in this so innerly a manner, if they enter into you, the Father who by nature holds the first place in these operations, will unite you to Him, from whom proceeds all fecundity and might, drawing you by a grace of special filiation, burying you in His eternity of all perfections" (*Diary*, July 19, 1906).

From Union to Unity

It is not possible to imagine transformation into Christ as a static reality. Divine life, communicated to man in his earthly pilgrimage, is of itself in constant progress.

From the outset of all Christian life, by the new birth "of water and of the Spirit," transformation into Christ begins, but it is but an initial transformation, a seed which must grow.

Even on the summits of the spiritual life this vital progress continues. This life of union still mounts toward unity, of course not a unity in the order of being, but in the intentional order of knowledge and of love.

"Listen. There are many progressive degrees in the transformation. The highest degree on earth corresponds to a transformation of the creature not only in its manner of thinking and of acting which becomes divine, but which, in a certain sense, causes it to disappear and annihilate itself to give place to Me.

"This degree is the work of the Holy Spirit alone who becomes the soul of this soul and the life of this body.

"This point which leads to union, even more, to unity, is the point of perfection which approaches most to the Trinity.

"The creature left to itself would be incapable of attaining this degree without the most powerful aid of Him who is the inexhaustible Source of graces, the Holy Spirit. The mystical incarnation attracts the Holy Spirit, loving, mighty and divine of the Word who possesses the soul. Transformation is in the innermost part and the most noble of the creature" (*Diary*, Aug. 6, 1912).

Lights About the Unity of the Trinity

"Today, in my prayer, the Lord gave me some radiant lights clarifying the Unity of the Most Holy Trinity. What abysses of perfections! What delights in God! What will heaven be, my God?" (*Diary*, April 9, 1913).

"Today, the Lord enveloped my soul in the depths of His uncreated light. He made me penetrate into these abysses of light the perfection of the Most Holy Trinity. He told me: 'Look and pay attention. All God's perfections are infinite, but they are based on one alone: on Unity. This Unity contains all the eternal riches. The highest perfection of souls consists in simplifying oneself, eliminating the multiplicity of objects and of things, in order to approach thus this essential Unity, fecund in its eternity, which without movement multiplies itself in its immutability in one eternal instant. There are Three divine Persons but only one Essence, only one Substance, one eternal and indivisible Unity. Precisely in this Unity is found the secret of its fecundity. The more souls unify themselves with this Unity by union, the more these souls are fecund, since, in the measure they approach the Most Holy Trinity, is the superabundance of light, of grace and of gifts they receive from it. In this beautiful and divine Unity, the Three divine Persons and the blessed find their beatitude. In this Unity are contained all the goods of earth and heaven, all graces, all created beings, and all those which will be created in the future. It is the eternal hearth of all movement and of all being. It is Love. It is God.

'Simplify your spirit. Remove all complications coming from creatures and things. Love Me in Unity; live, breathe, act, bring about that all virtues and all dispoilings of yourself tend toward this Unity. . . . You must live in this essential Unity, in this Unique God, bringing together your spiritual life in one only Love: Him; in one only will: His. In this capital point of unity of wills consists the perfection of this Unity.'

"That is what the Lord told me during Mass, and during my prayer He added: 'The end of every creature consists in this unity in God. There is found peace and lasting felicity. Souls which tend more and more to identify themselves in this Unity, that is, to make themselves but one with the Incarnate Word, the prototype of every creature's perfection, and which let themselves be divinized by Him in the Holy Spirit and in the Father, these souls are the holiest since holiness depends on love and the more love there is the more likeness there is to God, the more Unity there is with Him, the more perfection and holiness.

" 'One of the secrets of the Holy Spirit for developing divine life in souls and consequently union, is simplifying them in unity, that is, enriching them by love which is the essence of Unity in heaven and on earth. Spiritual marriage tends to this Unity through the Holy Spirit. Mystical incarnation tends toward this same unity through the Word. It is crowned in heaven by the Father, the mover and cause of spiritual marriage and of mystical incarnation. . . . The whole economy and all the designs of redemption on souls, all the means of the mystical life, the role of the Incarnate Word who loves souls passionately and of the Holy Spirit who brings them to perfection for glorifying the Father in them, all this tends toward this Unity of which I speak. It is due to love which simplifies, which raises from the terrestrial to the divine, which unites and identifies the soul with the Divinity. The whole Christian life, the whole mystical life, tends to lead to this culminating point, toward this end offered to every

soul which wishes to be saved and to be sanctified toward Unity'"
(*Diary*, April 11, 1913).

With the mystique of the Cross we come to the highest summits of Transformation by the Holy Spirit who unites to the Word and leads to the Father.

The Fastest Road to Unity

"What is the fastest road to come to this unity? It is the Holy Spirit who unites to the Word, who gives testimony of Him, who leads us toward the Father, a mission which pleases Him to the supreme degree. By title of Sanctifier, He sanctifies; sanctifying, He simplifies souls, leads them to the Father, making them lovers of the Trinity.

"The Lord told me complacently: 'God is One, and it is at the interior of this Unity His perfections are reproduced to infinity. God is One, but He does not dwell alone. There are three Persons in this Being which is One, and this One does not remain inactive. He cannot remain inactive because of the super-abundant fecundity of His Being. He is One, but it is precisely from this Unity that He draws the force of His action, of His creative power, of His fecundity. He produces Himself in each act, I might say so that you understand me, as you would express it. Contemplate this abyss of light, approach Him. But know that in God, there is no succession of acts. He operates eternally in one only act of His Will which covers all times and eternity, and all creations, all things in one only instant, the eternal instant of Unity in which is reflected and exists always present, past and future. That is when eternities without end vanish in Him. You, you measure time by the succession of your acts, but in God there is no time. All His acts, all His creations of nature and of grace, He Keeps them as in a mirror in the purity of His Spirit, brings out and reproduces out of His bosom and of His immensity all worlds, recompenses, crowns and all the beings that glorify Him, without the slightest movement on His part, in one only act of infinite Might.

" 'God multiplies Himself while still remaining One and without the least change. Immutable, eternal, He rejoices, in the infinite instant of His Unity, of His Being and of His numberless perfections.

" 'The souls closest to Him in heaven are those who, on earth, are most united to Him, putting aside all that could be an obstacle. They broke all attachments of evil passions and all else by the exercises of virtues and by self-spoliation, those who by perpetual separations and a constant abnegation united themselves unconditionally to His will.'

"I saw abysses of light in this beloved Trinity. What depths, or rather what sublime perfections and what marvels!

"I said to Him: 'Lord, how would I be able to simplify myself?'

"He answered: 'By dying to your will and by making it one with Mine' " (*Diary*, April 11, 1913).

"The Lord continues to show the practical way to arrive at Unity: 'I insist that, for simplifying your acts in one finality, super-naturalizing them in God, you simplify your loves in one only love, in that of God, whence comes love of neighbor in the Unity of this God.'

"Learn to have but one only outlook, one only tendency, one only affection and will in God. Employ your existence loving God most simply, without detours, without complications, without seeking other ways or paths to come to Him, but seek only this essential Unity in which you must plunge yourself.

"The very virtues you practice, direct them all to this Center of love, to this Unique Being whence all grace and holiness come, to this unity which is God. The Holy Spirit, *one* with the Father and the Son will bear you on His wings up to the heart of this Unity, that you may understand, move, breathe and live in It. This divine Spirit, on spiritualizing you, that is, on unifying you, will make you penetrate into what is Spirit, that is, into the essential Divinity, having prior to this passed through Jesus Christ in your transformation into Him in virtues and through love.

"This is most sublime, but not impossible for the creature.

This is not an ideal perfection I ask of you, but a most practical perfection by means of the exercise of virtues. This implies renunciation, simplification for uniting oneself more closely with Simplicity itself: God, *one* in the spirituality of His substance, this One in Three and these Three in One, indivisible and all perfect.

"All that you do and practice, cast it as often as possible into this Unity which must bring you along by the infinite perfection of its ever new beauties and by its infinite love. Your pains, your sufferings, your joys, your acts of renunciation, your desires and your hopes, your needs and your feelings, cast them all into this Unity which by its contact will simplify your life, the essence of your life, until you come to make yourself like to this unity itself in the plurality of virtues" (*Diary*, April 15, 1913).

The secret for arriving at unity is to let yourself be conducted by the Holy Spirit since it is He who brings about Unity in God Himself.

"Loving is perfection and living with the love the Father has for the Son, that is, through the Holy Spirit—[this] is the most sublime perfection.

"Once transformation into Jesus is brought about in a soul, the Holy Spirit also becomes the spirit of the creature raised to a more or less higher degree according to the intensity and amplitude of transformation, which strictly depends on the growth of the soul in virtue. The Holy Spirit absorbs the creature's spirit in the course of transformation and fills it with this so pure love which is Himself. Then, it is with this same Love that the creature loves the divine Word, that is, with the same Love with which the Father loves Him, with absolute Love.

"Loving with the Holy Spirit is the grace of graces, the fusion of divine charisms, it is heaven itself placed at the disposition of that poor creature. The creature no longer acts, for it is the Holy Spirit who acts, whose heart beats, and who lives in it, and who loves with it and wholly surrounds it (*Diary*, April 17, 1913).

When the heights of this spiritual life are perceived it could be asked whether this ideal is reserved for some rare privileged souls or if it belongs to the normal development of the life of grace.

The Lord gives us the answer: "I did not choose saints to tell them Be perfect as your heavenly Father is perfect. I addressed Myself to all men, to the good and to the evil. All without exception are obliged to sanctify themselves" (*Diary*, April 15, 1913).

God Desires All Souls to Enter into His Unity

"To establish Himself in the innermost of souls, such is God's desire, God's need, granted the charity of His Being is avid to communicate what He is, infinite Love. He wants to possess souls, not only through His ordinary presence, which cannot be wanting to penetrate them, but according to a wish of love on the part of the creature, in order to render him happy. Therein is the sole ambition of God: to transform us into His Unity" (*Diary*, April 23, 1913).

When the Christian reaches Unity in so much as it is possible for a creature, he participates in God's goods, he comes to the intimacy of the Trinity.

"The Spirit who scrutinizes all" illumines Conchita's contemplative outlook, which is lost in divine depths.

"The Father does not proceed from anyone. He was not conceived nor engendered, but He exists of Himself, and He has always existed. He had no beginning. Eternally, and before all time, He was already God, eternal and without beginning. He did not produce Himself for He was already God. He has been forever, He will ever be God. He Himself not having another beginning, is the Beginning of all beings created by His fecund Being which produces all things, the natural world and the supernatural, for His creative might is eternal and inexhaustible. He produces in Himself all the happiness of which He is impregnated, the happiness of One who is wholly God. He produces, and brings together, this same happiness. He does not go out of Himself to be happy, for He is Happiness itself, Beauty and Holiness essentially. His happiness is in Himself, and all else is but radiations of His very Being. He is Love, and He loves Himself, in eternal ecstasy, in this love without beginning."

Conchita, faithful to her charism, put off transmitting fervently and delicately what Christ shows her in the Trinity, in particular the eternal generation of the Word. She marvelously described the Father's generosity, His happiness, His pleasure in His Son, and she adds: "Jesus told me: 'If I too rejoice, it is not because I am recalling these things, for they are ever present to Me. I do not have to bring back memories, everything is present reality for Me. But I rejoice on communicating to you a feeble ray of the Sun which I Myself am, and that you can appreciate the great generosity which the Father displays without going out of His own Self'" (*Diary*, Jan. 24, 1931).

Then — in marvelous continuity — this contemplation many months later comes to the *procession* of the Holy Spirit who proceeds from the Father and the Son, not as a fruit or a refulgence leaving its source, but through the necessity of the Father's and the Son's Being, for the Holy Spirit is love since He is God. They could not be without the Holy Spirit *who is infinite Love in Person*. The procession of the Holy Spirit was operated by the mutual Love between the Father and the Son, and this same Spirit is He who binds, unifies, is Life, between the Father and the Son.

"God feels a most special joy in His mysteries comprehensible to Him alone. What He communicates about them to man is but a minimal ray of His light. . . . But He gave him His Word, and with His Word made flesh, He gave him all since He gave Himself as a gift. The Church is the throne of the Trinity on earth, the only gate through which one can enter into eternal possession of God" (*Diary*, Sept. 9, 1931).

This most sublime and divine life is lived by Conchita most simply, in her daily life, in faithful carrying out of all her duties and commitments of family life. Those about her never suspected the work God accomplished in her. In Conchita all is interior.

Her spiritual director, Archbishop Luis Maria Martinez told her: "The teacher and model of this life, is Mary. Contemplate Her. Imitate Her and throw yourself into Her motherly arms" (*Diary*, Sept. 17, 1927).

I Must Live in Mary

"I must live within Mary, imitating Her virtues and Her love of the Most Holy Trinity.

"The mystical incarnation puts the soul in contact with the Three divine Persons. In Them and in Mary, I must find my life, not only my spiritual life but also my maternal life, letting it vanish in the offering of the Son to His Father. I must, centering everything on this same offering, eat, sleep, find joy, suffer, and simplify my whole life in this continual offering which glorifies the Holy Trinity. I must spend my whole life in union with Mary, without leaving Mary, imitating Her love for Jesus, Her total submission to the Father, acting only under the impulse of the Holy Spirit" (*Diary*, Oct. 27, 1925).

Conchita spent her whole life in perfect obedience to her Directors and to the extent she advances toward the perfection God asks of her, she becomes more and more docile.

She wrote: "I want to carry out the advice my Director gives me, raising everything to the supernatural plane, persons and things, making ideal my practical life with the splendid clarity of heavenly light, seeing in all creatures and events God's love, the trace of God, God Himself.

"I will fully penetrate the Divinity as Jesus wants. I will not close my eyes before the unfathomable secrets of the Most Holy Trinity. He teaches me. I will penetrate as much as He wants the divine mysteries, God's happiness, the eternal generation, the love of the Holy Spirit, these comings and goings of mercy and of goodness, the intimate communications of the divine Persons, His attributes, His so perfect Unity, the inner Sanctuary of the Trinity, when He will wish it and so long as He will wish it.

"Oh, what a unique union! What a singular relationship! What a unity in the three Persons! What a unique infinite God in this Unity of the Trinity" (*Diary*, March 11, 1933).

The Unity of the Trinity

"Unity is the center of the Divinity, the mystery dearest to God. It is God Himself, for God is the essence of Unity.

"The Trinity rejoices in this mystery which unifies the divine Persons, in this likeness of substance and of essence. All Three have but one will, one might. Still further, They are founded, I might say, in one only Divinity, in the very substance of this indivisible Divinity, in an infinite abyss, in a boundless immensity of perfections, and ever in its Unity.

"This Unity is what love achieves, since love unifies beings and wills in one infinite Center. In the Three divine Persons is the love which makes union and renders Them fecund in the fullness of its Being, for it is love which simplifies Them, and God is love, simplicity, unity.

"None of the divine Persons loves more than the other, nor possesses more than the other, nor wishes nor desires more than the others. There exists among Them a delightful accord which ravishes Them, which inebriates Them and which constitutes all Their delights, for the unity which envelops and penetrates Them is Their own Being.

"This eternal harmony vibrates not only among the Three divine Persons, but echoes and reechoes throughout Creation, unifying everything that exists.

"The Trinity stamps with its seal all that goes out from Itself, and imprints on It Its own characteristics of unity, but, although I say: 'all that goes out from God,' it does not go out from God, for all that is made fecund by God remains within God Himself. It cannot be otherwise, because of the Unity of God.

"This mystery is produced primarily in the eternal origin of the divine Persons, and then in all beings which receive fertility from the Trinity in Its Unity.

"It is a mystery of unity, multiplying itself infinitely and eternally within the Trinity. It is a mystery of unity, the most fecund through love, since all fertility proceeds from infinite love.

"Love engendered the Word in the very bosom of the Father. From the infinite love between the Father and the Son, with one only divinity, proceeded the Holy Spirit. The infinite intensity of this love personified Him, making of Him not another God but one other divine Person in God, that is, assimilating Him with the other divine Persons and forming one only Divinity, one only, eternal and indivisible Unity.

"Why? Because in God there does not exist three substances, three essences, three lives, three loves, but one only essence, substance, love and life in one only Unity, in one only Divinity" (*Diary*, April 3, 1933).

Trinity and Christian Mystery

The mystery of the Trinity is the most fundamental mystery of Christianity, the soul of the Gospel, the substance of the New Testament. It is the primordial Mystery, at the root and at the summit of all Christian mysteries.

Conchita contemplates in the light of the Trinity all the mysteries of faith in their marvelous connection and their admirable harmony. The Trinity is the mystery of a God who is Love.

The Mystery of God

God Love is by essence a gift, a communication "in Himself." It is the mystery of the innermost life of God who is Father, Son, Holy Spirit.

"God could not be alone, although He is Unique. He could not maintain Himself in one only divine Person, because He is God, that is infinite and not limited. On account of His infinite might in the order of charity, He had to communicate Himself with all His perfections, and this love, being such, so intense and infinite, could not be reserved, I might say, to one also wholly divine and infinite Person, in the Father Himself, but He had to produce the Word, and as if this might of love redoubled itself in the two divine Persons, Love had to personify itself in the Holy Spirit, producing then this Being of Charity, this Fire from the same fire burning between the Father and the Son, forming the bond of union which rejoices Them, delights Them and which unifies Them and reflects in all fullness Their perfections.

"The Three divine Persons communicate Their attributes and perfections which are Themselves, forming this Unity which is God, and with this word 'God,' all is said" (*Diary*, April 22, 1913).

Creation—Union

God Love is a gift, a gratuitous communication "outside Himself." It is the mystery of creation and of the participation in His divine life by creatures.

"From this fertile and infinite might of God which reflects and unites among Them the divine Persons in these eternal emanations of Eternal Charity, there is also derived His love for man and the gift of His Word to save him.

"As it was not enough for God to empty Himself, I might say, from within Himself, as if He did not want to be happy without man, He made him in His image, as His likeness. This bearer of the divine image attracted Him strongly from eternity. In fact, creation, redemption, all was present for Him in His intelligence. His very Being of so fecund charity impelled Him to seek the way to diffuse more and more His love, to be loved! That is why He created heaven and earth and millions of angels, and ever diffuses and gives Himself without sparing Himself.

"I said He diffuses His love to be loved. This is a property of love, to make love, to attract the one in whom this love springs up" (*Diary*, April 24, 1913).

Redemptive Incarnation

God Love makes a new creation of the universe, destroyed by sin, by sending His Son. This is the mystery of the Incarnate

Word and Redeemer "conceived by the Holy Spirit and born of Mary."

"And the Word was made flesh." Why? It was done to unify with God, culpable mankind, cleansing souls with His merits and His Blood. This was the purpose of the Incarnation of the Word, the object of the Redemption and of an entire life of example and of humiliation, to unite the earth with heaven.

"The law of love was the constant theme of My preaching. Every action of My life and even My death on the Cross, ended in the unification of souls in God.

"In the course of My pilgrimage on earth I always accounted for My miracles and teachings to the Father and to the Holy Spirit in whom I lived united. I carried out none of My actions independently of Them, and the entire Old and New Testament tended to render all souls *one* in charity and in unification with God" (*Diary*, April 26, 1913).

"Do you understand anything about God's love for man, about the divine Word's folly of love, becoming incarnate in Mary for receiving your blood, for becoming like you, for cleansing your sins, for being Mediator and for bringing you to heaven?

"Do you understand more and more the sublimity of this love which shines in creation, consumes itself with all the magnificence of a God in the Redemption, in the Eucharist and in union with each soul through the Holy Spirit?

"Do you understand anything about the grandeur of the sacrifice of the Cross and the infinite ardor of My Heart when I show it in these last times nailed on this same Cross?

"Do you see now the value of souls and what each of them costs Me, and the magnet which attracted from heaven to earth a God to become man, solely because they bear in them the image of the Trinity

"Do you see a God satisfying for the offense committed against this same God, taking on a human body to be able to suffer and expiate the crime of sin and thus be able to cancel the decree of condemnation, with Blood on the Cross?

"Do you now clearly see God's plan, in which His infinite love ever triumphs, and this whole succession of benefits brought about for the profit of an ungrateful world, only to attract it to unity?" (*Diary*, May 4, 1913).

"The Redemption was the mystery of the purest love, of the most tender condescension and the most lovable. An eternal explosion of love in the vehement desire of the Son and the concurrence of the Father and the Holy Spirit intervening in the beginning, during, and at the supreme conclusion" (*Diary*, Aug. 1, 1934).

"The Word offered Himself immaculate to the Father because His charity wanted to expiate the sins of a flesh which He desired to purify and save to recompense it eternally.

"Do you not contemplate Man's elevation through the contact of God's Word with human flesh, an incomparable and incomprehensible abasement, even in the purity of the immaculate womb of a woman?

"He became flesh in order that the flesh be divinized by Him, be elevated with Him, be purified in Him. He set therein His dwelling, He annihilated Himself to be man in order that man become, in a certain sense, God, consuming himself in His Unity." (*Diary*, June 24, 1928).

Mary in the Trinity's Design of Love

"Mary was the creature indispensable to the Trinity for carrying out its designs. In this Immaculate Virgin It hid the secrets and the mysteries which carried out Its design to save lost mankind.

"She corresponded to It from the first moment of Her being, increasing ever in grace, possessed by the Trinity. The Incarnation accomplished, She was Virgin Mother through the mediation of the Holy Spirit, with most pure fecundation of the Father, and She fulfilled Her role of mother with a perfection higher than that of all mothers, identifying Herself with Her divine Son. Mary never had a single thought, a single desire which was not directed to fulfilling the Father's will in Me. Even in a mother's natural acts toward her child, Mary was supernatural and perfect since She knew quite well that Her Son was God.

"At the foot of the Cross, She saw My Church born and accepted in John, all priests, in Her heart, in My place, and all—all mankind as its Mother.

"Then, through her martyrdom of solitude, She acquired in union with My merits all graces for these new children who must be born of My Mother.

"Why? Because She was Co-redemptrix, the first to continue My Passion on earth, she who founded the Church with My Apostles, the Protector and Mother of priests, the Queen of all saints.

"Mary knows most, Mary experienced most contemplation of the Most Holy Trinity thanks to the affinity which links Her to the Three divine Persons. She rejoiced, She finds Her delight in this unity of essence and simplicity of substance, since to Her, more than to any other creature, came luminous and profound divine clarities, which penetrated and encompassed Her. No one entered the sanctuary of the Divinity as did She and no one contemplated the divine ideal of the Trinity in Its Church and in Its priests as she did.

"Mary, Daughter and Spouse of the Trinity, is directly in charge of harmonizing this Church, unifying priests and perfecting them in the Unity of the Trinity" (*Diary*, April 7, 1928).

The Church of Love

God Love sends His sanctifying Spirit to be the Soul of the Church, the Mystical Body of Christ; "the people brought together in virtue of the unity of the Father, of the Son and of the Holy Spirit."

"The Holy Spirit is My promise, the Father's response on behalf of My Church and of all mankind, the condescension of the Father, that is, of Love giving Love itself.

"The Holy Spirit is for man the fruit of My prayer, of My

ardent request, that is, the ineffable cry of love from My Heart of God-Man, My greatest tenderness on behalf of the world.

"Without the Holy Spirit the Church would not be able to exist. But as She was eternally conceived and brought into being in the Mind of the Trinity, eternally, too, the Holy Spirit was designated by the Father to govern Her.

"What would become of the Church without the Holy Spirit? She would not exist. But God's infinite love for man, this vivifying and transforming Spirit, hovers over the world of souls.

"My Father engendered in His bosom the beloved Church. The Holy Spirit established and strengthened the Church on earth upon redemptive foundations, taking in Me, what was His. The Church consequently is love, her laws and all her teaching are love, pure love.

"The Holy Spirit did not come for only a day, nor for a fixed time, not even for centuries upon centuries, but to remain eternally in the Church" (*Diary*, Aug. 29, 1928).

Stars Shine in the Night

Conchita mentions the effects these divine lights produce in her in the night of her "solitude."

"On writing these so sublime things about the Trinity, I experience in my soul how there springs up in it and in my mind, I do not know whence, the mysteries, the lights and the beauties of this eternal Trinity, which drowns me in Its depths, blinds me with Its splendors, shining like the stars in the darkness of the sky" (*Diary*, Dec. 27, 1927).

"At a simple contact of the Most Holy Trinity, God flooded me with a dazzling light? What I come to be able to express under Its impulse is like a shadow, but Its vast expanse remains within me" (*Diary*, Oct. 15, 1935).

The spiritual life is like an ever ascending spiral of shadows and lights. Conchita experiences this marvelous contrast and writes: "I sense in my soul with great clarity mysteries above all that of the Most Holy Trinity. It is as if a veil was lifted before my eyes, as if a most brilliant hearth of light suddenly illumined unfathomable secrets, and there I contemplate most clearly, most profoundly, most minutely, I might say, the abyss of perfections in God.

"All this on the one hand, and on the other pains filled with desolation and inmost sorrows. I love God, but with a love filled with tears. How is it that this should come to pass when I sense Him so near and should be happy?" (*Diary*, May 20, 1930).

"Why do I undergo at the same time suffering in the midst of light? The Lord instructed me on this mystery: 'Because it is as it was with Me. I underwent on earth light and sadness, love and sadness, joy and sadness' " (*Diary*, May 27, 1930).

It should not be thought that life in intimacy with the Trinity here below is lived in a happiness without shadows, a prelude of heaven.

Genuine holiness is configuration to Jesus who, while being One with the Father, consummated His existence in the abandonment and destitution of the Cross. Love is an oblation, an immolation, a service, the giving of life for the redemption of many.

The consummation of the spiritual life is found in the perfect joy of full association to the mystery of the Redemption of the world through the Cross.

HER MISSION IN THE CHURCH

"A new Pentecost through the Cross"

On finishing these pages in which we have wished to present, though incompletely and imperfectly, Conchita's person and doctrine, a synthetic view, an over all view is demanded.

A theologian must above all pose this question to himself: "What then did God intend to bring about through His humble servant for the benefit of His entire Church?"

The Greatest Degree of Holiness is Attainable for Everyone

"Being a wife and a mother was never an obstacle to my spiritual life," she asserted. Speaking as a woman to one of her daughters-in-law, she stated: "I have been very happy with my husband."

In the last conversation with her husband when he was gravely ill, she asked him: "What is your last wish in regard to me?" He replied: *"That you be wholly given over to God and wholly devoted to your children."*

The Lord Himself told her one day: "You married in view of My great designs for your personal holiness, and to be an *example* for many souls who think that marriage is *incompatible* with holiness."

The most sublime mystical graces described by spiritual masters are not privileges confined to souls consecrated to God the priestly or religious life. They are offered to all Christians no matter what their state of life.

It seems that God wanted to give us through Conchita a living historical proof of this truth.

Vatican II clearly and forcibly testifies to it (cf. ch. V, especially # 40, *Lumen Gentium*): "Thus it is evident to everyone that all the faithful in Christ of whatever rank or status are called to the fullness of the Christian life and to the perfection of charity."

There are no second class Christians. We are all called to seek the greatest holiness.

Conchita received the eminent graces of nuptials and of the spiritual marriage described by the great mystics, in her state of "poor wife," as she called herself.

An instrument of God, Conchita, as she was familiarly called, has a prophetic mission for today's world.

The Lord Himself has announced to her that she would be a model wife and mother, but that her mission would extend far beyond to make shine the sanctifying might of Christ and of the Holy Spirit "in all states of life." Yes, indeed, she is a model wife, mother, teacher, but she is also one of the greatest mystics of the Church, leading souls to consummation in the Unity of the Trinity.

Her message calls the entire laity, married men and women, to the highest sanctity.

A New Type of Holiness

There is no question here of a type of holiness departing from the Gospel, but rather of a resource taken in view of a new application of this same Gospel.

To depart from the spirit of the Gospel and from the teachings of the Cross would be to deny Christ. We are speaking in the same sense Thérèse of Lisieux spoke of a "wholly new way." We are incontestably in a new era of spirituality.

What constitutes its newness is:

1) a calling of *all*, even of the laity, even of married people, to *the greatest holiness.*

2) Through *transfiguration of daily life*, the sanctification of the profane, divinization by faith, by love and by the spirit of sacrifice *in ordinary life.*

3) *the greatest holiness*, Transcendance of the message of the Cross. Even the most banal actions are made of value to the infinite by the offering of love in union with Christ, in imitation of the last years on earth of the Mother of God, in the service of the nascent Church.

In the evening of her life the Lord asked her to begin a new work on behalf of the sanctity of homes.

"I am going to ask you one thing: a *Crusade of victim souls* to the glory of My Father, following the spirit of the Cross.

"I want many acts of expiation for the DIVORCES which are the source of so many evils in homes, harmful to spouses, children, in society.

"I ask expiation for so many hidden sins and for so many sins of omission in the Christian formation of children.

"I want a *"Crusade of victim souls"* for the sanctification of homes" (*Diary*, Oct. 31, 1935).

Who does not see how providentially opportune is this work?

You Belong to My Church

"Each soul bears its own mission on earth. Yours, on account of My bounty, is the sublime mission of offering yourself as a victim for My Church, of pursuing your life of loving sacrifice on behalf of the Church, especially of her Shepherds."

Conchita's mission par excellence is to offer herself for the Church, for the sanctification of priests.

"You no longer belong to yourself, you belong to My Church, and the Word will make use of you for His sake. Alone you are worth nothing, but in union with Me, God will do great things through you. Repeat often: 'I am the Lord's servant' " (*Diary*, Feb. 5, 1911).

From the beginning of her spiritual life, she felt a particular attraction for the grace to sacrifice herself for priests, yet to the extent her spiritual life developed, the Lord's will made itself more and more manifest.

"Do you not want to save the world? Did you not ask Me it, by your blood, even before the Works of the Cross existed? Why have these Works come into the world? Very well, if you want to save souls, there is only one and powerful means: *holy priests.*

"Yes, here we have the crowning of the Work of the Cross. This will truly be a solace for My Heart, giving Me holy priests. Tell Me you accept, that you will belong with Me to priests always, since your mission on behalf of them will continue in heaven.

"Yet here you have another martyrdom. What priests will do against Me, you will feel, since it is in this that basically *associating yourself* to My priesthood consists, in that you feel and you suffer because of their unfaithfulness and wretchedness.

"In this way you will glorify the Trinity. We will have the same reasons for suffering" (*Diary*, Nov. 29, 1928).

The central grace of the mystical incarnation has as its ultimate purpose to carry out this mission.

She offers herself as a victim and the worth of this oblation does not come from herself but from Christ who lives in her soul.

The Chain of Love is a source of graces for the Church.

In the last years of her life, the Lord confided to her the great message and the great call to priestly holiness which the Lord Himself called "Confidences," since there was question of the most private secrets of His Heart and they contain a priestly doctrine extremely relevant.

I think along with many Mexican bishops and some theologians that when the whole world will learn of these writings, it will marvel and exclaim: "This does not come from a woman, but from one inspired by God, from a doctor of the Church." Here, in Mexico, she was examined by the authorities of the Church, many times, by theologians and persons of high standing. All concluded that it was the spirit of God which inspired her. In Rome, in 1913, even more strongly, they said in high esteem: "It is something extraordinary in the extraordinary!"

At present, the Church of Rome is examining her virtues and her writings. The Church is the sole judge. Henceforth we adhere faithfully and wholeheartedly to her decision. *The Church's judgment will be for us God's judgment.* But we have the firm hope that, in keeping with the magnificent expression of Cardinal Miguel Dario Miranda: "There will be found in Maria Concepcion Cabrera de Armida *a new star* in the firmament of the Church and the communion of saints."

Yet Conchita's so very personal a mission is also a message for all Christians, since she makes manifest the innermost aspect of the mystery of the Church which is *communion*, as well as the close relationships her diverse participation in the unique priesthood of Christ possess.

Conchita's mission in relation to the Church and especially in regard to the ministerial priesthood shows that essentially every Christian may become holy.

Without any doubt the layman is sanctified in *secularity* which is a specific field, but the deepest value of the Christian being, is to be a living member of Christ by the common grace of divine filiation; higher then the sanctification and ordination of the temporal reign is the mystery of grace and of sanctification.

He is a *brother* and the spiritual support of the ministerial priesthood (cf. *Lumen Gentium* # 32; *Presb. Ord.* # 9). It is he who, in turn, is the servant of the people of God, the service he should perform in love and in holiness of his life.

The "new" in Conchita's mission in the "old," is to bring out clearly the fundamental action of the laity in the salvific design: each Christian participates in the priesthood of Christ and has the mission of collaborating in the salvation of the world.

Conchita was a model mother, wife and teacher of her children, which is supplementary. She has told us that more than anything else a Christian existence is worthy of being lived when it is not lived *for itself* but for the Church.

This seems to me one of the most original aspects of her mission, particularly eloquent at the present moment.

Conchita teaches us *how to love the Church*.

To love the Church is not to criticize her, not to destroy her, not to try to change her essential structures, not to reduce her to a humanism, a horizonalism and to the simple service of a human liberation.

To love the Church is to cooperate with the work of Redemption by the Cross and in this way obtain the grace of the Holy Spirit come to renew the face of this poor earth, conducting it to its consummation in the design of the Father's immense love.

Conchita, a simple laywoman, far from criticizing priests, *gives her life* for them.

In a sublime elevation of the Trinity she cries out: "I deliver into Your hands by an absolute, total, unconditional donation, all my being on behalf of priests.

"I want to carry in my heart Our Holy Father, charged with the whole burden of the Church, the cardinals, the archbishops, the bishops, the parish priests, the priests, the seminarians who waver and struggle in their vocation.

"I myself am worth nothing, but I possess You and I beg you to utilize me for the good of the beloved Church and of all her hierarchies which I love and respect with all my heart."

Then, as did Thérèse of Lisieux who prophesied: "I want to spend my heaven doing good on earth," Conchita ends her prayer saying to Christ, after having offered up her life even to her extreme agony for priests: "I will offer up my life for them on earth and I will spend my time in heaven in their service for Your love" (*Diary*, Nov. 30, 1928).

The Gospel of the Cross

As were Thérèse of Lisieux or John XXIII, Conchita is a grace of God for His Church. From an objective study of documents, one conclusion is demanded of theologians: Conchita is "a Word of God for our times."

Providence has entrusted to a laywoman a prophetic message for today's world. Her mission in the Church is that of announcing a "new Pentecost," the reign of the Holy Spirit in our godless epoch, and to recall to men, for saving them, the Gospel of the Cross.

When the Lord began to carry out His work in Conchita, He manifested to her in a synthetic vision the whole doctrine, or rather, the *Gospel of the Cross* in the symbol of a cross crowned and illumined by the Holy Spirit. "A large, a very large cross," she wrote, "and in its center the pierced Heart of Christ."

What does it signify, this mysterious cross?

It signifies that the Cross has changed its meaning, that suffering and death are no longer malediction and condemnation; that the Cross constitutes the *first fruits* of the definitive liberation of man and of the universe.

The symbol of Conchita's spirituality, her message and her mission is the "Cross of the Apostolate." It was a very large Cross. At the center was the Heart of Jesus, the Love of the Incarnate Word. Over all this are wings of light and fire of the Holy Spirit, the personal Love of God.

This message has a universal dimension. Never before has man suffered so much as in the present moment. Never as today has all this suffering been so futile. The present day world is under the empire of the cross, but unfortunately it is not the Cross of Jesus since it is a cross without love.

All men suffer, but rare are those who know how to suffer. Human pain must be transfigured by love. Starting out from that moment, it is transformed into a dynamic force, constituting a New Universe. The Cross, transfigured by love is a Cross illumined by hope which is certitude for our complete liberation. It brings us to the glory of the Resurrection.

The message of the "Cross of the Apostolate," gives us the key for understanding the spirituality of the Cross which is a recalling of the Gospel. The Spirituality of the Cross demands holiness, a holiness which is "apostolic," and at the service of others, not turned to self, not even to the states of soul and the operations of God in purified souls. It is a holiness on the horizons of the Church and of Catholicity, associated with their *raison d'etre* and their finality: the salvation and sanctification of men, and so a holiness leading to a total oblation of self on behalf of priestly holiness; a holiness carried on in the fidelity of simple existence, so a holiness accessible to all, whether at home, in the family or at work. Holiness amid daily trials and tribulations in the primacy of love, but under the seal of the Cross and of the spirit of sacrifice.

This meaning of the Cross is the base of the Gospel. All holiness is accomplished on the Cross. But each one, according to his place and his mission in the Church, his personal cross which is embossed on the web of a human life which is lived in evangelical simplicity and in perfect docility to the Holy Spirit.

Only the Holy Spirit illumines the meaning of the Cross of Jesus and introduces us to its mystery, revealing to us its salvific value, transfiguring it and making it stand out in splendors of glory.

The history of the world has its center on Golgotha where the Cross of Christ is ever raised between *two crucified humanities*, one in hate, the other in love.

Christ invites every human generation to share His Cross.

It is in his response to the call of the Crucified that each man enjoys his destiny.

The spirituality of the Cross is not something doleful, is no longer something passive. It is an active collaboration in salvation, a cooperation in the construction of the "new world."

Thus, what is most admirable in the doctrine the Lord manifested to Conchita is not found solely in the meaning of the Cross as expiatory suffering (reparation of the fault by a compensatory offering of love, to render to God the Father all glory in exchange for the offense of sin), not only as simple *satisfaction*, but as purification for sinful man.

There is question in a profound sense of a redemption by love, of a sanctification, a transfiguration and a configuration to Christ who "has loved us to the end."

In summary it is to rediscover the Cross of Christ, its value for salvation; it is to enter into the depths of the mystery of the redemption, it is a call to understand the innermost cross of the Heart of Christ, to honor it, and to share in it, and therefore to become personally involved in the co-redemption of men for the glory of God.

"That one associate souls to My redemptive sacrifice is an honor of predilection, but that the giving of these souls be perfect I must transform them into Me so that in this way, on integrating themselves in My perfect Mystical Body, they be one only thing with Me for the Father's glory" (*Diary*, Nov. 10, 1935).

Since it is the Cross of *Jesus*, it brings with it as fruit the effusion of the Holy Spirit.

A New Pentecost

Our secularized and desecrated world is dying on account of the absence of God. It is steeped in the spirit of comfort and pleasure. There is but one remedy: the Spirit of God, the Holy Spirit. He alone will be able to *revitalize* the Church and *revivify* her by a "new Pentecost."

John XXIII, the Vicar of Jesus Christ, proclaimed it vigorously: the Church needs a "new Pentecost."

Fifty years before the Council, after 1911, Conchita kept on writing again and again: "The Church and the world has need of a 'new Pentecost,' a second Pentecost, a priestly Pentecost, an interior Pentecost."

The Servant of God who had an ardent devotion toward the Blessed Virgin assured us: "The Holy Spirit and Mary will save the Church."

Yes, Conchita's prophetic mission is that of recalling to the modern and materialistic world, avid for liberty, that it will be saved only by a NEW PENTECOST and by the GOSPEL OF THE CROSS.

This new Pentecost, this sanctifying action of the Spirit, must begin with priests and extend itself to the entire People of God, as on the first Pentecost the Holy Spirit descended on the Apostles and on the whole community assembled in the Cenacle.

"I want to come back to the world in My priests. I want to renew the world of souls on manifesting Myself in My priests. I want a powerful impulse in My Church on infusing upon Her the Holy Spirit as on a new Pentecost" (*Diary*, Jan. 5, 1928).

But the Holy Spirit cannot descend to the world save by Christ's Cross since both missions, that of the Son and that of the Spirit, are inseparable.

"The Holy Spirit will reign the day when My sacrifice of suffering will also reign: the Cross in hearts. In so far as the Cross will not reign in souls, the Holy Spirit, He too will not reign" (*Diary*, May 26, 1901).

May Mary, the Mother of Jesus and Mother of the Church, intercede that this prodigy of Pentecost be renewed, and that the Church, this "people brought together by virtue of the unity of the Father, the Son and the Holy Spirit" carry out the design of love which springs from the Father: may She truly be the *Holy Church!*

APPENDIX

1) *Principal dates in the life of Concepcion Cabrera de Armida*

December 8, 1862	Birth.
December 10, 1862	Baptism.
December 8, 1872	First Communion.
September 16, 1881	Desire of perfection.
November 8, 1884	Marriage.
	First spiritual retreat.
January 14, 1894	Inscription of the Holy Name of Jesus.—Birth of the Works of the Cross.
January 23, 1894	"Total self-surrender."—Spiritual nuptials.
May 3, 1894	Erection of the first Cross of the Apostolate.—Birth of the Apostolate of the Cross, first of the five Works of the Cross, which bring together the People of God: to unite her own suffering and labors to those of Christ for continuing His salvific work in the world.
February 9, 1897	Spiritual marriage.
May 3, 1897	Founding of the Religious of the Cross of the Sacred Heart of Jesus, second work of the Cross: contemplatives of perpetual adoration who offer their lives for the Church, especially for priests.
September 17, 1901	Death of her husband.
February 4, 1903	Meeting with Father Felix Rougier.

March 25, 1906	Grace of the mystical incarnation.
November 30, 1909	Founding of the Alliance of love with the Sacred Heart of Jesus, third work of the Cross, for persons who in their own state of life commit themselves to seek perfection according to the spirituality of the Cross.
January 19, 1912	Founding of the Apostolic League,— fourth work of the Cross, for bishops and priests who want to live in this spirituality and help other works of the Cross.
August-December, 1913	Pilgrimage to the Holy Land and to Rome.
November 17, 1913	Audience with Pius X.
April 10, 1914	Founding of the Dominical Communion on behalf of priests.
December 25, 1914	Founding of the Missionaries of the Holy Spirit, fifth work of the Cross: a clerical religious Congregation specially devoted to priestly works and dedicated to the spiritual direction of souls.
February 2, 1917	Last stage of her life: meditation in depth and special devotion to the "solitude" of Mary during her own solitude.
October 31, 1935	Founding of the Crusade of victim souls on behalf of homes: in their own state of life they offer themselves, in the same spirituality of the Cross, for the glory of the Father and for expiating sins in marriage and in society.
March 3, 1937	Holy death.
September 29, 1959	Canonical opening of the Process of Beatification in Rome.

2) *Her spiritual directors*

1) First director: Father Alberto Mir, S.J. (Dec. 13, 1852-Dec. 22, 1916). He directed her for ten years, from the beginning of the year 1893. With his profound knowledge of the ways of the spiritual life, he rooted her solidly in the ascetical way, especially in the virtues of obedience and humility.

2) Father Feliz Rougier, S.M. (Dec. 17, 1859-Jan. 10, 1938). He confirmed her in her deep love for the Church and her representatives and in the most simple and heroic obedience, of which he himself was a living example. His direction was interrupted on Aug. 25, 1904, by his voyage to Europe to undertake the founding of the Missionaries of the Holy Spirit. His religious superiors kept him there for ten years. On Dec. 25, 1914, he finally founded the so desired Congregation and his cause for beatification was introduced in Rome.

3) Canon Emeterio Valverde y Tellez (March 1, 1864-Dec. 26, 1948) afterwards named bishop of the diocese of Leon. He directed her from September 22 to May 1905. He was very cultivated.

4) This direction was then continued by Father Maximino Ruiz (Aug. 19, 1875-May 11, 1949), after the month of June 1906 until that of September 1912. He was a great theologian and jurist of his time. Named bishop of Chiapas, then auxiliary bishop of Mexico.

5) Msgr. Dr. Ramon Ibarra y Gonzalez (Oct. 22, 1853-Feb. 1, 1917), first bishop of Chilapa, then bishop of Puebla, then first archbishop of this same diocese. A brilliant student at the Roman Universities: Doctor of Theology, in Ecclesiastical and Civil Law and also in Philosophy. Personally appreciated by Leo XIII. His direction began in October 1912 and ended the day of his death Feb. 1, 1917. His cause of beatification was introduced in Rome.

6) Once more Msgr. Emeterio Valverde y Tellez, after 1917 until 1925.

7) Her last spiritual director was Msgr. Luis Maria Martinez (1881-1956), auxiliary bishop of Morelia, then archbishop-primate

of Mexico and in charge of the Affairs of the Holy See at an extremely difficult period in the country. A famous author of spiritual theology; he himself, a great mystic, directed Conchita from July 7, 1925 to the more mature period of her spiritual life, until the day of her death March 3, 1937. As a theologian he explains the doctrine of the Cross.

An Interesting Thought

The publication you have just finished reading is part of the apostolic efforts of the Society of St. Paul of the American Province. A small, unique group of priests and brothers, the members of the Society of St. Paul propose to bring the message of Christ to men through the communications media while living the religious life.

If you know of a young man who might be interested in learning more about our life and mission, ask him to contact the Vocation Office in care of ALBA HOUSE, at 2187 Victory Blvd., Staten Island, New York 10314. Full information will be sent without cost or obligation. You may be instrumental in helping a young man to find his vocation in life. *An interesting thought.*